Wild Party

Planning an expedition to wild and wonderful Iceland starts with a phone call to Twickenham Travel. You'll find helpful, experienced Iceland enthusiasts who like nothing better than hearing your ideas and putting them into practice. For everything you need to know about arranging a party to Iceland's wilderness, and group discounts, call the UK market leaders on 01·221 7278 right now.

☎ 01-221 7278
TWICKENHAM

T W I C K E N H A M ' S · I C E L A N D

TWICKENHAM TRAVEL LIMITED · 33 NOTTING HILL GATE
LONDON W11 3JQ · TELEPHONE 01-221 7278 · TELEX 922889
GLASGOW TELEPHONE 041-204 0242 · ABTA/ATOL 1337

i

ICELAND
A HANDBOOK FOR EXPEDITIONS

by

TONY ESCRITT

Foreword by
Birgir Thorgilsson
Director, Iceland Tourist Board

Published by
The Iceland Information Centre Ltd
LONDON

To Nicholas and Catherine

First published March, 1985
Second edition August, 1986
ISBN 0 948192 00 3

ᶜ The Iceland Information Centre Ltd
   Expedition Advisory Centre
   Royal Geographical Society
   Kensington Gore
   London SW7 2AR

Printed by Ambrose Printing Limited, Granby, Bakewell, Derbyshire, England.

Cover photograph: Eruption in Gjástykki, North Iceland, September 1984. (Tony Escritt)

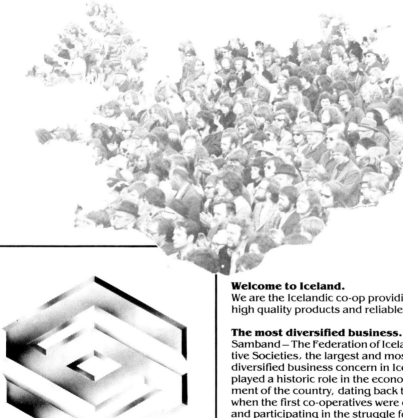

FOREWORD
Birgir Thorgilsson
Director, Iceland Tourist Board

In Iceland the forces of nature have competed for dominance in what has become a very fragile landscape. It has taken thousands of years to achieve even a delicate balance that is easily upset by short-term events, such as a volcanic eruption, heavy winter snowfall, or early spring melt. The picture now becomes more complicated by man's intrusion into the field of conflict through engineering, tourism, and curiosity. Our knowledge of the long-term effects of this intrusion is in its infancy but we can be certain that if we are not careful we run the risk of endangering the very landscape that we come to enjoy. The early settlers, though party to the early denudation of Iceland's vegetation, were in many ways more adapted to, and understanding of their environment than we are today.

I therefore welcome the publication of a handbook which lays stress on the conservation of landscape and an understanding of the background of the Icelandic settlement as priorities in the planning and execution of field study, exploration and recreation in our wild areas. The author has known Iceland since 1962, is a regular visitor, and is widely travelled. He has observed the evolution of research and educational visits to Iceland perhaps more closely than many others and is well qualified to comment on the "do's and don'ts" of back-country travel in Iceland.

I commend his advice to you and hope that your visit will prove valuable both to yourselves and to the stock of knowledge about landscape evolution in its broadest sense. Above all, please help us to conserve a landscape for future generations of travellers to enjoy.

PREFACE

Over the years so many individuals have directly or indirectly contributed to the contents of this Handbook that it is difficult to single them all out by name. If their names are omitted from this list then I apologise because sincerest thanks are due to everyone. The Iceland Unit of the Young Explorers' Trust was founded in 1972 and would never have come into existence but for the generosity of Harrow School in awarding me a sabbatical term, Nial Macdiarmid who provided me with some administrative finance, and Icelandair — notably Jóhann Sigurdsson and Bob Miller. A great deal of assistance was also given by Terry Mattingley (now Mrs Stavnem) then director of the former Anglo-Icelandic Travel Agency. The Anglo-Icelandic Field Research Group had ceased to exist but its former secretary, Paul Sowan, was still very active in things Icelandic and had an astonishing ability to seek out bibliographic material. This he still does and I owe him an enormous gratitude. The continued support of Icelandair ensures the survival of the Unit and I am grateful to their various officers in London, but particularly to Jóhann D. Jónsson.

In Iceland the help and encouragement has been no less forthcoming. Over the years the Youth Council of Reykjavík (Hinrik Bjarnasson, Ómar Einarsson, Ketil Larsen) have always welcomed me to their offices and allowed me to base my work there. I cannot underestimate the value of their kindness and support. The late Professor Sigurdur Thorarinsson was always in strong support as was the late Dr. Finnur Gudmundsson. These were two great men to whom I looked up with enormous affection. In 1972 I discussed the idea of the Unit with one Vigdís Finnbogadóttir. Her views on Iceland and the conservation of Icelandic culture and landscape have remained with me and I hope that not only are they evident in this Handbook but that those who follow will pursue the conservation ethic in its widest sense.

Throughout the Unit's development the National Research Council (Rannsóknaráð Ríkisins), notably Gunnar B. Jónsson, and the Nature Conservation Council (Náttúruverndarráð), notably Árni Reynisson and Jón Gauti Jónsson have advised the Unit in various ways. I am enormously grateful for continuous support from the Iceland Tourist Board (Birgir Thorgilsson) and The Iceland Tourist Bureau (Kjartan Lárusson). Gratitude is also extended to Aevar Petersen (ornithology), Eythór Einarsson (botany and conservation), Hannes Hafstein (rescue services), Gudjón O Magnússon (mountaineering and conservation), Gustav Arnar (radio communications), Helgi Björnsson (glaciology), Helgi Hallgrímsson, Hördur Kristinsson (botany), Ingvar B. Fridleifsson (geology), Péter O. Thórdarsson (accommodation), Sigrún Helgadóttir (conservation), Sigurjón Rist (hydrology).

Perhaps the greatest single 'thank you' should go to Brian Holt, formerly Her Majesty's Consul in Reykjavík where he still lives and, happily, is still very active with in-bound groups. His advice, admonishment, and kindliness has, over the years, provided the greatest encouragement.

To those with a direct input to the Handbook I must thank Dr. David Drewry (glaciology), Roger Smith (mountaineering), Dr. Ian Ashwell (Vatnajökull), Patrick Molony (Gaesavatnaleid), Edward Jackson (Human Geography), Jon Sandilands (food supplies), Olaf Richardson (Vatnajökull), Geoff Treglown (vehicles), Richard Moore (vehicles), Bryan Dawson (water supplies), Graham Derrick (radios), Dick Phillips (huts and many other snippets of information). Ted Grey (Chairman, YET), has run our successful annual gathering ("Þing") for a number of years, and Richard Moore has analysed the annual expedition questionnaires that have, yielded so much information for our files. Dr. Chris Caseldine has taken over the latter role and Linda Hine is now looking after the management of the bibliographic material supplied by Paul Sowan.

Tony Escritt

Illustrations

Illustrations are by the author except as indicated below:

Náttúrufræðistofnun	1 and 2.
Post and Telegraph Administration	20.
Náttúruverndarráð	7 and 8.
Landmaelingar Íslands	3 and 14.
Roger Smith	28 and 29.
Ian Ashwell	32 and 33.
David Drewry	6.
Hönnun h.f.	27.
Snaevarr Gudmundsson	30.

All the incidental line drawings are by Michael Weale (Wiltshire Schools Exploration Society).

LIST OF CONTENTS

HOW TO USE THIS BOOK

The Iceland Unit of the Young Explorers' Trust was founded in 1972 to help expedition leaders to find worthwhile projects and field areas within the limits of their budgets, and to provide a coordinated approach to the host country. Since its inception the Unit has advised most expeditions and fieldwork parties at some stage in their preparation, and has provided the opportunity for leaders to meet and to discuss their plans with those who have been before. This Handbook represents the amalgamation and rewriting of all the broadsheets published by the Unit. It is not intended to be read from cover to cover but used to help you to solve a particular problem be it a choice of area or a technical detail of expedition organisation. If you were to strictly adher to every single piece of advice then your expedition might never get off the ground!

The Handbook has been written in the belief that a leader wishes to put together his own unique expedition but one whose standards are high. High standards of expedition achievement may be attained by attention to detail and thorough pre-expedition planning. Why ignore the experiences of others? Expedition leaders will wish to refer to previous reports for ideas and advice. This can be difficult and so what we do here is to pull most of that information together into one tome. With this advantage the leader may now readily delegate the administration while he supervises the overall expedition plan and ensures a programme that neatly balances the requirements of science on the one hand and the needs of the members on the other. The Handbook will be invaluable when supported by two books that will be found in Chapter 18: "Polar Expeditions" (Renner), and "A Handbook for Expeditions" (Land).

Not surprisingly the Handbook will become 'out-of-date' in some small way the moment it is printed but it is easily updated by subscribing to the Iceland Unit Bulletin ISLAND which comes out three times a year. An application form will be found at the back of the book. Of course it can only be updated if you write to us with your observations and again a post-expedition questionnaire is included in Appendix L.

If the idea of an Iceland expedition is still in the germination stage then we suggest the following:

> 1. Read Chapter 1 and, if interested in mountaineering, Chapter 14. These should help you to formulate a general idea of what you wish to achieve.

2. With a field programme in mind read Chapter 3. to locate an area which may seem to suit your particular blend of expedition. Reference to Chapter 2. on Conservation is always relevant at this stage, especially if you may be operating close to a protected area. This may also be the time to be in touch with the Iceland Unit and to acquaint them with your ideas as they will be able to put you in touch with others in the same position or with experience of your proposed field area or activities. Write to:

> The Iceland Information Unit
> Young Explorers' Trust
> c/o The Royal Geographical Society
> 1 Kensington Gore
> LONDON SW7 2AR

3. Obtain maps and read Chapters 4. to 8. This will enable you to formulate an itinerary such that Tour Operators will be able to offer you quotations. It will help you to obtain a realistic quote if you can present all your requirements in detail.

4. If you live in the United Kingdom (or even if you do not!) plan to attend the annual February gathering, or "Þing", of the Iceland Unit. It is always an excellent way to gather ideas in a short space of time.

5. The more detailed planning outlined in Chapters 9. to 11. must now be undertaken and a training programme put together for the expedition members. Emphasis must be laid on conservation and safety as outlined in Chapters 2. and 13. If this is a young expedition, parents will want to know more about the itinerary and some of the details in Chapter 12. will be useful if put to them in a Newsletter.

6. Even before the expedition leaves for Iceland read Chapter 16. The success of the follow-up may well depend upon successful delegation prior to departure.

If this Handbook has been of any use to you we do hope that you will let us know its strengths and weaknesses. Its continuation and re-publication depends upon you the user. Have a good expedition.

SAFE JOURNEY   GÓÐA FERÐ!

1 WHY ICELAND? — The Scientific Framework

INTRODUCTION

Iceland has served as a North Atlantic stepping stone ever since it was created on the mid-ocean ridge. Mankind has been resident for over 1100 years and has evolved a culture that has remained largely intact inspite of outside influences. Today the forces that strive to destroy a nation's identity are as real in Iceland as anywhere else but there exists a national consciousness to do battle with them. The language remains almost pure old Norse; the sagas, passed on from generation to generation are still recounted and permeate the literature; attention is drawn to ancient Viking sites revered as much by Icelanders as foreign visitors. But as the pace of life becomes faster and faster so the need to secure these traditions becomes even more pressing and we all have a responsibility to conserve what could so easily be swamped by thoughtless misuse. Iceland is first and foremost a land of people with a rich tradition. We come not to stare but to participate in a living phenomenon in the full realisation that we will be experiencing and learning from involvement in something far more precious than a summer holiday.

That the Icelanders happen to live in one of the strangest landscapes known to man is no accident. The island occupies a unique position in the north Atlantic straddling the mid-ocean ridge and serving as a stepping stone for vegetation and birdlife. Ornithologically it has drawn many of the famous names including Sir Peter Scott who studied the pink-footed geese colonies and G. K. Yeates who recorded his ornithological adventures in 'The Land of the Loon'. The late Dr. Finnur Guðmundsson was much respected in the world of ornithology. Botanists and ecologists have extensively studied the expansion of vegetation into the newest of this planet's environments which include land released from frozen ice, fresh lava surfaces and the island of Surtsey. Here Sturla Friðriksson and his colleagues continue to study the evolution of an island ecosystem. Early glaciological studies involved Iceland in a study of ice in the north Atlantic region and records for Icelandic glaciers go back to the saga books. Processes operate so quickly here that many students of geomorphology have used Iceland as their living laboratory for studies of periglacial phenomena, landslides, rock glaciers, and soil erosion.

But the principal attraction must be the outstanding location for studies in geology and geophysics. Our knowledge of tectonic processes has evolved so rapidly over the last twenty years that it seems but yesterday that we were saying that it looked as though Wegener wasn't so far wrong after all. Iceland can boast an eruption every 7-10 years to provide fodder for each new generation of geologists and vulcanologists. At the focus of this rapid growth was the late Professor Sigurður Thorarinsson who has so many papers to his name in the scientific literature for Iceland (and a song in the

Icelandic hit parade!). His "Thousand Years Struggle Against Ice and Fire" is a classic in this collection. It was he who developed the study of tephrachronology that has been such a useful tool in unravelling the history of the Icelandic landscape. It is not surprising that Iceland now hosts the United Nations Geothermal Training Programme with an Icelandic director and a host of Icelandic lecturers whose expertise is sought world-wide.

Iceland's history has been carefully documented from the first settlement to provide an invaluable tool for the demographer. Iceland itself is developing very rapidly while trying to resist the worst of outside influences. Its developments in agriculture and industry, and the changing patterns of settlement are of interest to the human geographer.

Icelanders may be amused or bemused by the annual flock of 'expeditions' to their island but it is not so surprising when so much of interest is on their doorstep.

What follows is a review of the principal fields of study by, mainly, young expeditions. For more detailed information we must refer you to "The Handbook for Expeditions" (Butterworths) and "Polar Expeditions" (Expedition Advisory Centre). At the end of each section we list up to two past expedition reports that have proved useful to expeditions. This is mainly for the benefit of UK expeditions who should be able to view them at the Iceland Unit or the Royal Geographical Society. Further bibliographical material will be found in Chapter 18.

Putting pure research on one side we suggest that field programmes be kept as simple as possible in view of the time available in the field and the inevitability of outside factors such as weather intervening to upset the work.

FIELDWORK OPPORTUNITIES IN ICELAND
BOTANY:

Botanically Iceland leans towards the European continent but with a third of the plants termed arctic-alpine. Of interest is the island's relative isolation and the thesis that half of the vascular plants are survivors of the last ice age. Numerous expeditions have attempted to study the development of the vegetation in the wake of a receding glacier. It is frequently astonishing to see how plant life clings to the most precarious of habitats, rooted to cracks, gravel banks or loose sand, and in danger of being swept away by ever-changing stream courses. Today's climate is probably less important than that of the glacial period and the present paucity of vegetation cover is in large part due to destruction by early settlers. Examination of todays woodlands reveals a remarkably rich flora beneath the shade of the birch.

There are ample opportunities for pure and applied botanical work. But care must be taken to ensure the conservation of flora in what is a sensitive environment. There are a number of species protected by Icelandic law and the current list appears in Appendix A. The study of Icelandic flora is a very specialised task and it would help if groups will send or leave a copy of

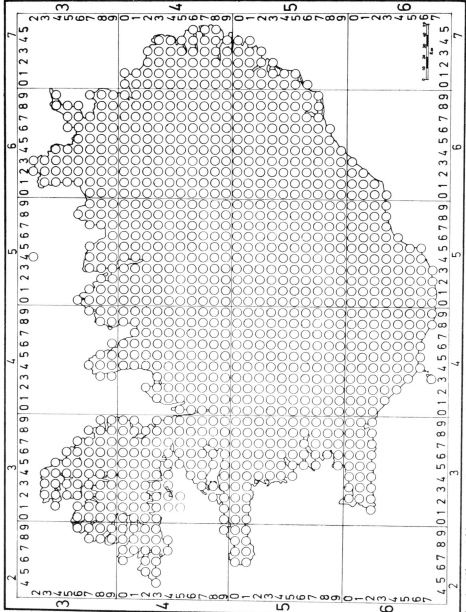

Fig. 1. 10km grid base map for mapping plant distributions.

their collection lists to the Natural History Museum in Reykjavik for checking before publication in reports. This would take no time at all, and would ensure no serious errors. Those working in the north should know that the Natural History Museum in Akureyri is staffed by botanists who also have a field centre to the north of Akureyri at Vikur Bakki. The herbarium of the museum houses a collection of some 19,000 vascular plants, 9000 specimens of fungi (mainly mushrooms), and about 7000 specimens of lichens. The bulk of this material is from Iceland, but some collections from neighbouring countries are kept for the purpose of identification and comparison.

A botanical atlas of Icelandic flora along the lines of the British version using ten kilometre squares is being compiled. The base map and a copy of the recording card are shown in Figures 1. and 2.

Examples of botanical projects recently carried out include:

The effects of increased visitor pressure on the footpaths within the Skaftafell National Park (Brathay Exploration Group).

Measurement of the altitudinal limits for selected species, with regard to aspect and distance from the sea (eg. Betula spp., Juniperus, Vaccinium).

Phenologic studies of some species — flowering times, fruiting etc. at different altitudes.

Description of overall aspect of the vegetation in relation to slope direction and slope angle, snow cover, wind direction etc.

Lichen distribution in relation to glacial retreat.

Measurement of crop yield of selected species to compare with specimens in Britain or mainland Europe.

Ecology of small lacustrine islands isolated from sheep populations.

Comparative studies of different systems: eg. sand dune, lake margin, open water etc.

Useful Reports: BILBOROUGH COLLEGE (1979): Mývatn
                        U.C.N.W. ABERYSTWYTH (1977): Thórvaldsdalur

ENTOMOLOGY

Expeditions are not so aware of the insect life in Iceland as in other parts of Europe. Moths, harvestmen, and wolf spiders perhaps catch the eye but few expeditions have undertaken entomological work in view of its specialist nature. However it is simple enough to install pitfall traps, use pooters, or sweep nets, to sample a variety of habitat (eg. hayfields, lake margins, lava, heath etc.). It has been suggested that observations and studies of the occurrence of bumble bees would usefully contribute to our knowledge of the species. The Oxford expedition referred to below investigated the dependence of plants on insects for pollination by means of exclusion experiments. Several expeditions have looked at the insect populations in the vicinity of hot springs.

REITUR	STAÐUR	NAFN/DAGS.
		H. Y. S.

ACHILL	her	rost	aci	ama	dry	**MYOSOT**	**POLYST**	sag	**TARAXA**
mil	int	ruf	pal	aur	phe	arv	lon	sub	spp
AGROST	sta	sal	pau	cam	**LATHYR**	pal	**POTAMO**	**SALIX**	**THALIC**
can	ver	sax	uni	det	mar	str	alp	cal	alp
sto	**CALLUN**	sub	**ELYMUS**	ten	pal	**MYRIOP**	fil	her	**THYMUS**
ten	vul	vag	are	**GERANI**	pra	alt	gra	lan	arc
ALCHEM	**CALTHA**	**CARUM**	**ELYTRI**	sil	**LEONTO**	spi	nat	phy	**TOFIEL**
alp	ral	car	rep	**GEUM**	aut	**NARDUS**	per	**SANGUIS**	pus
fær	**CAMPAN**	**CATABR**	**EMPETR**	riv	**LEUCOR**	str	præ	off	**TRICHO**
vul	rot	aqu	her	**GLAUX**	alb	**OPHIOG**	pus	**SAXIFR**	cæs
ALOPEC	uni	**CERAST**	nig	mar	**LIGUST**	azo	**POTENT**	aizoid	**TRIENT**
æqu	**CAPSEL**	alp	**EPILOB**	**GLYCER**	sco	**OXALIS**	ans	aizoon	eur
gen	bur	arc	als	flu	**LIMOSE**	ace	cra	cæs	**TRIFOL**
pra	**CARDAM**	cer	ana	**GNAPHA**	aqu	**OXYRIA**	ege	cer	rep
ANGELI	bel	fon	col	nor	**LINUM**	digy	pal	cot	**TRIGLO**
arc	hir	glo	hor	sil	cat	**PAPAVE**	**PRIMUL**	fol	mar
sil	nym	**CHAMÆN**	lac	sup	**LISTER**	rad	str	hir	pal
ANTENN	**CARDOP**	ang	pal	uli	cor	**PARIS**	**PRUNEL**	hyp	**TRIPLE**
alp	pet	lat	**EQUISE**	**HARRIM**	ova	qua	vul	niv	mar
ANTHOX	**CAREX**	**COCHLE**	arv	hyp	**LITORE**	**PARNAS**	**PUCCIN**	opp	**TRISET**
odo	ade	off	flu	**HIERAC**	uni	pal	mar	riv	spi
ANTHYL	atr	**COELEO**	hie	isl	**LOISEL**	**PEDICU**	ret	ste	**UTRICU**
vul	bic	vir	pal	spp	pro	fla	**PYROLA**	ten	min
ARABIS	big	**CORALL**	pra	**HIEROC**	**LOMATO**	**PHIPPS**	grand	**SEDUM**	**VACCIN**

alp	bru	tri	var	odo	rot	alg	min	acr	myr
ARCTOS	can	**CORNUS**	**ERIGER**	**HIPPUR**	**LUZULA**	**PHLEUM**	**RAMISC**	ann	oxy
uva	capil	sue	bor	vul	arc	com	sec	ros	uli
ARENAR	capit	**CREPIS**	hum	**HYDROC**	mul	pra	**RANUNC**	vill	vit
nor	cho	pal	uni	vul	spi	**PHYLLO**	acr	**SELAGI**	**VALERI**
ARMERI	dia	**CYSTOP**	**ERIOPH**	**ISOETE**	sud	coe	gla	sel	off
mar	dio	frag	ang	ech	**LYCHNI**	**PINGUI**	hyp	**SESLER**	sam
ATHYRI	ech	**DACTYL**	sch	lac	flos	vul	pyg	coe	**VERONIC**
alp	flacc	mac	**EROPHI**	**JUNCUS**	**LYCOPO**	**PLANTA**	repe	**SIBBAL**	alp
fil	glac	**DESCHA**	ver	alp	alp	lan	rept	pro	ana
ATRIPL	glar	alp	**ERYSIM**	arc	ann	maj	tri	**SILENE**	fru
gla	hel	cæs	hier	art	sel	mar	**RHINAN**	acau	off
pat	kraus	fle	**EUPHRA**	big	**MATRIC**	**PLATAN**	min	mar	scu
BARTSI	lach	**DIAPEN**	cur	bul	mat	hyp	**ROEGNE**	**SPARGA**	ser
alp	lim	lap	fri	cast	**MELAMP**	**POA**	bor	ang	**VICIA**
BETULA	lyng	**DRABA**	**FESTUCA**	fil	sil	alp	can	hyp	cra
nan	mac	alp	rub	ran	**MENYAN**	ann	**RORIPP**	min	sep
pub	mag	inc	viv	squ	tri	gla	isl	**SPERGU**	**VIOLA**
BLECHN	marit	niv	**FILIPE**	trif	**MERTEN**	lax	**RUBUS**	arv	can
spi	mic	nor	ulm	trigl	mar	nem	sax	sal	epi
BOTRYC	nar	**DROSER**	**FRAGAR**	**JUNIPER**	**MILIUM**	pra	**RUMEX**	**STELLA**	mon
bor	nig	rot	ves	com	eff	tri	acetos	cra	pal
lan	nor	**DRYAS**	**GALIUM**	**KNAUTIA**	**MINUAR**	**POLYGO**	acell	gra	riv
lun	oed	oct	bor	arv	bif	amp	lon	hum	tri
CAKILE	pan	**DRYOPT**	nor	**KOBRES**	pep	avi	**SAGINA**	med	**VISCAR**
mar	pil	ass	ver	myo	rub	per	cæs	**SUBULA**	alp
CALAMA	pulch	dil	**GENTIA**	**KOENIG**	str	viv	int	aqu	**WOODSIA**
neg	pulic	fil	niv	isl	**MONTIA**	**POLYPO**	nod	**SUCCIS**	alp
CALLIT	rar	**ELEOCH**	**GENELL**	**LASTRE**	fon	vul	pro	pra	ilv

Fig. 2. Botanical species recording card.

8

Useful Reports: OXFORD UNIVERSITY (1973): Mývatn
NEWCASTLE UNIVERSITY (1973): Arnavatnsheiði

FRESHWATER BIOLOGY

Iceland has a great many small and large lakes of interest to the biologist. Work in and around Lake Mývatn has been extensively written up but this is not an area to which expeditions would be encouraged to go on account of its protected status. Expeditions would do well to make comparative studies with other lakes. Expeditions wishing to undertake freshwater biological studies must contact the Natural History Museum in Reykjavík with their proposals. Recent work has included:

Collection and study of crustaceans, rotatoria, algae etc.

Measurement of chemical and physical quality of the water to compare with species.

Studies of the photosynthesis and respiration (dissolved oxygen measurement) of lake plankton to find an overall productivity.

Studies of Nostoc productivity.

Bathymetric survey by plane table followed by sampling of the three major trophic groups: herbivores, carnivores, and detritus feeders. Sampling of plankton, littoral and sublittoral habitats.

Studies of food concentrations for diving duck.

Useful Reports: UNIVERSITY OF NEWCASTLE (1973): Víkingavatn
WEYMOUTH GRAMMAR SCHOOL (1981): Víkingavatn

GEOLOGY

The youthful and dynamic nature of Iceland's geology makes it a 'Mecca' for geologists and geophysicists and it is important that all work be coordinated through the National Research Council. Broadly speaking the island consists of a Tertiary basalt province split in two by a neovolcanic zone (Figure 3) in which eruptions occur at regular intervals. Currently the vulcanological interest is focused upon the Krafla area, north-east of Lake Mývatn, where a section of the neovolcanic zone is being subjected to infusions and injections of magma that periodically appear at the surface along fissures as long as 9 km. The tectonic adjustments are of great interest as the blocks of crust are shunted around by earthquake and eruption activity. The results of such activity may be seen all over Iceland and there is plenty of scope for the geological enthusiast or student to interpret the patterns. Excellent air photographic coverage for a landscape largely devoid of vegetation is enormously helpful in interpreting the tectonics (Chapter 4).

If you wish to do more than 'look and see' which is perfectly legitimate for many types of expedition, then it is necessary to focus down on a specific topic of relatively small scope. Those undertaking a geological tour should

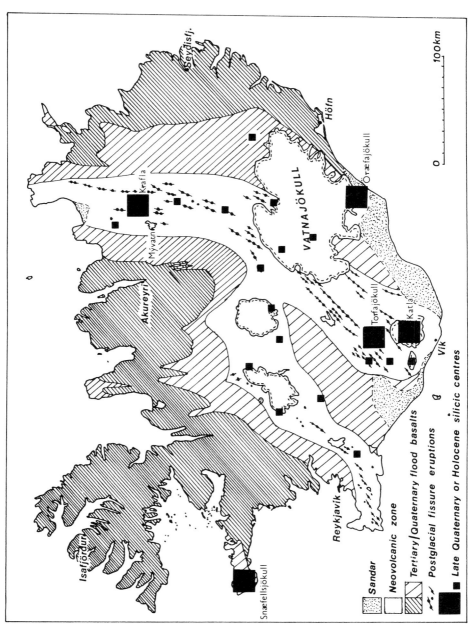

Fig. 3. Simplified geological map of Iceland (after Saemundsson, 1973).

Snæfellsjökull
Ísafjördur
Reykjavik
Akureyri
Mývatn
Krafla
Seydisfj.
Höfn
VATNAJÖKULL
Öræfajökull
Torfajökull
Katla
Vík

Sandar
Neovolcanic zone
Tertiary/Quaternary flood basalts
Postglacial fissure eruptions
Late Quaternary or Holocene silicic centres

0   100km

10

employ the same code of geological practice as is used in Britain but with especial attention to the conservation of sites. It is illegal to export rock speciments from Iceland without the express written consent of the National Research Council (see Chapter 10).

Recent work has included:

Mapping and study of individual flow units in the Tertiary basalts or in the neovolcanic zone.

Exploration of lava tube features (see Speleology below).

Interpretation of glacial and fluvio-glacial landforms.

Measurement of groundwater temperatures.

Studies of the morphology of lava flow forms.

Those considering a geological tour may contact the Iceland Unit for suggestions and advice.

Useful Reports: BILBOROUGH COLLEGE (1979): Mývatn
                      QUEEN MARY COLLEGE (1977): Mývatn

GEOMORPHOLOGY

Iceland is a perfect laboratory for field examination of geomorphological processes. The high humidity and prolific frost action on bare rock and detrital surfaces result in rapid activity in spring and autumn, the results of which may be observed in summer. Particular reference should be made of:

Landslides : these are especially notable in the Tertiary basalt country where post-glacial collapse has resulted in many fine examples.

Solifluxion forms : Polygons, stone stripes and lobes are common in the highlands and on the plateau surfaces within the Tertiary basalt zones. In the interior, eg. near Tungnafells, the extreme winter temperatures have caused tundra cracks to form.

Pro-glacial landforms : Some glaciers, but not all, are suitable as classrooms for studies of moraines, eskers, kettles, and erosional features. Some advice is necessary, perhaps from the Iceland Centre, since the proliferation of glacial debris enhanced by volcanic deposition can make such studies difficult to unravel. Till fabric studies, though tedious, can produce quick and interesting results.

Slopes : Comparative studies can be made to differentiate between, say, moraine, ice-cored moraine, scree, dirt cone surfaces (see Glaciology below), landslips and pro-talus ramparts.

Desert landsforms : The centre of Iceland, especially the tract between Askja and Dettifoss has developed some fine desert features including dunes, faceted pebbles and boulders, stoney pavements, and buttes. Detailed mapping and study of a specific area could be very rewarding.

Coastal Landforms : Most of these are perhaps too large for the majority of expeditions but Iceland has some fine haf and nehrung coastlines as well as

Fig. 5. Air photograph of Skaftafellsjökull and Svínafellsjökull. The National Park camp site lies centre left. © Iceland Geodetic Survey. Photo 5216G. 1982.

raised beaches and old clifflines.

Snowpatches : The detailed study of the surround of a snowpatch as it recedes through the summer with respect to soil, vegetation, moisture, weathered surfaces.

Soil Erosion : The effects of water and wind are prolific and have resulted in remnant soil structures (an equivalent to desert rock pedestals), deflation hollows, deflation surfaces, and, in some areas, redeposition as dunes.

Useful Reports: UNIVERSITY OF SHEFFIELD (1973): Sólheimajökull
                        EXETER/ST. ANDREWS (1981): Tröllaskagi

GLACIOLOGY

Iceland's glaciers are attractive to the young explorer because of their accessibility. Even the Vatnajökull attracts large numbers of enquiries (Chapter 15). But one must remember the maritime location of Iceland and the humid nature of the climate which means that the weather is very changeable and the wind chill conditions very severe inspite of the relatively low altitudes.

Iceland possesses a wide range of glacier type from cirques to icecaps and piedmont tongues. Of particular interest are the rock glacier forms that are to be found in the alpine mountains of the north, and the surging characteristics of a number of glaciers, both alpine and from icecaps. The glaciers are close to their melting point and possess a large amount of water both on and below their surfaces. They are also covered by much debris derived from volcanic eruptions. This debris creates distinctive dirt cone features.

Generally speaking the length of an expedition is too short for any really worthwhile work to be done on a one-off expedition. However, even a short period can produce results if the work is a follow-up to previous studies. The Iceland Unit keeps records of past expeditions and their work. The Iceland Unit ran a scheme in conjunction with the Science Institute in Reykjavik to build up a glacier inventory for Iceland. This concentrated on the area known as Tröllaskagi but there is no reason why, in conjunction with the institute, other groups should not carry out similar ground truth work in other areas.

The North Iceland Glacier Inventory programme (NIGI) is now concluded but work can still be done within the field area to build up on earlier work. The manual referred to in Chapter 18, written especially for NIGI, is applicable to all areas of Iceland.

The movement of many Icelandic glaciers is measured annually from a set of stakes (jöklarmerki). The number of stakes will vary, but the maximum is a straight line of four, laid out as follows:

No: 1. 700-800m from the snout.
No: 2. 200m from the snout.
No: 3. 20-30m from the snout.
No: 4. At the snout itself.

The annual measurements are taken by scientists, field workers, or local farmers and published annually in 'Jökull' the journal of the Iceland Glaciological Society. Records and station descriptions are kept at the Iceland Power Authority (Orkustofnun). Every stake has a number.

In most cases there are no up-to-date large scale maps of the snouts marking the position of the 'jöklarmerki' or that record the actual movement along the snout as a whole. In view of this there are ample opportunities for field parties to undertake this type of survey work. Some glaciers are already the preserve of existing groups, but enquiries through the Iceland Unit will reveal 'vacant' glaciers!

Expeditions should ensure that their studies are not made in isolation, but in the full understanding of the glacial system as a whole. This is best appreciated by study of the book 'Glaciers and Landscape'. Ideas for projects are outlined in the chapter on Glaciology in 'A Handbook for Expeditions', and in the Polar Expeditions manual (see above).

An outline plan for glaciological work in Iceland will be found at the end of this chapter.

Useful Reports: BRATHAY (1969): Skaftafell
BSES (1977): Tröllaskagi

HUMAN GEOGRAPHY

Most expeditions to Iceland seem to concern themselves with studies of the physical environment. This is to be regretted in a country with a fascinating human geography. To most this is an afterthought because it is rather harder to set up the programme before arriving in Iceland. We would advocate that all expeditions should have had a reconnaissance the previous year but this is not always within the bounds of costs. What we should be aiming at is a well considered piece of fieldwork rather than a "let's have a look at the local farms" at the end of a period studying glacial deposits. This should be research devoted specifically to the pattern of settlement and related questions. This is of intrinsic interest and, if one is a little more ambitious, can help us to understand some broader questions about human occupance in general.

There are compelling reasons for doing 'human' research, the main one being the fascinating but relatively simple pattern of settlement and its history. Before Iceland was settled in 874 AD, it was more or less virgin landscape, but, more important, this means that we can trace back, through 1100 years to its initiation, changes in the pattern of rural settlement. Surely there are few other areas in the world where we can do this with any degree of certainty. Admittedly there are no records for early settlement which are both complete and accurate for the island; for certain areas though, it is possible to gain an idea of distribution of farms from a careful reading of the sagas (see, for example, the map of Fljótshlíd in Njál's Saga). From the end of the seventeenth Century, complete records do begin to become available, and exist for the dates 1695, 1840, 1849, 1920, 1930, 1938, 1957 and

14

1965. A first task of fieldwork would be to bring these lists up to date by identifying the locations of all operative and abandoned farms in the chosen area. This would then give rise to the opportunity of tracing in considerable detail the ways that Icelandic farming has changed in terms of distribution and siting over a period of almost three hundred years. And a clear idea of the spatial pattern of change provides a framework for studies of agriculture and land use patterns.

In addition, Icelandic population statistics go back to 1703, and again we have an opportunity to examine changes in population patterns, for a whole nation, for a longer period of time than is probably possible anywhere else in the world.

Those wishing to undertake studies of patterns of current farming practices may like to use the questionnaire in Appendix D. It was designed for use in North Iceland and therefore it may not be wholly applicable to all parts of the island. Although it includes a translation it does really need an Icelandic speaking member of the group to explain the questions or to discuss the questions in more detail. Very often there are town children working on the farms during the holiday who may be able to help if the farmer speaks little English. Without this assistance misunderstandings may arise.

The more unusual industries may be of interest: aluminium smelting, geothermal energy, hydro-electric power, or the processing of fish, seaweed, and meat products.

Useful Reports: TORONTO UNIVERSITY (1973): Vestur-skaft.
EVESHAM HIGH SCHOOL (1975): Tröllaskagi.

HYDROLOGY

Hydrological studies may be interesting in relation to meteorology or supra-glacial studies. A study of the morphometry of small supra-glacial drainage basins is easily established as well as the various parameters of the well-defined meanders that develop on ice under almost ideal laboratory conditions. Pro-glacial hydrology is less easy because the streams respond to so many parameters and the drainage basins are not easy to define. Furthermore the streams are very turbulent and unstable making discharge measurements difficult to obtain. The most reliable method may be found in the article by Östrem.

For small streams you could exploit your expedition skills to construct a portable V-notch weir using wood and polythene.

There is a need for bathymetric surveys of many small lakes all over Iceland in a similar way to those carried out by Brathay in the Lake District (see "The Handbook for Expeditions"). Some of these are in unusual situations. In addition to the bathymetric survey it should be possible to carry out fresh or saltwater biological projects.

Useful Reports: BSES (1977): Tröllaskagi

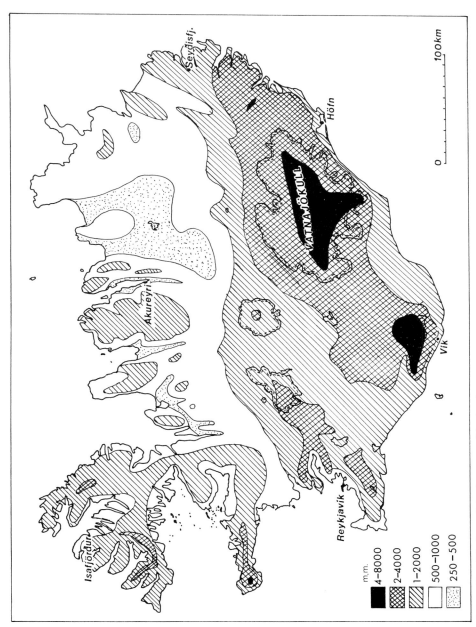

Fig. 4. Simplified precipitation map of Iceland.

16

METEOROLOGY

Iceland's situation, south of the arctic circle and athwart the passage of trans-Atlantic depressions, results in very variable weather conditions especially in the south of the country where the highest precipitation is to be found (Figure 4). But because of the pattern of relief interesting local variations of weather may be observed as, for example the fohn effect of the Öraefajökull massif protecting the farms on the Skaftafell side. The wide expanse of inland plateau north of the Vatnajökull is a veritable desert as much for the porosity of the substrate as the rainshadow effect of the mighty icecap. Glaciers and icecaps generate their own weather conditions and in Iceland steep pressure gradients develop between ice and bare sandur below resulting in frequent dust devils blowing across the plains. The effects upon soil erosion are readily appreciated. Those in steep-sided glacial valleys will soon appreciate the effect of aspect on temperatures.

Expeditions have kept meteorological records in connection with glacier ablation studies and soil erosion studies. The work of Dr. Ian Ashwell is recommended reading. Dr. Ashwell maintains that projects are rarely suitable as a main expedition aim, but rather connected to the main aim (eg. the study of glacier hydrology). Alternatively, well-conceived studies of small events may be successful (eg. air flow on slopes relative to farm sites, or widespread coverage of a fohn wind, mapping of a fohn wind, the effect of different types of surface (ice, moraine, grass etc) on the air temperatures above them, katabatic winds).

Meteorological studies are quite inadequate for a study of glacier mass balance *per se*. The period in the field is far too short and the accuracy of the measurements too unreliable.

Meteorology does provide the opportunity for members to use a little initiative in designing and building their own equipment: eg. rain gauges out of old washing-up liquid bottles, wind vanes from old bicycle hubs, wheatstone bridges for electrical thermometers. With such simple and cheap equipment one can saturate an area to obtain a great deal of valuable data.

The Iceland weather bureau (Veđurstofnun) publishes monthly statistics and an annual summary. The Iceland Unit holds copies of two complete years and averages from 1930 to 1960. We also have access to monthly averages from 1960.

Those with an interest in acid rain and atmospheric pollution may be interested in records kept by Iceland's National Centre for Hygiene and Environmental Protection which came into existence in 1982. However there has been a recording station 60 km east of Reykjavik since 1960 measuring rain water contaminants, sulphur dioxide, sulphates, chlorates and so on. This has been run by the Meteorological Institute. The station is deliberately situated well away from any indigenous pollution sources so as to try to detect pollution from abroad. A new station is nearing completion in Reykjavik.

ORNITHOLOGY:

Iceland's mid-ocean position provides habitat for birds that are at the extreme edge of their north American or European range as well as the truly Arctic species that many will come to see. Most are migrants or visitors while only 73 nest regularly on the island. The Lake Mývatn area probably has the world's largest concentration of breeding ducks, notably the Barrow's goldeneye. Perhaps the attraction to the visitor is the tameness of the birdlife.

An Act of Parliament provides for bird protection in Iceland. All birds, their nests and eggs are protected with certain exceptions within defined seasons. The law applies particularly to eider duck and special permission is required for the taking of photographs or film of eagles, gyr falcon, snowy owls, and little auk in or near their nests. Only the Icelandic Museum of Natural History has the right to ring or mark wild birds and no rings other than those issued by them may be used. It is absolutely illegal to possess birds, eggs, eggshells, or nests let alone export them from Iceland. The full text of the law can be viewed at the Iceland Unit.

That many Icelandic birds are on the endangered list may be attributed to a number of factors including a general warming of the climate, drainage of wetlands, escaped mink, poisoning, egg collecting, and disturbance by visitors on the breeding grounds.

A recent survey (Petersen Æ. 1984) presented in Icelandic to the Nature Conservation Council includes four categories of birds which include recent, and perhaps temporary immigrants such as the brambling and wood sandpiper.

Threatened by extinction: little auk, grey phalarope, water rail.

Recent immigrants with low populations: snowy owl, pochard, house sparrow, fieldfare, barnacle goose, wood sandpiper, brambling.

Endangered species: white-tailed eagle, slavonian grebe.

Rare, or common only to particular locations: gyr falcon, shoveler, short-eared owl, great northern diver, Barrow's goldeneye, harlequin, gadwall, goosander, storm petrel, Leach's petrel, manx shearwater.

Please do not write asking for bird rings. The limited supply is reserved for groups known to be ringing large numbers of birds of a single species. Expeditions wanting to ring birds must be **ringing expeditions** with no other commitments, and should have the recommendation of the Ringing Section of the British Trust for Ornithology or its equivalent.

Generally speaking the expedition season is too short for any worthwhile scientific projects to be recommended to youth expeditions especially if the party lacks a really experienced ornithologist leader. Many suggested programmes are much too specialised for the time available, the personnel involved, or the type of expedition. Expeditions generally have diverse interests, and this again makes it very difficult to select areas where all the interests can be satisfied.

With only a small staff the Icelandic Museum of Natural History cannot deal effectively with the annual flood of requests from all over the world. They suggest that:

(a) Enquiries of a **specific** scientific nature should be sent direct to them.

(b) Enquiries of a more general nature should be sent to the Iceland Unit.

(c) Anyone wishing to call at the Museum is most welcome to do so. This is probably the quickest way to obtain the answer to your request. The Museum is at Laugavegur 105. It is a research establishment, and not a museum in the usual sense of the word.

Studies that involve least disturbance to colonies include:

Behavioural studies, feeding activities at different hours, predation etc.

Colony counts.

Useful Reports: NEWCASTLE UNIVERSITY (1973): Arnavatn/ Vikingavatn

PEDOLOGY

Icelandic soils tend to be light and friable and derived principally from weathered basalt, wind-blown loess deposits, or volcanic ash. A feature of many Icelandic soils is the ash (tephra) layers from the past eruptions which, when dated, indicate the rapid growth of loessal soils. Their destruction since The Settlement Period has left surfaces open to wind and water erosion. Katabatic winds off glaciers and icecaps, drawn across unvegetated sandar result in powerful destructive winds. Many plateau areas have been affected by frost heaving to produce frost hummocks (púfur) which, especially where heavily grazed, show their own brand of soil deterioration.

The mapping of soils and studies of their profiles, composition, and texture is interesting when related to other studies such as post-glacial plant colonisation, tephra studies, soil organisms, vegetation, hot springs, soil erosion etc. Simple BDH soil testing equipment will yield adequate results.

Please note that the Icelandic soils are fragile and take a long time to recuperate. The digging of soil pits should be avoided.

SPELAEOLOGY

Iceland has a number of caves, or tubes, formed within lava flow units. They represent the channels occupied by fast flowing basalt beneath a solidified crust. When the effusion from the vent ceases the flow stops and the tubes drain of their lava. The resultant forms are of great interest and while most studies have taken place on Hawaii Iceland's rather smaller versions (as yet) do show a variety of forms. The three best known tubes are Surtshellir, Stefánshellir and Raufarhólshellir.

Useful Reports: SHEPTON MALLET CAVING CLUB (1970): Raufarhólshellir
SOMERSET YOUTH SERVICE (1972): Grettishellir

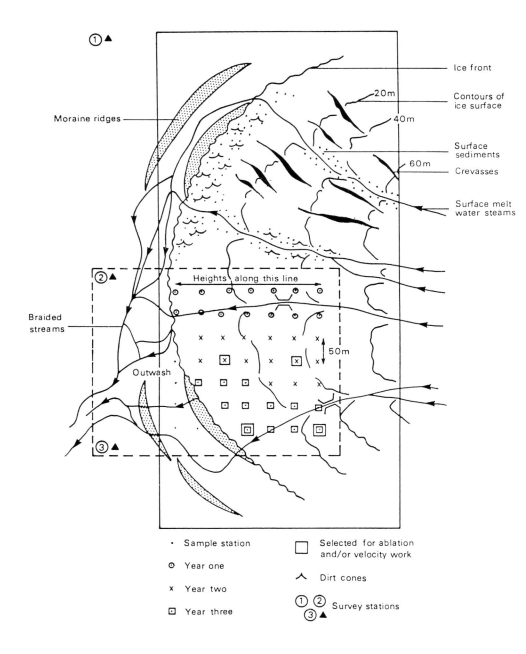

Fig. 6. Model base map for a glaciological fieldwork programme.

ZOOLOGY

The fauna of Iceland has been described in a series of papers published by the Museum in Copenhagen. These papers are in English and describe the distribution of most species and details of their biology. Identification of specimens is often a specialist task, but useful survey work can be carried out with the minimum of equipment. The 24 hour cycle of daylight of the Icelandic summer is of interest in the study of activity cycles, especially when comparisons can be made with specimens of the same species in Britain or mainland Europe. Other topics have included:

Observations of mice, and their activities (Mus. silvaticum)

Snails (there are rather few easily identifiable species).

See also the sections of Ornithology and Entomology.

A GLACIOLOGICAL FIELDWORK PROGRAMME

This outline was originally prepared for the Brathay Exploration Group to provide a framework within which to place their studies in S.E. Iceland where the glacier tongues are rather large. Brathay used to visit the Skaftafell National Park every year and were therefore able to build up on their own groundwork. Nevertheless the same principles can apply to one-off groups who would like their own work to lead on to something else. If they have done the groundwork then others can follow on and a useful job will have been done. A National Research Council permit is a prerequisite to any such study.

THE FRAMEWORK:

The framework is designed to be relatively straight forward, cumulative and suitable for the training of up-and-coming expedition leaders.

We suggest the detailed examination of a **section** of a glacier over a number of years. A typical glacier snout envisaged for this sort of survey is shown in Figure 5. Most glaciers are far too large for small expeditions to tackle as a whole. The study should take place at two scales:

1. **A Large Scale Map** : this should be of the whole snout area (1:5,000 or larger) showing the ice margin, general areas of crevassing, dirt cover, meltwater streams etc.

2. **Detailed Survey** : this should be of a smaller area within the mapped area referred to above and may be only 400m. x 400m. to include both ice margin and outwash (see Fig. 6), and designed so that sampling may take place on a grid pattern with points 50m. apart. The grid would be used to obtain an objective distribution of sample points, obtain an easy basis for mapping a measured property afterwards (eg. contouring), and to instil a scientific approach in those undertaking the experiments.

MEASUREMENTS:

These do not have to be taken at every sampling point (grid intersection) every year, nor do all data have to be collected from every grid intersection. The most important thing is to build up the programme in a logical manner. Do not progress on to stage two or three until the previous stage has been completed.

THE PROGRAMME:

Stage One : Establishment of good primary ground control on peripheral rock or moraine. Rock is preferable for control points.

Stage Two : Selection and mapping of stations to be used for data collection.

Stage Three : Recording of data and/or re-mapping according to equipment available, numbers in the party, expertise, and the inclination of the expedition leaders and members.

DATA COLLECTION:

The following data could be included within the programme:

Annual mapping of glacier surface streams (course, depth, width etc.)

The above used to determine discharge measured daily and/or hourly on at least one occasion during the expedition.

Measurement of conductivity:

(i) melted ice samples taken on a grid pattern over the area.

(ii) melt stream water sampled 'in situ'.

Repeated profiles up and across the selected area using the grid intersections as datum points. Profiles should be along flow lines in the ice.

Sediment concentration: filter and weigh sediment from a quantity of melted ice. Retain samples for mineralogical analysis.

Ice density measurements.

Ablation measurements.

Mapping of stake net movements.

Dirt Cone studies. The mapping of dirt bands and studies of their particle size and shape.

IMPLEMENTATION:

The starting point for novices is the chapter on 'Glaciology' in "The Expedition Handbook".

The North Iceland Glacier Inventory: Manual for Field Survey Parties is also a useful starting point because it places basic mapwork studies within an overall framework of recommended procedures as layed down by the International Commission for Snow and Ice.

2 CONSERVATION IN ICELAND

BACKGROUND

The conservation of the Icelandic landscape is one of the most important expedition responsibilities. All expedition members should have the opportunity to be exposed to the principles of conservation in this ecologically sensitive environment and to this end the Iceland Centre has produced a video programme that may be borrowed for educational purposes (see Appendix H).

The Icelandic landscape represents the product of a tenuous balance between land and natural forces. The climate in this northerly latitude is unpredictable and often extreme. Rain, snow, and high winds can lash the rocks with great ferocity. The rocks and soils are young and often unconsolidated so that their fragility may be revealed by wind and water erosion. It is thought that when the first settlers came to Iceland more than half of the total land area was covered in vegetation. Human settlement and annual grazing eventually led to the destruction of the woodlands and the deterioration of the soils and vegetation. Today only about 25% of the land is vegetated of which only 1% is wooded. The geographical isolation of the island results in a paucity of flora so that 31 of the 475 species of wild vascular plants are protectd by law. If we add to this picture the periodic damage caused by falls of volcanic ash, the ravages of 'glacier bursts', and the not inconsiderable effect of tourism we can appreciate the concern in Iceland for nature protection.

The need for conservation meaures were recognised in the last century and truly began in 1907 when the Althing enacted "A Law on Forestry and Erosion Control" and the State Soil Conservation Service was created. Many small projects were tackled in the years that followed but not real progress was made until the 5-year plan of 1975-79 which tackled large areas between 100 and 400 m. above sea level and bounded by exclusion fences.

NATURE CONSERVATION ACT

In April 1971 the Althing passed the Nature Conservation Act with three clearly expressed purposes:

1. To encourage the intercourse of Man and Nature in such a way that life or land be not heedlessly wasted, nor sea, freshwater or air polluted.

2. To ensure as far as possible the course of natural processes according to their own laws, and the protection of exceptional and historical aspects of Icelandic nature.

3. To enhance the nation's access to and familiarity with Nature.

The Act also clarified the public's right of access to land as follows:

1. Everyone is entitled to free passage through, and stay in, areas lying outside the property of registered farms for legitimate purpose.

Fig. 7.   Map of protected areas in Iceland.   1. Country parks, 2. National Parks, 3. National monuments, 4. Nature reserves.

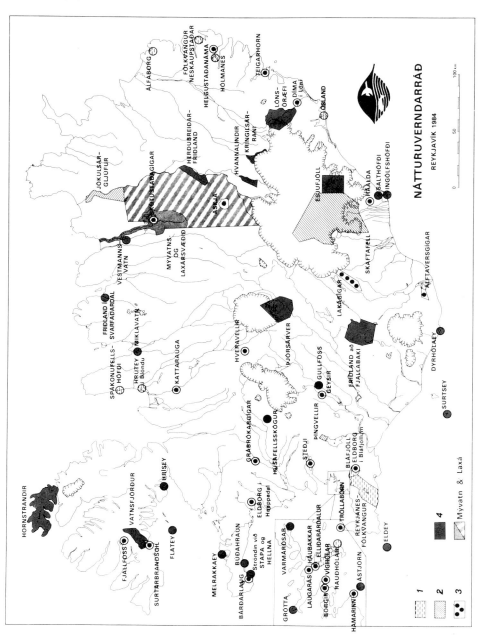

2. Walkers may pass through privately owned ground, provided it is uncultivated and unfenced, and also provided that their stay does not disturb livestock or cause inconvenience to those holding legal rights to the land.

3. On fenced ground, the permission of the owner is required for the purpose of passing through or staying on the land. The same applies to cultivated land.

4. Everyone shall take care to avoid unnecessary damage to the nature of the country. Damage to nature in an illegal way, whether intentionally or inadvertently, is punishable.

5. It is the duty of the Council to prohibit all unnecessary driving outside roads and marked trails, where this can cause the ravage of nature.

6. In the open countryside it is prohibited to throw away or leave behind refuse which can constitute danger or defilement, or deposit such waste or refuse into the sea, on beaches or sea coasts, into rivers or on river banks, streams or stream banks. Rest areas and camping grounds shall at all times be left clean and tidy, and nothing must be left behind which despoils the environment.

7. Vegetation must not be damaged or ruined unnecessarily, either by the tearing up of moss, heaths or shrubs in any manner, nor shall water supplies, whether rivers, brooks, lakes or wells, be polluted.

8. Wherever a fire is lit in the open, this shall be done either in a specially prepared hearth, or on soil of a type where there is no danger of its spreading. Care shall be taken that the fire has been entirely extinguished before leaving the site.

NATIONAL PARKS AND NATURE RESERVES (Figure 7)

Following vigourous activity by the Nature Conservation Council (Náttúruverndarráð) Iceland now has three National Parks (Thingvellir, Skaftafell, and Jökulsárgljúfur), and one area, Mývatn-Laxá, that has been designated by special law (1974). Of the National Parks only Thingvellir is not managed by the Council as it was established separately by the Althing in 1928. In addition there are:

> 10 Landscape Reserves (eg. Gullfoss)
> 17 Wildlife Reserves (eg. Surtsey)
> 23 Natural Monuments (eg. Geysir)
> 9 Nature Parks (eg. Bláfjöll ski area)
> over 200 areas designated as worthy of protection

Figure 7 shows the distribution of these parks and reserves but the 1984 report of the Nature Conservation Council also shows a further 36 sites singled out for priority protection in the next three years and another 230 sites that are in need of protection. In this handbook we refer to these as Category 2 and Category 3 sites respectively. (Figure 8).

These figures will almost certainly be out of date by the time that you read this paragraph. However the message is still clear: expeditions must be

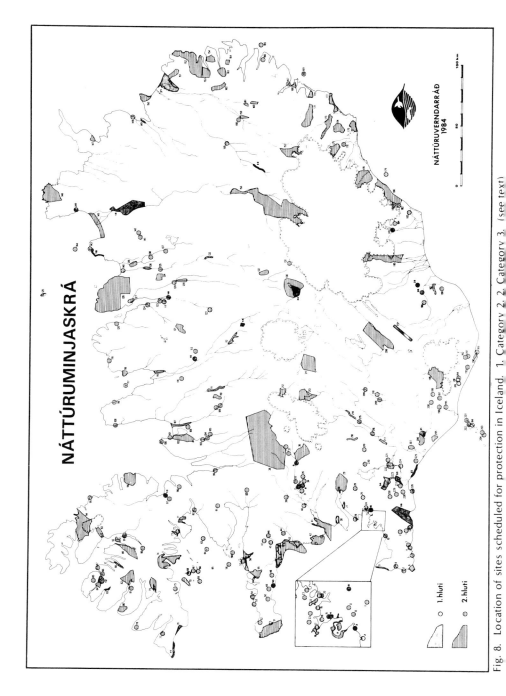

NÁTTÚRUMINJASKRÁ

NÁTTÚRUVERNDARRÁÐ
1984

100 km

o 1.hluti
⊕ 2.hluti

Fig. 8. Location of sites scheduled for protection in Iceland. 1, Category 2. 2, Category 3. (see text)

26

aware of the location and status of reserves in an environment that is ecologically sensitive to over-use.

To enable Iceland to maintain its existing vegetation and to reclaim that which has been destroyed requires the help and understanding not only of Icelanders but of visitors and especially large groups who by sheer weight of numbers are capable of irreparable damage.

The full list of protected areas is given in Appendix B.

AN EXPEDITION CODE

The code that follows applies to movement in any part of Iceland, not only in the parks and reserves.

1. If working within or close to a reserve you must have the permission of the Nature Conservation Council and, where appropriate, the landowners.

2. Do not camp within reserves without special permission.

3. Take nothing but pictures, observations and measurements without the express written consent of the Nature Conservation Council and National Research Council (see Chapter 10)

4. Pack out what you take in. Do not drop or bury litter.

5. Keep all water clean. Others will be using it after you.

6. Do not damage vegetation of any kind, or disturb wildlife and livestock. People's livelihood may depend upon it.

7. Do not light fires.

8. Keep to the track when driving cross-country. Tyre marks on virgin ground will be visible for many years.

9. Keep to marked footpaths when requested to do so.

10. Observe the conservation rules and heed wardens' advice.

11. Always treat your surroundings with respect.

PROTECTED PLANT AND BIRD SPECIES

The list of protected plants is given in Appendix A and the laws applying to the protection of birds and geological sites are referred to in the relevant sections of Chapter 1. and Chapter 10. In some instances the penalty is imprisonment.

Fig. 9. Expedition locations, 1962-82.

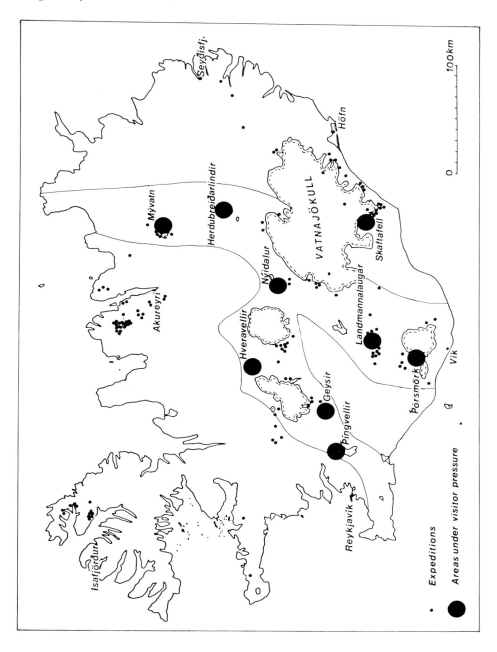

3 FIELDWORK AREAS

INTRODUCTION

Over the years it has become apparent that expeditions tend to concentrate in certain areas. These areas are now so visited by groups and tourists that they are ceasing to be ideal expedition venues. Expeditions will undoubtedly wish to visit the classic sites such as Skaftafell or Mývatn but we would suggest that by seeking alternative locations for the main part of the expedition you will be more likely to find the 'expedition experience' that your members have in mind.

The Iceland National Research Council, the Iceland Nature Conservation Council and the Iceland Unit have jointly agreed to consider proposals for alternative sites. As these are likely to vary from year to year it is felt inappropriate to include them in this book. Expeditions are therefore invited to write to the Iceland Unit. Figure 9. shows the principal locations chosen by expeditions between 1962 and 1982 but excludes those groups who were touring from place to place. By implication the black spots are those to avoid although this is not strictly true because some areas have a greater capacity than others. The honeypots of the central highlands and plateau areas are the most sensitive because their season is short both for tourists and for vegetation growth so that the intensity of use is higher than the coastal areas or the more alpine Tertiary basalt zones.

Any expedition will wish to experience a much of Iceland and its culture as is possible in a short time. Costs will preclude extensive tours so itineraries need to be designed so as to take in different routes in to and out from the base camp.

CLASSIFICATION OF AREAS

Preusser in his "Landscapes of Iceland" devised a nine-fold division of Icelandic landscape types which we have used as the basis for our divisions. However his system is not wholly applicable to one designed for expedition logistics and so we have had to considerably modify his primary and secondary boundaries. His primary divisions are:

    I.   Vegetated Lowlands
    II.   Sandar Plains
    III.   Fjord Landscapes
    IV.   Tundra Plateau
    V.   Highlands
    VI.   Desert-like plateaux outside the Young Volcanic Landscape
    VII.   Young Volcanic Landscape
    VIII.   Glaciers
    IX.   Islands

Bibliographic material may be found in Chapter 18

Fig. 10. Expedition Regions (based on Preusser, 1976).

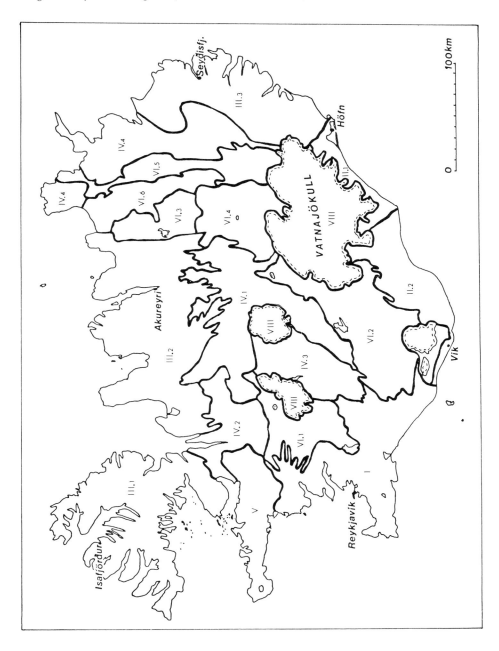

I. VEGETATED LOWLANDS

1. South-west Iceland

The area here termed south-west Iceland is defined more by distance from Reykjavík than any particular landscape type. Broadly speaking it consists of the coastal lowland areas, which by their occupied nature make them unsuitable for most expeditions, and the Reykjanes peninsula which strictly belongs to a young volcanic province.

The region comes into its own at Easter when field study groups may base themselves at Reykjavík or, say, Hella and undertake a variety of excursions. Hella is well placed for visits to a number of the Icelandic 'must sees' such as Gullfoss, Geysir, and Thingvellir. Excursions might include:

Thingvellir and Kaldidalur: site of original Viking parliament, rift valley, step faulting, shield volcano, lava forms, cold desert.

Thjórsardalur: basalt formations, Hekla ash deposits, Viking settlement, hydro-electric power station.

Gullfoss and Geysir: waterfalls, geysers, desert margin.

South coast: glaciers, Skógar folk museum, sandar outwash plains, cliffs and beaches.

Hveragerdi: geothermally-heated greenhouses, Kerid explosion crater.

Reykjanes Peninsula: Krîsuvîk hot springs, palagonite ridges, lava fields, Graenavatn explosion crater, Grindavîk fishing village.

The Reykjanes peninsular, although close to Reykjavík, will afford an 'expedition experience' to the group on a low budget. It is an area much used by Icelandic schools for fieldwork in geology and botany. The Icelandic Scout Association has a camp site at Úlfljótsvatn (south of Thingvallavatn) which, subject to their permission would be ideal for both field studies and hill walking.

The actual lake Thingvellir is included in this area but most interest lies on its northern shores in region VI.1.

The northern part of this south-west region includes the very attractive Borgarfjördur which on the face of it is typical strandflat country with ice polished rocks riding a level plain fringed by myriads of small rocky islands. The district includes some fascinating volcanic vents and lava flows, notably Eldborgarhraun and Gullborgarhraun and in the north-east corner the Grábrók craters and moss-covered flows. All are under the protection of the Nature Conservation Council.

II. SANDAR and their fringing mountains

1. Austur-Skaftafellsýsla

This must be one of the most outstanding wilderness areas in Iceland on account of its high mountains, glaciers, and vast outwash plains. The three are inseparable. Iceland's highest mountain, Hvannadalshnúkur rises from sea level to 2119 m. in a horizontal distance of only nine kilometers. From the lofty crater of Öraefajökull the glaciers cascade over 1,000m icefalls to re-form with magnificent ogives. It is no wonder that the Skaftafell district has been designated a National Park. Further east the ice approaches the coast in the broad tongue of the Breiðamerkurjökull which discharges icebergs into the lagoon Jökulsárlón. Once past the outlet the country again becomes mountainous with large valley glaciers descending between bold, jagged mountains.

For many years the Brathay Exploration Group have carried out annual programmes here. Their principal interest was the colonies of arctic tern and great skua but their work has included repeated surveys of glacier tongues (notably Falljökull), studies of sand dune orientation on the Ingólfshöfdi headland, and, most importantly, monitoring of the vegetation changes within the National Park as a contribution to long term management plans. Their reports are available for study by contacting the Group at Brathay (see Appendix F). Numerous other glacier studies have been carried out further east by both Brathay and the British Schools Exploring Society.

Although very dynamic and attractive access to the western part is in some ways limited. Within the National Park camping is restricted to the official site. Outside of that the available ground for base camps is limited and often privately owned grazings. East of the Jökulsárlón however the situation changes a little because the approach valleys are longer and more remote. Acess is not too difficult and approval for expedition work would be readily obtained.

Access by road can be achieved on the daily bus from Reykjavík to Höfn or by chartered bus through tour operators. Regular domestic flights go to Höfn but no longer to Fagurhólsmýri.

2. Vestur-Skaftafellsýsla (incl. Eyjafjöll)

The western end of this district is probably the most interesting especially where access to the mountains is possible. The glacier Sólheimajökull has attracted much attention but it should not be too swamped by visitors as the landowners are not keen on seeing too many people within their grazings. Note that its outwash stream discharges sulphur from the subglacial volcano Katla which last erupted in 1918 causing floods and devastation on the plains below. This and other glacial outpourings have gradually extended the coastline to include former offshore islands which stand like fortresses from their sandar. Birdlife is a feature of this zone and the cliffs and beach at Dýrhólaey, near Vík, are a must for a visit.

Apart from the glacial interest this area has not received much attention from expeditions, perhaps because it is well populated or rather narrow in extent. West-east travel in the hills is more difficult than south-north. One notable route is that between Mýrdalsjökull and Eyjafjallajökull. As you travel east the mountains pull back from the coast and larger glacial tongues descend from the Mýrdalsjökull. Streams and dust storms become the major obstacles to access. Once across the desert-like Mýrdalssandur the scenery is dominated by the Skaftáeldar lava flows of 1783 until you reach Kirkjubaejarklaustur. East of here the mountains change again and separate the coastal strip from the western edges of Vatnajökull. The ice-dammed lake Graenalón has been visited in the past and provides a fine expedition setting but it is difficult of access and requires good planning.

There is an excellent folk museum at Skógar which includes rebuilt turf houses and innumerable artefacts. The tranquility of the site enables one to appreciate Viking Iceland.

III. FJORD LANDSCAPES

1. Vestfirdir

The Vestfirðir peninsula is in the old grey basalt province and offers some of the best opportunities for a true expedition. The peninsula has a low population, is remote and offers a range of fieldwork possibilities between coast and icecap. Hitherto, expedition attention has focused on the north side of Ísafjarðardjúp where Sugden and John (op cit) carried out studies of the Kaldalón and the small glacier at its head. Several expeditions have followed up this work or have concentrated on the deglaciation vegetation sequences. More recently (1973-75) Durham University had a programme investigating Pleistocene temperature gradient changes for the North Atlantic. This work covered the entire peninsula and include work on the margins of the diminishing Drangajökull icecap.

From a purely recreational point of view the coastline between Baeir and Norðurfjörður is marvellous hiking country. You can approach from either Baeir or Ingólfsfjörður whence a six day hike will bring you to the manned lighthouse at Látravík.

Expeditions have explored Drangajökull and have also canoed the extreme north-west coastline. Although largely abandoned with respect to permanent dwellings the farmhouses are still in private ownership, are used in the summer and should not be entered under any circumstances.

It would be a pity to ignore the opportunities afforded by the rest of the peninsula, especially the south coast from Reykjanes to Látrbjarg (Barðaströnd). The scenery together with the opportunities for botanical, ornithological, geological and geomorphological work make this a very attractive area for expeditions. The district does include several locations singled out for protection but they are in Category 2 (see Chapter 2).

The route out and back to the Vestfirðir can be balanced in a number of ways to provide expeditions with a broader experience of Iceland and its landscape. The direct route out can take in the whaling station (Hvalfjörður) and the neo-volcanic district of Kólbeinsstaðahreppur which includes the impressive Eldborg crater (30 mins walk from the farm Snorrastaðir). An alternative route, perhaps camping at Húsafell on the way, incorporates the old parliament site and rift valley (Thingvellir) and the glacial-volcanic desert along Kaldidalur. The Húsafell district (see Area IV.2) is of great interest.

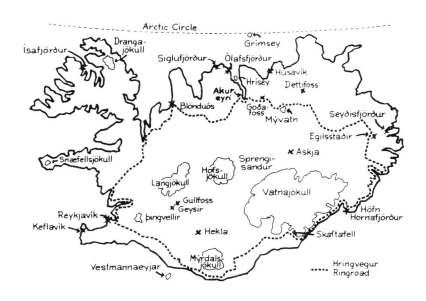

Experts on Excursion Organizing
in
Northern Iceland

Daily buses from Akureyri to Myvatn

15th May — 15th September

Special Transport and Sightseeing for Expeditions and Special Interest Groups easily arranged.

2. Northern Highlands

The four peninsulas of Skagi, Tröllaskagi, Flateyardalsheiði and Tjörnes constitute this northern sweep of Iceland. Tröllaskagi is well-known and was much visited by groups that were working on the North Iceland Glacier Inventory between 1973 and 1978. It is an ideal expedition location which offers high mountain country, numerous manageable, small glaciers, and interesting proglacial features. In itself, apart from the tip of the Skagi peninsula, it does not offer the truly volcanic side of Iceland but this dimension can be added with a visit to Mývatn or to volcanic sites closer to Reykjavík.

It is also good trekking country but care should be taken in route planning because the maps cannot always be relied upon where the slopes are extremely steep. The basalt is very loose and often coated in slippery mosses. Air photographs can be of great assistance to supplement the maps. Shadows cast by low angled sunlight often reveal sharp pinnacled ridges that quite clearly are impassable.

Skagi is not so well known yet would be interesting for a small expedition with geological (Pleistocene volcanics), botanical, or limnological inclinations. This might represent a focal point for one phase of an expedition programme. Access is easy via Blönduós where all services and a camp site are available.

On account of its landscape, vegetation and birdlife the entire Flateyardalsheiði peninsula has been designated for protection in the near future. It has been abandoned by a permanent population since the mid-1950's but is still extensively used as sheep grazing and the farmers are not too happy about its use by groups. Since access is principally along north-south valleys with no east-west connection it is not suitable for large expeditions anyway. Very small research parties with specific objectives and pemission from the land owners may be permitted.

The coastal scenery of Tjörnes peninsula is very striking but not very suitable for expeditions as the shore is largely inaccessible because of cliffs or private land. Should you visit any of the geological sites there you are urgently requested to respect them even though others have wrought enormous damage.

Apart from the Quaternary flows of Skagi this region is one of Tertiary flood basalts similar to those elucidated in Eastern Iceland by Walker and others. A long-standing geological problem is the status of the highest summit lavas in the peaks around Akureyri and Hörgardalur. These overlie tuffs both north and south of Hörgardalur but their equivalence has yet to be demonstrated or disproved. Detailed mapping of the sub-summit lava tuffs of the Glerádalur-Öxnadalur region to the north and west would be a valuable exercise as yet only partially attempted (Sowan, 196). At lower levels, detailed work on zeolite zoning, particularly in the north would be useful.

The northern fjords are easily reached by air to Akureyri or Sauðarkrókur, or by daily bus to Akureyri. Many groups vary their outward and return journeys by combining bus and air travel or by travelling the coast road on the outward journey and the Kjölur or Sprengisandur route through the interior on the return.

Base camp would almost certainly need to be on a farm. A reconnaissance would be the best way to check this but local contacts can sometimes be achieved through the Iceland Unit.

3. Eastern Highlands

The mountains of Eastern Iceland rise abruptly from the coast to between 1100 and 1200m. In the 1960's the story of these impressive geological piles unravelled by G. P. L. Walker then at Imperial College, London. Since then very little work has been done by expeditions except that by Clapperton and Croot on the surges of Eyjabakkajökull.

Because they are so precipitous and loose the mountains themselves are not very accessible from the coast. Long hikes up the many valleys are necessary. These valleys lead to the edge of the plateau which then slopes gently west towards Fljótsdalur. However those valleys which dissect the western side of the ancient plateau, east of Skriðdalur for example, look interesting from a geomorphological point of view. Reconnaisance of the air photographs would reveal a number of sites for studies of landslides and associated phenomena. The only permanent ice is in the southern part on Þrándajökull and Hofsjökull both of which merit examination. An expedition landing at Seyðisfjörður or Egilsstaðir could approach up Fljótsdalur and then have access to both these ice masses, the eastern edge of Vatnajökull and peaks such as Hornbrynja (961m) and Snaefell (1833m).

IV. TUNDRA PLATEAUX

1. Central Plateau

The plateau lies at about 1000m sloping gently southward from the heads of the valleys of Eyjafjörður and Skagafjörður. Other than for very specific research this area is unsuitable for most expedition purposes. Remote, yes, but largely featureless and barren. Furthermore there is considerable Icelandic research interest there in view of proposals for a new hydro-electric scheme in the western part. The western part is rather wetter with a number of lakes some of which have been studied.

If planning a west-east traverse of Iceland on foot the north side of the Hofsjökull is a difficult area to cross on account of the numerous, ever-changing stream courses. These are glacial, turbulent and cold. When the RAF team crossed here in 1972 and finally arrived at the east coast they mey with some vehicle-borne Icelanders who reassured them that "It's quicker by road, you know."

On the basis of landscape this zone also extends into Region IV.3 but from an expedition point of view we treat this separately. However the west flank of the Sprengisandur route is included. This is a mononously flat area inhabited by thousands of greylag geese. Access by way of the Sprengisandur route is rarely possible before the middle of July.

2. West Central Plateau

This represents the dying edges of the previous region where the monotonous plateau is dipping towards the north and west coasts. In few areas is the ground free from thick coatings of moraine but it does include numerous small lakes and pools and isolated clumps of vegetation taking refuge above the general swampiness. In the southern part of the area a series of dry valleys have been interpreted as subglacial fluvial channels (Ashwell).

3. Central Highlands

Because of its centrality and proximity to two icecaps this area has always attracted attention. It is eminently suitable for true expedition work subject to the following observations:

(a) The route through the middle (Kjalvegur/Kjölur) is well used in the summer and this automatically eliminates the hot spring site at Hveravellir on account of the number of visitors. The pressure at Hveravellir is such that large groups are advised not to base themselves there.

(c) Thjórsaver, the area south and east of the Hofsjökull is a protected area for pinkfooted geese and permission will not normally be granted for expeditions to stay there.

This therefore leaves the following:

The Kerlingarfjöll Mountains : These snowclad rhyolite peaks with their small hot spring areas make a very dramatic landscape. In the summer months there is a ski school here at Ásgard and therefore quite a lot of people in the vicinity of the huts. Too much activity here is to be discouraged but camping may take place lower down the track and expeditions can move in to the camp area north of here towards Blágnípa where the ice from Hofsjökull descends to provide an interesting proglacial area. The climbing potential of this area is covered by Chapter 14.

Hagavatn : The changes in the margins of Langjökull have long been a source of interest at this point. There is an interesting series of overflow channels and evidence of periodic glacier surges which have influenced the shape of the lake. This is also the source region of the sand which is periodically blown over the farmlands that lie to the south-west. Problems of soil erosion can be studied here. This is good expedition country for geology, geomorphology and glaciology.

Geysir-Hvítarvatn : Several groups, with vehicle support, have walked this challenging route with its desert landscape and impressive lines of volcanic ridges (Jarlhettur). Recommended.

4. North-east

This area is rarely visited and one must be honest and say that at face-value it does not look too attractive for anything other than the true research expedition. It is an undulating tundra plateau crossed by numerous small streams and frequented by many small lakes and bogs. This is predominantly a Tertiary basalt area with Old Grey basalts in the west and north-west. The most northerly part of Iceland the Hraunhafnartangi peninsula is interesting for its truly tundra vegetation, periglacial landforms (polygons), and its geology which includes palagonite and post-glacial volcanism.

Aircraft fly from Reykjavík and Akureyri to Raufarhöfn. Buses depart from Húsavík and Egilsstaðir.

V. HIGHLANDS

1. Snaefellsnes

The Snaefellsnes peninsula is a little difficult to classify within our system because it consists of both highland and coastal lowland. In many ways it is similar to the fjord landscapes but without the indented coastline. It also fits into all the geological zones having both older Tertiary basalts and younger volcanism. Hitherto it has not received enough attention from expeditions although it is very attractive. On the one hand it offers a transect from coast to icecap (Snaefellsjökull — 1446m), and on the other a mountainous backbone that is geomorphologically and botanically interesting. Access is easy yet once away from the road you are remote. The area is therefore ideal for Duke of Edinburgh Award type expeditions. And expeditions wishing to blend a variety of disciplines.

There are a number of Category 3. (Chapter 2) conservation areas in this district of which the area referred to as 'Undir Jökli' is the most sensitive; notably around Búðir (vegetation) and the Arnastapi headland (birdlife).

Volcanic craters and lava flows are found at numerous sites around the peninsula notably on the southern approach (Eldborgarhraun and Gullborgarhraun) and on the north coast, the Berserkjahraun. Snaefellsjökull occupies the crater of a composite volcano. The mountains contain several cirques that were apparently occupied by remnant ice in the 1930's.

For routes into and out of Snaefellsnes refer to the last paragraph of Area III.1 Vestfirðir. There are daily buses from Reykjavík to the principal towns of the peninsula.

VI. YOUNG VOLCANIC LANDSCAPES

1. South-west

To date expeditions have largely ignored this district but for a few Duke of Edinburgh Award-type groups for whom it is eminently suitable. Húsafell is a good point for a base camp from which to undertake exploratory acclimatisation hikes. It has the advantage of good access, proximity to Reykjavík, considerable landscape interest and the opportunity for remote expeditions within the glacio-volcanic interior. Tour parties regularly use the route from Thingvellir to Húsafell (Kaldidalur) which would be your means of access but it still has considerable interest and once you move away from the road you are quickly into another world, especially east of Húsafell between Eiriksjökull and Langjökull.

The woodland at Húsafell is protected. The hot springs and magnificent waterfalls of Barnafoss-Hraunfossar are scheduled for protection but in any case these are not strictly sites for expedition work. The lava caves of Surtshellir and Stefánshellir are Category 3 sites and it would be advisable to seek permission for any work there.

Expedition interest is varied and includes geological interest in the lava morphology, especially that of lava tubes. Two notable shield volcanoes, Skjaldbreiður and Ok dominate the Kaldidalur route. Geomorphologists will be interested in the desert features, landslides and periglacial phenomena, and especially the effects of wind-blown sand. Ice is all around, though difficult of access because of the steep approaches. Nevertheless the icecaps are crossable by experienced parties. Vegetation may not seem too apparent to many but the colonisation by plants is something short of remarkable in this severe environment.

Access can only be by road and best by chartered vehicle. There are no regular services beyond Thingvellir in the south but there are daily buses to Reykholt and Húsafell.

2. South-central

This area is very attractive to expeditions because it is so close to Reykjavik and combines a variety of landscape types into a small area. In the eastern part the features of the mid-ocean ridge are well displayed along the Laki and Eldgjá fissures where the grain of the country is seen to run south-west to north-east and under the Vatnajökull glacier. Explosion craters, eruptive cones, and lava flows abound. This grain is also followed by streams, some of which are turbulent and flow through steep-sided gorges undiscernable from the maps. The best source of navigation information in this area is Dick Phillips (Appendix E) who maintains his hostel and library at Fljótshlíd.

However, the area is increasingly visited by tourist groups at certain locations such as Landmannalaugar and Eldgjá, and it contains a growing number of reserves some of which are very sensitive. The Landmannalaugar area (Fjallabak), especially is heavily used and groups are encouraged to avoid spending any length of time there. The Fjallabak reserve (47,000 ha) is one of the largest in Iceland after Hornstrandir, Mývatn-Laxá, and Skaftafell). Under no circumstances should groups camp within the reserve without the express written consent of the Nature Conservation Council.

The key locations in the western part are Hekla, Torfajökull and Tindfjallajökull.

This area also contains a number of huts (see Chapter 8), a list of which is available from the Iceland Unit. However as a general principal these should not be used by expeditions except in extreme emergency.

Similar comments apply to the Laki fissure and to the Thórsmörk area even though it is a Category 3 reserve. It is accessible only by four-wheel drive vehicle because of the river Krossá which is exceedingly dangerous. Single vehicles with inexperienced drivers are not recommended to try it.

The East part is especially barren and remote and centres on the Jökulheima hut owned by the Iceland Glaciological Society. It is from here that they make their annual Whitsun snowcat crossing of the Vatnajökull. Access to the ice in this part is prohibited by the Tungnaá river but once north of the Kerlingar access is possible via Sylgjujökull (unnamed on the maps). The glacier that descends between the Kerlingar peaks makes an interesting expedition location. Sylgjujökull is a surging glacier, the evidence for which is quite plain. The outwash zone, though difficult, is interesting geomorphologically (dirt cones, cryonite holes, supraglacial stream and debris flows).

The strip of country hard up agaist the Vatnajökull is very difficult of access and only negotiable by four-wheel drive vehicles travelling from west to east. They should travel in pairs on account of the quicksands, steep slopes and snow patches. The route is described in Chapter 16.

The mountain oasis, Nýidalur (Jökuldalir) and the area surrounding Tungnafellsjökull is in part a Category 2 reserve and in part Category 3. Because of its altitude and the brevity of the season there the vegetation is very sensitive to overuse. The Nature Conservation Council wish to discourage groups from using it and special permission must be sought.

3. Mývatn-Gjástykki-Jökulsárgljúfur

There can be no doubt that the Mývatn district (Mývatnsveit) deserves the special protection that it has been given in Icelandic law. Ornithologically, botanically, and geologically it is unique among landscapes. The majority of expeditions will visit as tourists but with a proprietory interest in the natural history. They camp on the official camp sites (Reykjahlíd and Skútustaðir), and happily join in the general appreciation of the district. Camping **is** restricted in the most visited and farmed area but permission can be obtained to camp further afield where the general public do not go (eg. the approaches to Bláfjöll beyond the Lúdent craters). Objectives must be quite explicit.

Perhaps of greatest recent interest has been the volcanic activity (1976 onwards) associated with the Krafla central volcano and the fissured district (Gjástykki) that runs north to Axafjördur. These are described by Escritt in several Geographical Magazine articles.

It has happened that groups wishing to undertake biological work have been diverted to other areas within this region. Such areas have included Víkingavatn and Vestmannsvatn where similar vegetation and freshwater studies could be carried out. The Kelduhverfi district is interesting although access is to some extent limited by farms and farmland. It is here that the northernmost fissures of the Gjástykki (Krafla) tectonic activity are well displayed. There is also a haf and nehrung coast with skua colonies and small lakes. The Nature Conservation Council are not averse to groups undertaking work within the Jökulsárgljúfur National Park which is, geologically and botanically interesting and a unique place to be. A base camp can be set up at Ásbyrgi and an advance camp in Vesturdalur whence journeys may be made in all directions. No-one could fail to be impressed by this place or at least by the mighty power of the river Jökulsá á Fjöllum as it dives over Dettifoss.

4. Ódaðahraun

South of Grímsstaðir you enter the glacio-volcanic desert of the Ódaðahraun. You are still within the vast reserve of Mývatn-Laxá where permission must be sought. An expedition in this area would need careful planning and logistical support. Equipment would have to be good because the wind can blow unabated, whipping up powerful sandstorms that can be very unpleasant, especially to the bespectacled. Water is scarce, having sunk down into the sand, gravel and lava. The area is also very sensitive and at Herdubreiðarlindir, for example, is in danger of severe erosion owing to visitor pressure and camping around the hut. Vehicles crossing this rough terrain must be prepared for loose sand and lacerated tyres.

Interest revolves around the periglacial features, desert landscape and the volcanic landforms exemplified by the Askja caldera, Herdubreid (palagonite mountain), Trölladyngja (shield volcano), and Kverkfjöll (hot springs, and ice caves adjacent to and within the icecap).

5. Palagonite Ridge Highlands

The east side of the Jökulsá valley is bordered by palagonite hills stretching some 200km northwards from the Vatnajökull. They rarely exceed 500m. in height. At their southern end they abut onto the icecap at Brúarjökull which is one of the surging type. In 1963/64 the glacier advanced 8km in three months. Its outwash zone is a model for proglacial landforms.

6. Jökulsá á Fjöllum Region

This area really falls into no clear landscape slot. It is bordered by young volcanics to the west and palagonite hills to the east. Its thread of continuity is the mighty river itself which, in its northern section, flows through the impressive Jökulsárgljúfur National Park. This is where the Iceland Breakthrough team canoed to the Dettifoss waterfall before negotiating the fall itself with motorized hanggliders. It is also an area that receives regular dust storm debris from the Ódaðahraun. The national park and the area to the south contain several interesting grabens, craters and crater rows (Hrossaborg and Sveinar). The system includes now dry canyons where the river formerly flowed, the most notable of which is the canyon at Ásbyrgi where two small, deep ponds mark the spot where the river once tumbled over a 100m-high waterfall.

In the southern desertified section the landscape is impressive for its openness and the expanses of gravel and sand. Former courses and levels of the river can be seen here.

VII. GLACIERS

Iceland possesses far more permanent ice than the maps would suggest. In the Tröllaskagi peninsula, for example, there are over a hundred small glaciers of one kind or another. Icelandic ice is close to its melting point and therefore referred to as temperate ice which possesses a great deal of meltwater both on and within it. Meltwater streams, outwash streams and moulins are common features which make navigation hazardous for the explorer. Snow cover varies greatly from year to year and there are no hard and fast rules. On Vatnajökull the permanent snowline is at about 1100m. on the south side but at 1400m on the north side where the fohn effect melts ice at a higher altitude. All Icelandic glaciers are hazardous at anytime because the weather conditions, especially on the icecaps can be so severe. Even experienced alpinists are astonished at the weather that can be flung at them. The damp, cold air makes the conditions much more severe than at equivalent heights in the Alps.

In 1972 the North Iceland Glacier Inventory programme (NIGI) was initiated and its accompanying Manual for Field Survey Parties (Escritt) serves as a useful handbook for glacier-bound fieldworkers. This study highlighted the existence of numerous rock glaciers and related phenomena in the northern highlands.

Details of the Vatnajökull and its adjacent Öraefajökull are given in Chapter 15.

VIII. ISLANDS

There are really only two principal islands, Grîmsey and Heimaey. Grîmsey, is reached by air or by boat from Akureyri (m.s. Drangur). The principal attraction is the fact that it straddles the arctic circle and provides 24 hours daylight for the sun worshippers. The cliffs are well-known for their seabird colonies. Few expeditions have visited Grîmsey in recent years, perhaps discouraged by its lack of surface water, but comparisons with older work would now prove interesting.

Heimaey is reached by daily aircraft from Reykjavîk or boat (m.s. Hérjólfur) from Thórlakshöfn. Heimaey is one of the windiest places in Iceland and aircraft landings are often not possible so if planning a one-day excursion to view the 1973 eruption centre be prepared for disappointment. It is best to book this for early in the trip so that if postponed you still have another chance to get out there. Those intending to stay for longer than a day will find the camp site adequate and the hostel accommodating. One or two expeditions have carried out local human geography surveys, but most come simply to view the eruption centre and effects upon the island community. Certainly worth a visit.

The volcano Surtsey, 20 miles south-west of Heimaey, is still the subject of extensive study to see how the bare lava develops a vegetation cover and how new communities come into existence. Expeditions, other than from research institutions, will not receive permission to land.

M.H.WEALE .83.

4 DEVELOPING THE IDEA

GATHERING IDEAS:

Iceland is such an exciting country that it is tempting to want to see it all at once. However, scale and distance are hard to assess and you soon discover that costs are becoming prohibitive. Don't give up, it will all happen but in the event your final choice of venue and itinerary will be constrained by several factors other than cost:

The Type of Programme:

Your flexibility increases as you move from a pure research expedition, to an educational fieldwork expedition, to a purely recreational or social expedition. We assume that research demands the pursuit of a very explicit scientific objective which in itself will pinpoint the venue; the relative sophistication of your equipment will influence the choice of transport. Research expeditions usually start with the question 'where should I go to find the ideal situation for this type of investigation?' That question is relatively easy to answer. Less easy, and more frequent, is the sort of question which says "we want to do something in the field of glaciology, what do you advise?" At this point we must ask questions about the following:

Numbers:

At the bottom end of the scale you may find that you must have at least ten people to enable you to qualify for a cheap group ticket; 20 people may bring further reductions on internal transport costs. This may however be too many people to satisfy either the leader:member ratio, or the demands of the field programme. People with nothing to do can ruin an expedition. If hiring self-drive vehicles then a seating constraint comes in to it. A microbus, for example, only has 9 seats.

Type of Area:

The specific areas of Iceland have been discussed in Chapter 3. but it is worth asking what the expedition members would like to get out of the visit whether it be for research, fieldwork or recreation or a combination. Is it necessary for example, to travel into the interior which would require a 4-wheel drive vehicle? A 10 seater Land Rover, for example, is very expensive and in reality on rough tracks does not seat 10 people as well as their food and equipment. If you plan to bring a non-4-wheel drive vehicle from home or to hire on in Iceland you are automatically debarred from using the interior tracks. To do so would be foolhardy and costly. How necessary is it to set foot onto a glacier? If the outwash area will suffice it will save on insurance and equipment costs. In any case most Icelandic glaciers are so covered in volcanic debris that they look better from a distance!

The Iceland Experience

A visit to Iceland is no mere holiday, it is an experience of a lifetime. No where else on earth can one observe so much natural beauty in so small an area.

Planning your Iceland Experience is like putting together a rather complex jig-saw puzzle. Just leave out a few pieces and the final picture is incomplete. There are so many travel options, from simple 'go-as-you-please' arrangements, right through to fully inclusive guided tours of the island. Suffice to say, in order to get the best out of your holiday, you may need the assistance of those who have travelled the same path before, and have up-to-date information on the many choices available.

At Arctic Experience we pride ourselves in being able to tailor a holiday, or expedition, to the exact requirements of the individual.

The Arctic Experience Iceland and Greenland brochures include a diverse selection of holidays and travel ideas, which may well give you food for thought. The advice we give is of course free, and the prices for services we arrange are very competitive. We also carry an extensive range of maps on Iceland and Greenland. For further details please telephone or write to me today.

Clive Stacey

ARCTIC EXPERIENCE LTD.

29, Nork Way, Banstead, Surrey SM7 1PB.
Telephone: (07373) 62321; Telex: 897807 Arctic G.

ATOL 2013

ICELANDAIR

Age and Experience:

For many groups this may be the first overseas visit and their first experience of an extended camp anywhere, let alone in a wild, often inhospitable area. This must affect the itinerary and locations. In most cases the use of young members to suit the ambitions of the leader does not work very well.

Period in the Field:

When do you wish to travel? Departure dates affect air fares; they also affect access to the interior. The road across the centre of Iceland (Springisandur) is rarely open before mid-July; on the other hand you may be able to achieve your objectives at Christmas or Easter time when costs are considerably lower. Several cultural and recreational expeditions have chosen that time of year. Fieldwork may also be influenced by departure dates; a late spring may seriously affect glaciological or botanical work. Ornithology and glaciology are generally incompatible; the one requires an early season location, the other a late season when all snow has melted. Furthermore the length of time that you can spend in the field will affect the amount and type of fieldwork that you can achieve. The question 'is there any useful research work we could do for anyone?' is unrealistic for anything less than a month in the field and as soon as you plan to stay longer than one month the air fare soars to the full annual figure.

Equipment:

If you do not already own sufficient equipment you will need to budget for acquisition or renting in Iceland. (See Chapter 13).

Insurance:

See Chapter 10.

JOINING ANOTHER EXPEDITION

If after all these considerations you are beginning to think that you have no hope of getting together an expedition why not join another expedition or expeditionary tour? Iceland is a safe enough place for two people to do their own thing provided that they are sensible and do not go too far off the beaten track. Tour operators offer sensibly priced fly-drive packages or campers' do-it-yourself packages. In Chapter 8 details of tent and equipment hire in Iceland are referred to. In Iceland there are a number of expedition-type trips either on horseback or on snocats across the Vatnajökull. Bus companies run camping tours throughout the season and Ferðafélag Íslands (The Touring Club of Iceland) offer a wide range of low-priced tours that you may join in Reykjavík. Details of these are usually posted in the youth hostel. As a last resort you could try asking the Iceland Unit to publish your existence in the bulletin 'Island' but do give bibliographic details as well and don't be too hopeful.

Iceland.
Go with
The A-Team.

Scanscape may be the newest and fastest growing operator covering Iceland but our specialist staff have been involved in arranging university, school and group expeditions to Iceland for many years.

We not only know the landscape thoroughly but most important we know the best people on the ground over there and work with them as a team.

The result – apart from a superb range of Icelandic tours covering special interests and the best the country has to offer, we will also tailor a tour to your own special requirements. After all Iceland is a very special country.

Call us for our comprehensive colour brochure.

68½ Upper Thames Street, London EC4V 3BJ
Telephone: 01-248 0431.

ATOL
2122

PREPARING A PROSPECTUS

Before approaching advisors or tour operators it is worthwhile preparing a preliminary prospectus that is brief and to the point, and which answers all the questions that are likely to be asked of you (see Table 1). Armed with this information the quality of all the advice that you receive will be greatly enhanced.

We realise that at this stage you may not have all the information to hand in which case the following sections should assist you. Undoubtedly your initial concern will be to obtain a costing to enable you to sell the idea to potential members, parents, or sponsors. When seeking quotations bear the following in mind:

1. Group fares apply to groups of 10 or more people and cheap fares are for a maximum of one month. Beyond that you pay a full annual fare or a cheaper Apex fare. Midweek fares are cheaper than weekend and, at the time of writing, August fares are cheaper than July fares. See Chapter 6 for more details.

2. All air fares are subject to a Departure Tax payable in advance.

3. As Keflavîk airport is 40 km south of Reykjavîk you will need to cost in an airport transfer.

4. It is worth spending your first and last nights in sleeping bag accommodation in Reykjavîk. See Chapter 8.

TABLE 1: TYPES OF INFORMATION NEEDED TO HELP YOU GET STARTED

| | Needed for: | |
| | Advisors: | Tour Operators: |
Type of information:		
1. Type of Group (school/univ./scout)	★	
2. Type of Activity (research/Fwk/rec.)	★	
3. Age (of main group)	★	
4. Numbers (how many leaders/members)	★	★
5. Approx. dates	★	★
6. Length of Stay	★	★
7. Departure (midweek/weekend)		★
8. Equipment (taking or renting)	★	★
9. Transport: (i) To Iceland — boat/air	★	★
(ii) In Iceland — air/bus etc.	★	★
10. Insurance (ordinary/mtneering/rescue)		★
11. Type of Area: (i) interior/coastal	★	★
(ii) glacial/desert/volc.	★	
12. Field Interests (glaciol/geomorph/botany etc)	★	
13. Experience: (i) Leaders	★	
(ii) Members	★	

The Iceland specialists who'll tailor make your group tour.

If you're planning a group tour to Iceland there are three good reasons why you should be talking to Sonicworld.
— Being leading specialists in Iceland we know it like the back of our hand.
— We have also specialised for some time in taking over university, school and youth groups.
— We have the flexibility to put together a tour that meets your individual needs and your budget.

So for your group encounter with the scenic experience of a lifetime contact our Student and Youth Group Tour Dept., at the address below.

Fred. Olsen Travel

11 Conduit Street, London W1R 0LS
01-409 3275 Inclusive Tours

TRAVEL ENQUIRIES:

The Iceland Information Unit:

The Iceland Unit is coordinated by Tony Escritt and located wherever he is based. Currently, while teaching at Harrow School, his address is Kennet Cottage, Harrow Park, Harrow on the Hill, Middlesex (01-422 2825). However, his address may always be obtained from the Expedition Advisory Centre at the Royal Geographical Society, 1 Kensington Gore, London SW7 2AR (01-581 2057).

The Unit exists to assist expeditions by maintaining up-to-date information on travel, fieldwork areas, literature, previous expeditions, etc. One visit to the Unit could save you weeks of correspondence.

Icelandair:

Icelandair is the only airline with regular scheduled services to Iceland's Keflavik airport. They are able to supply general information leaflets about Iceland but the special group tickets for expeditions must be obtained through the specialist Travel Operators (see below). Details of air fares are given in Chapter 6.

Travel Operators:

By and large your High Street travel agent knows little about Iceland, especially when it comes to the oddities of expedition needs and costs. However several companies specialise in Iceland or have Icelandic departments. These are listed in Appendix E, and we recommend that you contact them having drawn up a prospectus based on the ideas referred to earlier in this chapter and in Table 1.

Shipping Companies:

When your plans are further advanced and you have decided to send freight or a vehicle by sea, you should contact the agents of the Icelandic shipping company whose regular sailings come closest to you (see Appendix G). They are able to offer special educational discounts to 'bona fide' educational expeditions. See also Chapter 6.

Smyrill Line:

This Faeroese car ferry line operates between Europe, Britain, the Faeroes and Iceland (Seydisfjördur). At the time of writing the situation is rather 'up in the air' and you will need to contact the Travel Operators to find out the current situation. At the time of writing their m.s. Nörrona travels between Denmark (Hansholm), Norway (Bergen), Shetland Islands (Lerwick), Faeroes (Torshavn) and Iceland. This is covered in more detail in Chapter 6.

Iceland Tourist Bureau (Ferdaskrifstofa Rikisins):

Generally speaking there is little that they can do to help expeditions that cannot be done by one of the bodies already referred to (see also the

section on Fieldwork Enquiries). In Britain the offices of Icelandair distribute their literature.

The Icelandic Embassy:
The Embassy can offer little help to expeditions in the planning stage, and in most cases will refer enquiries direct to the Iceland Unit. They do however have a stock of films which may be useful for promotional exercises (see Appendix H).

SOURCES OF GENERAL INFORMATION:

Iceland Unit Publications: publishes broadsheets, Icesheets and a quarterly bulletin.

Icelandair publications: useful pamphlets on geology, weather, bird life, and flora of Iceland.

Bus Timetables (Leiðabók): this is the bus timetable for Iceland which may be purchased from the Iceland Unit or Dick Phillips or, when in Iceland, from the Long-Distance Bus Station (Umferðamiðstöd). Its currency is May to May, and the issue covering the summer is never available until after it comes into operation. One therefore has to plan on the basis of the last year's edition. In practice the details change very little from year to year. The Iceland Unit can advise.

Telephone Book (Símaskrá): the Icelandic telephone directory: Very useful for locating names and addresses. The Iceland Unit always holds a current edition.

Guide Books: until 1985 there was a paucity of useful guidebooks for Iceland but there are now several available through the Iceland Unit or Dick Phillips (see Appendix E). The Iceland Road Guide, contains useful descriptions of routes and points of interest along them. Those with their own vehicles will find this very helpful. For good general background reading on the history of Iceland we recommend Magnússon's 'The Northern Sphinx'. This is not a guide book but a very readable account of the history. A number of other background references are given in Chapter 18.

MAPS:

At an early stage you should acquire the 1:750,000 Tourist Map of Iceland as a starting point for forward planning. Individual group members may prefer to purchase the smaller Little Touring Map at 1:1,000,000. For more detailed planning you will need some of the following:

1:250,000: (c.3.95 miles: 1 inch) in 9 sheets. These are good quality touring maps with considerable detail and available as single or double-sided sheets. The reference numbers are shown in Figure 11. The double-sided combinations are 1-2, 3-6, 4-7, 8-9.

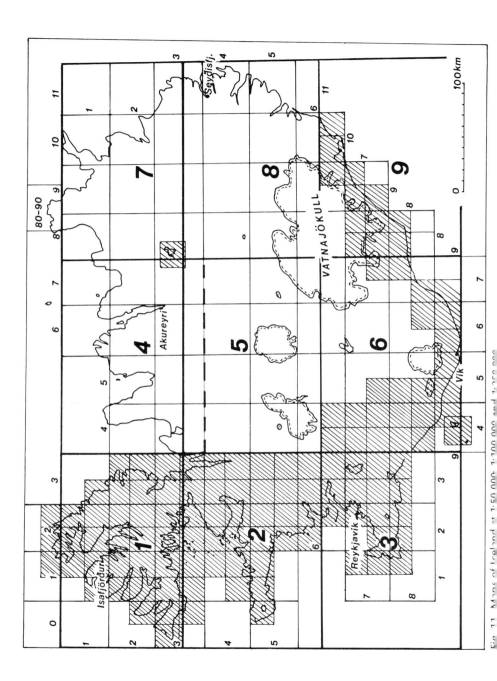

Fig. 11. Maps of Iceland at 1:50 000, 1:100 000 and 1:250 000

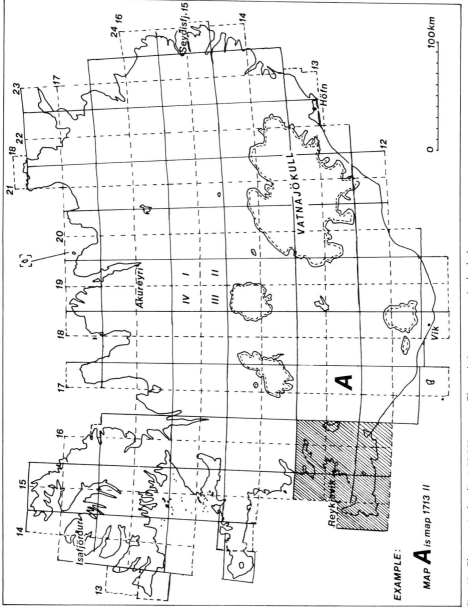

EXAMPLE:

MAP **A** is map 1713 II

Fig. 12. The new Icelandic 1:50,000 maps. The existing coverage is shaded.

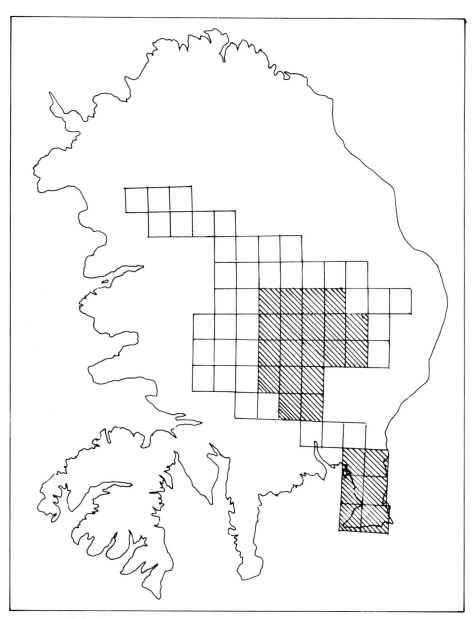

Fig. 13. Published vegetation maps of Iceland (shaded) (1966-68).

1:100,000: (c.1.6 miles: 1 inch) These were originally made by the Danish Geodetic Survey but have been extensively updated by the Icelandic Survey. See Figure 11. Special maps have been produced at this scale: Hornstrandir (N.W. Fjords), Skaftafell National Park (includes a map at 1:25,000), and Húsavík-Mývatn-Jökulsárgljúfur.

1:50,000 (Icelandic): (c.0.8 miles: 1 inch) Originally mapped between 1902 and 1914 these represent(ed) one quarter (NW, NE, SW, SE) of every 1:100,00 map. Most are now unavailable except for the west and south coast areas and are being phased out to be replaced by a completely new series of which only the extreme south-west area has been covered. (See Figure 12). However there are several special maps at this scale: Hekla, Mývatn, and Vestmannaeyjar.

1:50,000 (American): The U.S. Army mapped the island from air photography in 1949. These maps provide a very useful tool for fieldwork as in many respects the topographic detail is more accurate. Some are still available from the Iceland Geodetic Survey.

1:25,000: Two special maps have been produced at this scale: Thingvellir and the map of Skaftafell that is published jointly with the special map at 1:100,000.

Geological Maps: These cover the same areas as the 1:250,000 maps except maps 4, 8 and 9 have not yet appeared but are in preparation.

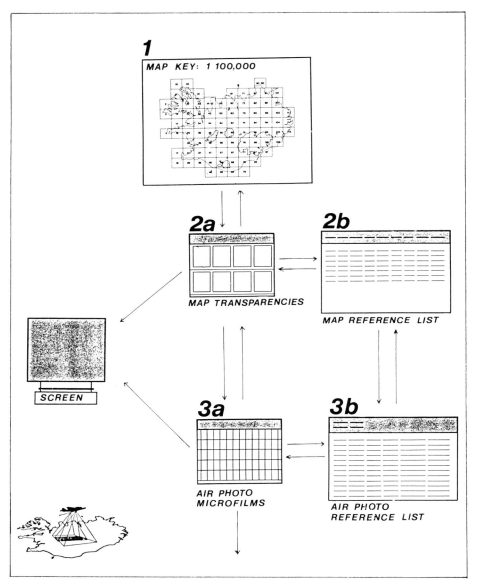

Fig. 14. The aerial photograph microfilm system developed by Thorvaldur Bragason at the Iceland Geodetic Survey.

Vegetation Maps: These cover a belt of country from Reykjavík east and north towards Mývatn (see Figure 13). Not surprisingly many of them do not have a vast amount of information but they are quite useful for early planning and selection of likely field sites.

To obtain all these maps the best sources are the Iceland Unit or Dick Phillips (see Appendix E) who offer an all-year-round service. Because they do not have to charge the tax normally levied on sales in Iceland they can supply almost all current maps, at or around Reykjavík shop prices.

AIR PHOTOGRAPHS:

Iceland has been photographed at various times since 1937. The U.S. Army did a major revision in August 1960 and the Icelanders have updated many special areas since then. Expeditions may obtain stereo cover but this is not normally approved without a National Research Council research permit or "Announcement' (Chapter 10). The office of the Iceland Geodetic Survey (Landmaelingar Islands) is at Laugavegi 178, Reykjavík (Tel: 8-16-11). The quickest, cheapest, and most efficient means of obtaining photographs is to call in and use their microfilm library. Photos can be produced quite quickly but not so quickly that you could arrive in Iceland, select, and then take them into the field with you. There are two options:

1. Call in during the winter while on a reconnaissance visit using one of Icelandair's special winter "Breakaways".

2. Send a photocopy of the area for which you require coverage indicating precisely the area and whether or not you want stereo coverage. You can discover the current price from the Iceland Unit. Landmaelingar will normally send photographs cash on delivery with an official order. Sales Tax is not imposed on orders paid in foreign currency.

It is possible to obtain prints of the mosaics flown for particular areas that were flown by the original U.S. flights. The Tröllaskagi peninsula, for example, is covered by four such index sheets.

Using the microfilm library: The microfilm and scanner are located in the reception in the office at Laugavegur 178. It is very simple to use by following the procedures below (Fig. 14):

(i) Study the reference map which depicts Iceland divided into 115 squares which correspond to the 1:100,000 maps.

(ii) The maps corresponding to these squares have been placed onto 35mm transparencies which may be viewed on the scanner and flight paths and flight numbers determined. These maps are also listed on the adjacent map list.

(iii) Use the flight paths to find the reference numbers for the appropriate air photographs. At the moment the references refer to the actual air photograph library but it is intended eventually that all the air photographs will also appear on microfilm.

FIELDWORK ENQUIRIES:

Notes on specific types of fieldwork are given in Chapter 1.

THE ICELAND UNIT:

The Unit can always be contacted through the Royal Geographical Society. Assistance to leaders can take several forms:

Bulletin: "Island": This comes out three times a year and keeps expeditions in touch with developments affecting Iceland expeditions, recent literature, expedition news, reports on field research, problems of transportation etc.

Regional Meeting (Þing): This is held in February each year to enable leaders and members of past and forthcoming expeditions to meet and to compare notes. In addition a more formal conference will be arranged from time to time at which specialist speakers will present aspects of field research in Iceland.

Access to Records: The records include maps, air photographs, expeditions reports, offprints, journals and over 3,000 references. Expedition reports are a particularly useful source of information and ideas.

Liaison with Iceland: Leading Icelandic scientists act as consultants to the Unit which also holds copies of the Research Permit Application Form that is required to be sent to Rannsóknaráð Ríkisins, the Iceland National Research Council.

Correspondence: A visit is far better than correspondence but the Unit can provide specific information, contacts at home and in Iceland, suggested programmes of fieldwork etc. The Unit can also comment upon the suitability of various routes for different types of vehicle.

ICELANDIC SCIENTISTS:

In the past many expeditions have written to Icelandic scientists and to Ferðaskrifstofa Ríkisins (The Iceland Tourist Bureau) but with little success. The former are too busy to cope with an annual flood of requests and would prefer enquiries to be directed to the Iceland Unit first (unless you already have a contact in Iceland of course, and the enquiry is of a specifically precise nature). The latter do not specialise in this type of enquiry and would refer you to the former, or to the Iceland Unit.

ICELAND GLACIOLOGICAL SOCIETY:

Expeditions planning glaciological research should be in touch with the Society. Those planning to cross icecaps would do well to seek their advice as well as that of the Iceland National Lifesaving Society (Slysarvarnafélag Íslands). See Appendix G. for addresses.

A FEW TIPS FOR ADVANCE PLANNING:
PRELIMINARY

Air Fares: Do thoroughly investigate the various air fares referred to in Chapter 6. It could save you a lot of money.

Travel within Iceland: Remember that every time that you move it will cost you something, so weigh up the options very carefully and, if necessary, ask for comparative quotations from the Tour Operators. See the earlier section in this chapter.

Insurance: The lack of a reciprocal agreement with the British National Health Service means that hospital treatment is expensive. Do be adequately insured. This topic is dealt with in Chapter 10.

Food and Fuel Costs: Remember that food costs will be expensive and that careful logistical calculations will be necessary. See the discussion in Chapter 9.

Letters to Iceland: Icelanders will openly admit that letter writing is not one of their strongest points! It is therefore important that you make letters very specific. Be prepared for your Research or Educational Permit application to take a while to be processed — it may have to be passed around to numerous individuals before being sanctioned. If you are sponsored by your local Rotary or Lions Club you may wish to contact them (see Appendix G).

MORE ADVANCED:

Itinerary: Be sure not to plan any major refuelling or revitalling on the first Monday in August which is a Bank Holiday. Distances and movement are hard to assess from an armchair at home. Be conservative in your estimates. See Chapters 7 and 13.

Accommodation: We recommend that you spend your first and last nights in sleeping bag accommodation in Reykjavík. See Chapter 8. for a discussion of this.

Equipment: Wet and low nightime temperatures will be your principal enemies. See Chapter 13.

Radios: Are radios necessary? Generally the answer is 'no' but read Chapter 11.

Passports and Currency: See Chapter 10.

Involving Young Icelanders: While fully supported as an excellent principle it is not easy to guarantee this because young Icelanders have a sixteen week Summer holiday during which most of them obtain jobs to boost their pocket money and to help pay for their education. Periodically groups such as The Brathay Exploration Group have successfully involved one or two young people but all too often this has been a last minute arrangement because the Icelanders could not commit themselves. Any projects, involving questionnaires in human geography (see Chapter 1) really do need Icelanders and this has usually been arranged 'on-the-spot'.

This is not very helpful to the leader who wishes to have a watertight programme. As summer jobs become more difficult to obtain it is possible that Icelanders may be more receptive to the idea of an expedition.

PRE-DEPARTURE:

For young parties especially we would recommend a series of informal sessions supported by film, video and slides (see Appendix H) designed to encourage good expedition organisation and a better understanding of the host country. Topics might include:

1. **Safety:** (see Chapter 13)

Homesickness: some people can become physically ill on their first trip away from home, even to the point of repatriation.

Perception of Scale and Distance: distance from assistance lowers the margin of safety.

Navigation: palaeomagnetism within the basalt rocks can affect compass bearings. Beware map inaccuracies (binoculars sometimes of more use than a compass). Naismith's Rule (3 miles per hour plus 1 hour for every 1500 ft. of ascent) is not applicable.

Clothing: emphasis on cold and wet.

First Aid: stress the dangers of hot springs and treatment for cuts, burns, and dust in the eyes (Chapter 13).

Ropework: for glaciers **and** rivers.

2. **Physical Background:**
    (a) Geology
    (b) Soils and Vegetation
    (c) Climate

See Chapter 18 for recommended reading.

3. **Cultural Background:**
    (a) History
    (b) Political situation
    (c) Religion

See Chapter 18 for recommended reading.

4. **The Need for Conservation:** (see Chapter 2)

5. **Fieldwork Preparation:**
    (a) Background
    (b) Equipment preparation and operation
    (c) Techniques practicals

A FINAL SUGGESTION:

Be flexible: the pace of life and the social structure in Iceland will not easily accommodate the rigidly arranged expedition. Buses **will** be late; aircraft may not fly; your booking may not appear on the records; freight will be lost; it will rain! Anticipate that everything will go wrong. Happily Iceland is a delightful place where everything turns out alright on the day and it is usually better than you originally planned!

5 THE ICELANDIC LANGUAGE

Icelandic is a difficult language to master but worth looking at because it remains so close to Old Norse and the language spoken by the Vikings. If you attempt to read a scientific paper in, say, French or German, there is a good chance that you will get the gist of it because of certain similarities in words and constructions. Icelandic literature is not so comparable because so few foreign words have been incorporated into the language and indeed all new words are translated into a pure Icelandic form. A good example is that of the word 'ecology' (French: 'écologie'; German: 'Ökologie') which has been translated into Icelandic as 'vistfraeði' (literally: 'life study').

At first the Icelandic place-names will seem to be utterly unpronounceable. But if you apply a few basic rules and tackle them with determination they soon become manageable. That some place-names seem interminably long can be understood when you realise that in Icelandic several words may be linked together. For example:

-Breiðamerkurjökull	Breiður	(broad)
	- merki	(mark)
	- jökull	(glacier)
Kirkjubæjarklaustur	Kirkja	(church)
	- bær	(farm)
	- klaustur	(monastery)
Hveravellir	Hver	(hot spring)
	- vellir	(plain)

A number of words will crop up again and again and some of the most common are given at the end of this chapter.

The most important piece of advice is to lay the stress on the first syllable of the word. This rarely fails. If you then apply a modest knowledge of welsh and think of towns kike Llangollen such words as 'jökull' or 'fjall' (mountain) become easier to cope with. The word 'fell', incidentally, is pronounced as it looks (eg. Snaefellsjökull). There are several other combinations of letters which in Icelandic require their own intonation. For example there are plenty of banks in Iceland but 'banki' is pronounced 'bowngki'. In other words '-an' followed by a 'g' become 'owng'. The same applies if '-an' are followed by a 'g' as in 'langur' (long). 'ae' is pronounced as in the English 'eye' (eg. as in 'baer'). But be careful with names such as Vestmannaeyjar where the 'a' and the 'e' represent the last and the first letters of two separate words ('manna' and 'eyjar') 'ö' is pronounced as in the English vowel in 'turn'.

Now try saying 'Öraefajökull' (er-eye-va jerkle). The 'j' is like the 'y' in 'yoke'. If you still have difficulty try climbing it first and then have another go!

A few more rules:

1. The Icelandic letters 'þ' ('Þ') and 'ð' ('Ð') are pronounced as a hard and a soft 'th' as in the English 'the' and 'thorn' respectively.

2. Acute accents transform the pronunciation of 'a', 'i', and 'u' as follows:

'á' is pronounced as the 'ow' in the English 'down'. Since the Icelandic rivers are 'á' you are likely to trip over this one rather often.

'í' is pronounced like the vowels in the English 'been'. Try saying 'Reykjavík' which is two words with a rolling 'R' and the emphasis very much on the first syllable.

'ú' is pronounced like the 'oo' sound in the English 'moon'. The word 'stúlka' should materialise a young girl but in this case the '-lk' is palatized resembling the Welsh 'll' (the same is true of '-lp' and '-lt'). Perhaps easier (and safer) than 'stúlka' is this memorable ditty:

> Remember that in Icelandic
> A House is 'hús'   (hoose)
> A Mouse is 'mús'   (moose)
> And a Louse is 'lús'!!   (loose)

By now you will have looked up a few words in the dictionary and will have found words that look like the one that you seek but that they differ in some small degree. You are probably right. The problems are that:

(a) Icelandic nouns have nominative, accusative, dative and genitive cases in both singular and plural. As a generalisation the datives end in '-i' (plur. '-um', genitives end in '-s' (plur. '-a'), and nominative plurals end in '-ir' or '-ar'. For example ('hestur' a horse):

	Singular	Plural
nom.	hestur	hestar
acc.	hest	hesti
dat.	hesti	hesta
gen.	hests	hesta

(b) In many cases the whole word seems to alter as the noun declines. For example:

	Singular	Plural
nom.	jökull	jöklar
acc.	jökul	jökla
dat.	jökli	jöklum
gen.	jökuls	jökla
nom.	fjörður	firðir
acc.	fjörð	firði
dat.	firði	fjördum
gen.	fjarðar	fjarða

(c) Now the fun starts because the nouns that we have used so far have all been translated with the indefinite article. The definite article, 'hinn' also declines and is tacked on to the end of the noun except when an adjective precedes the noun. To take our horse as a simple example:

	Singular	Plural
nom.	hesturinn	hestarnir
acc.	hestinn	hestana
dat.	hestinum	hestunum
gen.	hestsins	hestanna

Simple isn't it? Well not really, because 'hestur' is a masculine noun and Icelandic also has feminine and neuter nouns, and the appropriate definite article declines accordingly!

(d)   This is not a teach-yourself-Icelandic primer and so we go no further except to mention that of course the verbs decline, and many are irregular (of course). The present and past indicative tenses of the verb 'að vera', 'to be', may be useful:

Person	Present	Past
eg	er	var
pu	ert	varst
hann	er	var
við	erum	voru
pið	erud	vorud
peir	eru-	voru

That's enough! If you want to know more get hold of a dictionary and the 'Teach Yourself Icelandic' book. Better still find a patient Icelander to help you with a few phrases and if you get the chance try communicating with a few Icelandic children. One of the best ways to learn to pronounce the language is to sing in church. Hymns are slow enough for you to hear and participate.

Góda ferð!

SOME WORDS COMMON TO ICELANDIC PLACE-NAMES

Note that in this list the nominative singular is given but in the example the plural may have been used to indicate an alternative form of the same word. The number in brackets indicates the number of words that comprise the placename.

Icelandic	English	Example	
á	river	Breiðá	(2)
ás	small hill	Ásbúðir	(2)
austur	east (eystri — eastern)	Austurhlíð	(2)
bær	farm, small settlement	Saurbær	(2)
bjarg	cliff, rock	Látrabjarg	(2)
borg	town, crag	Dimmuborgir	(2)
botn	head of valley	Leirbotn	(2)
breið	broad	Skjaldbreiður	(2)
brekka	slope	Lundarbrekka	(2)

brú	bridge	Jökulsárbrú	(3)
bunga	rounded summit	Háabunga	(2)
dalur	valley	Skíðadalur	(2)
djúp	deep, long inlet	Djúpivogur	(2)
drangur	column of rock	Hraundrangur	(2)
dyngja	dome	Trölladyngja	(2)
eld	fire	Eldfell	(2)
ey	island (pl. eyjar)	Flatey	(2)
eyri	sand spit	Akureyri	(2)
fell	mountain, hill	Sandfell	(2)
fjall	mountain (pl. fjöll)	Dyngjufjöll	(2)
fjörður	fjord (pl. firðir)	Eyjafjörður	(2)
fljót	large river	Markarfljót	(2)
flói	large bay, marshy area	Faxaflói	(2)
foss	waterfall	Gullfoss	(2)
gígur	crater	Lakagígar	(2)
gil	gorge, ravine	Brekkagil	(2)
gjá	fissure, chasm	Gjástykki	(2)
háls	ridge, saddle	Tröllaháls	(2)
heiði	heath, moorland	Lyngdalsheiði	(3)
hlíð	mountain side	Reykjahlíð	(2)
hnjúkur	peak	Hvannadalshnjúkur	(3)
höfði	promontory	Ingólfshöfði	(2)
höfn	harbour	Höfn	(1)
hóll	rounded hill (Pl. hólar)	Raudhólar	(2)
hólmur	islet	Stykkishólmur	(2)
holt	stony hill	Skálholt	(2)
hraun	lava	Eldhraun	(2)
hryggur	ridge	Tungnahryggur	(2)
hver	hot spring	Hveragerði	(2)
innri	inner	Innra-Höfðagil	(3)
jökull	glacier	Vatnajökull	(2)
kirkja	church	Kirkjabæjarklaustur	(3)
laug	warm spring	Laugavatn	(2)
lón	lagoon	Jökulsárlón	(3)
mýri	marsh	Fagurhólsmýri	(3)
nes	headland	Akranes	(2)
norður	north (nydri — northern)	Norðurá	(2)
öræfi	wilderness, desert	Öræfajökull	(2)
reykur	steam, smoke	Reykjavík	(2)
sandur	sand, sands	Skeiðarársandur	(3)
skarð	mountain pass	Námaskarð	(2)
skógur	wood	Hallormstaðarskógur	(3)
staður	place	Egilsstaðir	(2)
suður	south (syðri — southern)	Suðurárdalur	(3)
tjörn	small lake	Nykkurtjörn	(2)
tunga	tongue	Tungnahryggsjökull	(3)

67

vatn	lake	Grîmsvötn	(2)
vegur	route, way	Kjalvegur	(2)
vîk	inlet	Grindavîk	(2)
völlur	plain	Thingvellir	(2)
ytri	outer	Ytri-Bægisá	(3)

6 GETTING TO ICELAND

INTERNATIONAL AIR TRAVEL

Types of Fare

Your first question is going to be "What is the cheapest fare available to me?" The answer is that the fare structures change from year to year and you will need to seek advice from Icelandair and the Tour Operators (see Chapter 7 and Appendix E). However the following list of fares may help. Note that they are listed in rank order with the cheapest at the top.

Pex
Only the **Pex 1** fares are suitable for expeditions. They are the cheapest over-the-counter fares but full payment is required at the time of booking. Maximum stay: one month. **Pex 2** fares are for designated mid-week flights only. **Pex 3** only for December departures such as winter snowshoeing or skidoo expeditions.

Group Fare
Slightly more expensive but more flexible and reliable. Restrictions: Minimum group of ten people; minimum stay 5 days; maximum one month. Fares normally paid 8 weeks in advance and available only through Tour Operators.

Youth Fare
Normally 25% less than the Excursion Fare. Same restrictions. Applicable to anyone who is **less than 23 years of age.**

Excursion Fare
Available to anyone. Restrictions: minimum stay five days; maximum one month. If you send an advance party of two people to clear freight etc. they will probably have to use this fare.

Annual Fare
Vastly more expensive and generally not applicable to expeditions unless staying for more than one month.

"Breakaways"
These off-season "Breakaways" provide the opportunity for a small reconnaissance in the winter to enable you to meet and talk to Icelandic scientists and other contacts. Such a visit saves months of correspondence and serves to clarify your expedition aims and objectives. It may even save you money in the long run.

NOTE:

1. All fares, both international and domestic, are currently subject to an Icelandic Departure Tax. This is payable in advance when you purchase your tickets. It is not incorporated within the cost of the ticket so check that it has been quoted.

2. Fares vary as between midweek and weekend. Winter fares are cheaper than Summer fares when the rate varies with the month. At the time of writing the July fare is the highest followed by August and September. The fare is based upon your date of departure from your own country.

3. All international flights go to Keflavík airport which is 40 Km. out of Reykjavík. A transfer coach is layed on at additional cost.

Excess Baggage:

On all flights the personal baggage allowance is 20 kg per person (we presume that you will not be travelling Saga Class!). As a group you can usually check in together and spread the load between you. We reckon that by careful planning a group can take enough food and equipment for two weeks without incurring freight charges (see Chapter 10). However, should you exceed the 20kg per person the excess per kilo is approximately 1% of the annual return fare.

You may take bicycles (see Chapter 7) by air to Iceland if you remove the front wheel, protect the sharp corners and turn the handlebars through 90°.

Routes:

Icelandair maintains regular jet services to Iceland from London, Glasgow, Copenhagen, Stockholm, Gothenburg, Oslo, Amsterdam, Frankfurt, Dusseldorf, Luxemburg, Paris, New York and Chicago. **Eagle Air** operates scheduled flights from Zurich, Dusseldorf and Amsterdam. **Scandinavian Airlines System (SAS)** operates flights from Copenhagen to Narssarssuaq (Greenland) via Keflavík.

TRAVEL BY SEA:

At the time of writing the ferry system is in a state of flux. There used to be regular sailings to Iceland from Leith (Scotland) on the dearly loved m.s. Gullfoss but they ceased some years ago to be replaced by a Faroese service from Scrabster (Caithness, Scotland) to Seydisfjördur. This ship, the m.s. Smyrill, operated successfully until 1982 when a new line, m.s. Edda, opened between Newcastle (England) and Reykjavík. The advantages were obvious but the line lasted only one season. In the meantime, however, the Smyrill Line had moved its port of call from Scrabster to Lerwick in the Shetland Islands. That is the current situation but will the m.s. Edda return to Britain, and will the Smyrill Line return to the British mainland? In the meantime it continues to serve Hantsholm (Denmark), Torshavn (Faroes) and Lerwick.

If you are prepared to go to Aberdeen the trip is very attractive if you enjoy sailing. The new ship, the m.s. Nörrona, (8000 tons) is a fully stabilised car/passenger ferry with capacity for 250 cars and over 1,000 passengers. It has a first class restaurant as well as a cafeteria, and a night club with light

music and disco dancing. The journey from Lerwick to Iceland takes a day and a half via Torshavn. The return takes over four days because the vessel goes from Torshavn to Hantsholm and back again before proceeding to Lerwick. However you may stop off in the Faroes for a fascinating two days until the ship returns from Denmark. You may camp or use the youth hostels on Stremoy, Eysturoy or Nordoyar. In Lerwick there is a youth hostel and anyone considering a stopover in the Shetlands is invited to contact the Information Officer, Shetland Tourist Organisation, Information Centre, Lerwick, Shetland ZE1 0LU (Tel: 0595 3434).

To get to Lerwick you can either fly from Aberdeen, Inverness or Edinburgh or take the P & O Ferry m.v. St. Claire from Aberdeen. The sea journey takes about 14 hours and involves an overnight stop in the Shetlands in each direction.

Bookings: All bookings can be made through Tour Operators (Appendix E)

SENDING FREIGHT BY SEA:

Travel Operators cannot do this for you and you must make arrangements for yourselves. British groups can do this by taking their freight to the agents of the Iceland shipping companies at least three weeks before the departure of the main expedition. The freight will not take three weeks to get there but you must allow for strikes and hold-ups along the line. 'Bona fide' expeditions will be permitted an educational rate. Goods may be shipped to Reykjavík or to several other destinations around Iceland for no extra cost (eg. Akureyri, Ísafjörður, Höfn). This can save you a lot of time and paperwork because the settlements are so much smaller than Reykjavík. If for any reason, the freight is delayed while being transhipped in Reykjavík, the company will forward the goods overland in their own vehicles. You will need to contact the agents direct for sailing dates and current rates. Rates are quoted for the cost per 1000 Kg or cost per cubic metre whichever yields the greatest revenue. Remember also to allow for warehouse dues, handling charges, customs charges etc. It all mounts up, especially at the British end.

Icelandic warehouse charges are not excessive but as in any port anywhere in the world you must guard against pilferage. This means that your packages should be too large to tuck under the arm, robust enough to withstand rough handling, and give no external indication of their contents. Expeditions of the past who have listed the contents on the outside went hungry! It is worthwhile approaching a local firm to have your boxes steel or plastic banded. In this way two to four cartons can be banded together for freighting and readily separated at the other end for transport within Iceland.

When considering suitable containers you should also consider transport within Iceland. How many expeditions have had to sit on the quayside and repack their freight to suit the vehicle? Tea chests are not suitable for coach transport; they are too big for the luggage compartment and would damage the seats if taken inside the bus. The best sort of box is the army 'compo' ration type made of a weatherproof board with the box contained within a slieve.

When you deliver your freight to the dock do get there early. Late arrivals are not easily tolerated, especially on a Friday. If you can load all the gear yourself onto one pallet or into a container it will save you searching time in Iceland.

FREIGHTING VEHICLES:

The Iceland Steamship Company will take vehicles but note that the term 'unpacked vehicle' refers not to contents but to whether or not the vehicle has been crated for shipment. You will need to know the vehicle height and weight and it is advisable to arrange insurance cover while in transit. The agents at Felixstowe charge 1% of the value each way. When you go to the dock it is worth doing two additional things:

1. Obtain a Customs form ready for you to complete in advance of the return of the vehicle from Iceland.

2. Visit the import department at the agents office **before** departure so as to make a start on the paperwork.

For more information on taking vehicles to Iceland see Chapter 7.

FREIGHTING CANOES:

If sending canoes to Iceland, encase them in polythene to prevent people sitting in them and to stop people lifting them by the deck lines. Put plenty of ropes around them to help lifting and to spread the load. Uncrated they are relatively cheap to ship as they have a small volume and are light. Take paddles by air as part of your normal baggage allowance. If travelling on the m.s. Nörrona (Smyrill Line) the canoes may be carried free as 'hand luggage'.

STOP PRESS

In 1987 Lufthansa plans to start operating scheduled services between Munich and Keflavík via Dusseldorf every Sunday from May to September.

7 TRANSPORT WITHIN ICELAND

TRANSPORT WITHIN REYKJAVÍK

Buses

The cheapest and most efficient form of transport is the city bus service (SVR). Charges are the same however far you travel. Different types of ticket are available:

Midi (single ticket)   Simply place the appropriate amount of cash into the receptacle. Drivers do not give change.

Midal (bulk discount)   Nine tickets on a perforated card. Each time you travel, place a ticket in the receptacle.

Skiftamiðan   Put cash or a single ticket into the receptacle and ask for one of these. It enables you to use any two buses within 45 mins of issue.

It is also possible to obtain a tourist ticket valid for one week from the day of issue. This allows unlimited use of the bus system inside the city. For most expedition use it is probably cheaper to obtain 'midal'. These tickets are obtainable at the SVR terminals at Laekjatorg or Hlemmur. (Fig. 21)

Buses operate from 0700 hrs (Sundays and holidays from 1000 hrs) to midnight daily. Tickets on SVR buses will not serve on buses to Kópavógur, Garðahreppur and Hafnafjörður, which are run by separate companies. These companies do give change. They run from the east side of Laekjagata almost opposite the Iðnabankinn.

Routes are marked on the 1:15,000 map of Reykjavík. A small route map is also obtainable from the kiosks referred to above. Buses will only stop at those stops bearing their number and timetable. If you wish to stop at the next stop, press the button; a bell will ring and a red light reading "STANZAR" will appear above the driver. Route No:5 is in many ways the most useful for expeditions because it runs between the camp site, the centre of town and the domestic airport. It also runs close to the youth hostel in its present position in Laufásvegur (see Chapter 8).

Taxis

There are several taxi companies in Reykjavík that run a 24-hour service. There are direct lines to these, at no charge, from the foyer at Hotel Loftleidir (the terminus for your bus from Keflavík) and at Reykjavík airport. Just pick up the receiver, request a taxi and give your name. At other times their telephone numbers may be found in the yellow pages of the Iceland telephone directory under Bifreiðastöðvar.

Vehicle Hire

Expensive. But it might be worthwhile for a group of four or five wanting a visit to eg. Krîsuvîk or Thingvellir under their own steam, or to use to save time while trying to sort out the freight. Drivers must be over 22 years of age. Don't forget your licence. See also "Self-Drive Hire' below.

Van Hire (with driver)

Vans to move heavy equipment such as your freight from the docks to the airport or the overland lorry terminal, can be arranged by dialling 2-50-50, or look up "Sendibilastöd" in the telephone directory. These vehicles operate just like taxis.

Bicycles

One enterprising expedition shipped out a bicycle to help them get around in Reykjavîk while clearing goods through customs. They later used it in the field (see below). For a modest daily rate you can hire bicycles in Reykjavîk from Tjaldaleigan, the tent hire shop, opposite the long-distance bus station (Umferðamiðstöð) on Hringabraut.

TRANSPORT OUTSIDE OF REYKJAVÍK

Do not cling to the false assumption that plans laid well in advance are plans well made. Coaches etc. may not materialise when expected. Do go out to Iceland knowing what to do should anything like this occur. Make sure that you know which bus company or car hire firm you have reserved a vehicle with. It is advisable to check and double-check on everything. As a matter of normal practice Icelanders will always check with Icelandair that their plane departure is on time before they go out to the airport.

Coach Hire

For most expeditions this is probably the cheapest form of transport because you can arrange for yourselves and your goods to be transported almost anywhere in Iceland. A coach can drop you off and then return to pick you up, say, three weeks later at the same or another pre-arranged spot. If you plan your outward route to be different from the return you can extend your view of Iceland. You pay for the time and distance involved and so it would be expensive to have a bus with you for any length of time especially if the vehicle is to be idle for any lengthy periods of time, and you have to provide for the driver. The three companies — Arena Tours, Guðmundur Jónasson, and Úlfar Jakobsen — offer excellent facilities for camping tours with kitchen wagons. Coaches can be hired in advance through Tour Operators.

Bus Services

Public bus services (Figure 15) cover most of the main roads of the island although they are not necessarily timed to link with each other. Full details are published in the Leiðabók (see Chapter 4).

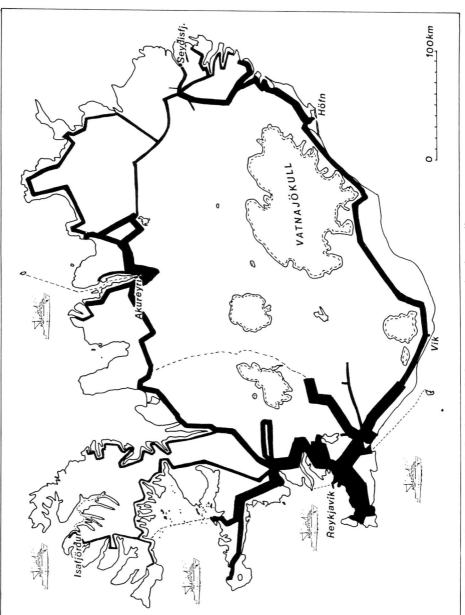

Fig. 15.   Bus and ferry routes in Iceland. Line thickness proportional to bus traffic.

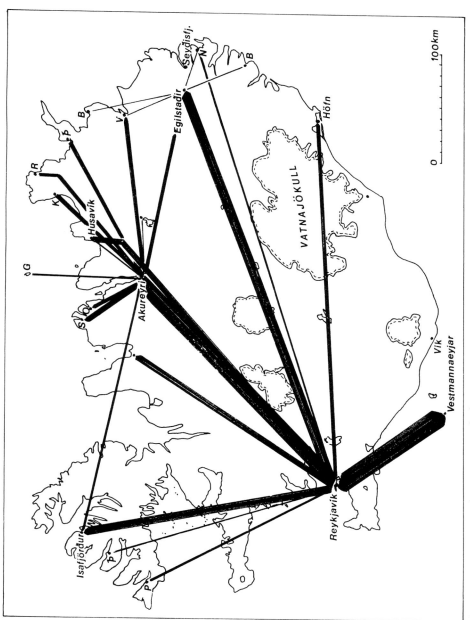

Fig. 16. Domestic aircraft routes. Line thickness proportional to traffic.

Buses depart from the long-distance bus station (Umferdamidstöd) on Hringabraut near to Reykjavik airport. As with everything else do check and double-check the times. Buses have been known to depart early!

Buses can carry quite a lot of luggage. Personal rucsacs and, say, a box of food/equipment each should be manageable. Large expeditions should not however expect to find places 'on spec'. Reykjavik-Akureyri and Reykjavik-Skaftafell-Höfn are two much used routes and groups could be disappointed. There are also two scheduled services through the centre of Iceland. Groups working in the north may like to consider travelling one way by air or by the coastal route and the return through the middle. These journeys are bookable through Tour Operators.

In 1985 an experimental budget camping tour is being offered by one tour operator whereby you can get on and off a bus at any point along a circular route around Iceland.

Aircraft (Icelandair) (Figure 16)

This is worth consideration by expeditions inspite of slightly higher costs. With the Group Inclusive Tour reduction the costs of air and land travel compare very favourably. Time is the main factor. Reykjavik-Akureyri, for example, takes 8 hours by bus and 55 minutes by air. There are regular services from Reykjavik to Akureyri (5/day), Egilstadir (1-2day), Höfn í Hornafjördur (5/week), Húsavik (1/day), Isafjördur (2-3/day), Nordfjördur (3/week), Patreksfjördur (3/week), Saudarkrókur (every weekday),

Vestmannaeyjar (3/day), Þingeyri (2/week). All departures are subject to a domestic departure tax. A number of special tickets are available for visitors that enable you to take a specified number of flights within a limited period. There are also special Air/Bus Rover tickets.

In addition to the scheduled Icelandair flights Flugfélag Norðurlands flies regularly from Akureyri to Egilstaðir, Grímsey, Húsavík, Ísafjörður, Kópasker, Ólafsjörður, Raufarhöfn, Siglufjörður, Vopnafjörður, Þórshöfn and Reykjavík. Flugfélag Austurlands flies from Egilstaðir to Bakkafjörður, Borgarförður, Breiðdalsvík, Höfn í Hornafjörður and Reykjavík.

Private Aircraft

There are now a number of private companies operating charter services. At Reykjavík airport these include Sverrir Thoroddsen and Helgi Jónsson. These companies are based at the old control tower alongside Hótel Loftleiðir. Helgi Jonsson flies a weekly service to Kulusuk (twice weekly in the summer). He has a self-catering guesthouse for up to 23 people which avoids the need for additional helicopter transport to the mainland. In Akureyri Flugfélag Norðurlands operate similar services. Expeditions have made use of small aircraft for reconnaissance purposes, aerial photography, and even for sightseeing. Helgi Jónsson and Flugfélag Norðurlands also fly expeditions to Greenland. Flugfélag Norðurlands have aircraft based in Greenland during the summer for the Danish government and have regular traffic between Akureyri and Mesters Vig.

Lorries

Expeditions with large freight loads may need to send their freight ahead by lorry. There are two main depots in Reykjavík that serve the principal towns in Iceland and the rates are quite reasonable. These are Vörflutningamiðstödin h.f., Borgartúni 21, Reykjavík Tel: 1-04-40) and Landflutningar, Skútuvógi 8, Reykjavík (Tel: 8-46-00).

Ponies

Ponies are not recommended for general expedition use. They are expensive to hire and difficult to feed in the interior. Unlike a vehicle they cannot be relied upon to stay in one place while you climb a mountain! An Icelandic guide would probably be needed to look after the animals. In short, they are probably more trouble than they are worth.

River Rafts

Since the Iceland Breakthrough expedition pioneered the use of rafts in Iceland a company offering rafting trips has opened in Reykjavík. Icelandic glacial rivers provide exciting possibilities for those with experience.

Mail Boats and Ferries (Figure 15)

Pamphlets about individual ferries can be picked up at the tourist bureau or travel agencies in Reykjavík. The principal ones are:

m.s. Fagranes	Ísafjörður-Vigur-Hvítanes-Ögur-Ædey-Baeir -Melgraseyri-Vatnsfjörður-Reykjanes -Arngerðareyri-Eyri.
m.s. Akraborg	Reykjavík-Akranes.
m.s. Drangur	Akureyri-Grímsey.
m.s. Baldur	Stykkishólmur-Flatey-Brjránslaekjar.
m.s. Hérjólfur	Thórlakshöfn-Vestmannaeyjar(Heimaey).

Cycling

Cyclists have been observed but both they and their cycles need to be robust! The expedition previously referred to found that riding a bicycle was preferable to walking across the sandur and a useful, cheap method of running errands. If you take one ensure that it is simple and sturdy, and has a well-sprung seat; and don't forget the repair kit and tools. See Chapter 6. concerning taking a bicycle by air.

Snowmobiles

The growth of interest in this form of travel does increase the possibility of their use by expeditions. (See Appendix G — The New Touring Club).

Walking

Hitching is possible but not for a whole expedition of course. Individuals are not advised to walk off the beaten track on their own although some certainly do. For an expedition, some sort of transport is required to get to a base camp or to act as a supply vehicle. However, you may find yourself in

Sound Links
in a Flexible Chain

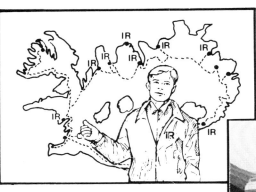

Our branches around Iceland are like
links in a chain — contacting one gives
access to them all.
Flexible service is our byword. You can
hire a car on a short- or long-term basis.
Just pick it up wherever you want and
return it to any of our branches.

interRent

need of hitching, eg. by missing the only scheduled bus for a week. Be prepared for long waits. One group spent 7 hours hitching out of Skaftafell and two days trying to get out of Djúpivógur. You may manage 14km one day and 300km the next. Cars will often stop but the journeys are often not very long.

Self-Drive Hire

Icelandic roads are a real test for any vehicle and it is not surprising to find that hire rates are high and that cars other than 4-wheel drive are not permitted off the principal road network. Costs are high and as a general guidance we suggest that self-drive be a last resort when you have calculated the cost of other methods. Of course a Land Rover, for example, may be the only way to achieve your objectives. In our view, vehicles do not give as much flexibility to movement as might be expected. Vehicles are always a liability, especially if they are not your own, and the penalties for damage are high. Do be sure to read the small print to see what you are signing for. Do remember that if you reserve a car from abroad, and it fails, the fault does not lie with your agent. You will have signed the documents on a contract between yourself and the Icelandic car hire firm.

In most cases, hired vehicles must be returned to their starting point. Both 7-seater and 12-seater Land Rovers can be hired but on Icelandic roads we would suggest that a loaded vehicle should take no more than 5 or 8 people respectively. It is also recommended that two 7-seater Land Rovers are a safer car hire than one 12-seater if you will be travelling in any of the remote

and difficult areas such as the Gaesavatnaleid, 4-wheel drive Bronco and Mitsubishi are also available.

9-seater microbuses are available but they are not suitable for roads in the interior on account of their low clearance, especially through rivers. A minibus **may** get through the Sprengisandur route; it probably would not get through the Kjalvegur (between the Langjökull and Hofsjökull), and definitely would not get through the Gaesavatnaleid, north of Vatnajkull. See Chapter 16 for a detailed description.

Drivers must be over 19 years of age and carry their current driver's licence. There are a number of car hire companies but few stock four-wheel drive vehicles. The largest company is Höldur h.f. (Inter-Rent). If in the height of the season you have difficulty in hiring a vehicle try some of the smaller companies listed in the Yellow Pages under 'Bilaleigur'. Tour operators offer attractive fly-drive schemes which may be worth investigating.

TAKING YOUR OWN VEHICLE TO ICELAND

It is beyond the scope of this book to discuss the acquisition of vehicles which we regard as a general expedition problem. As we see it the problem breaks down under three headings as follows:

1. **Four-wheel drive or Two-wheel drive?** The answer is simple. If you wish to go into the interior then it has to be 4-wheel drive. If you plan to tackle a route such as the Gaesavatnaleid, north of Vatnajökull, then two vehicles will be safer than one because you could well get stuck in quicksand or a river, or quite simply break down.

A Ford Transit, or similar, is wholly unsuitable to fording rivers or negotiating the potholes and boulders of the interior. Transits do not seem to like the low grade Icelandic petrol although they cope well enough with the principal roads.

2. **Petrol or Diesel** Diesel fuel in Iceland is cheaper than in Britain while petrol is more expensive. You gain more miles per gallon from diesel, in fact the consumption on the Icelandic interior tracks is better than for petrol on roads in the United Kingdom. Fuel prices, unlike in Britain, are standard all over Iceland, even in the interior. However there is a tax on imported diesel vehicles. The tax is not exorbitant and is based on vehicle weight and the proposed length of stay.

3. **Ferry or advance freight?** The ferry services have been dealt with in Chapter 6. Time is the principal factor here on both counts and a logistics exercise based on current fare rates, mileages and petrol costs will need to be carried out. For British groups to get to the ferry they must drive all the way to Aberdeen and transit to the Shetlands. The ferry then docks on the east coast at Seydisfjördur whereas the airborne party will arrive at Keflavík on the west coast.

To ship your vehicle out in advance will mean that it must be delivered to the port three weeks prior to your arrival in Iceland and you may not be able to spare it for so long. The same must be borne in mind for the return journey.

CALCULATING COSTS: A British group trying to calculate the relative cost will need to know the following:

FERRY

Fare:	Aberdeen-Lerwick (Return) Vehicle and Passengers
	Lerwick-Seyðisfjörður (Return) Vehicle and Passengers
Accommodation:	Two nights in Lerwick (see Chapter 6)
Fuel:	Home base — Aberdeen (Return)
	Seyðisfjörður — Reykjavík (Return) (744 Km)
Food Costs:	en route — esp. Faroes stop-over.
Insurance:	
Green Card:	

FREIGHT

Fare:	Runcorn/Felixstowe — Reykjavík (R)
Warehouse:	Dues in Iceland and UK.
Customs:	Charges in Iceland and UK.
Fuel:	Home base — port.
Insurance:	For the longer period away from home.
Green Card:	

LEGALITIES

Insurance: The Green Card applies to Iceland and so there is no longer the requirement that visitors should obtain Third Party cover with an Icelandic Insurance Company. However should you wish to insure your vehicle in Iceland you can do so with Almennar Tryggingar, Posthússtraetei 9, Reykjavík. Rates are reasonable. You will need to shop around at home to obtain reasonable cover but try The Guardian Royal (via A.A.?), and the Commercial Union. The A.A. Five Star Scheme includes Iceland.

International Driving Licence: The red print states that this is required for Iceland although we are unaware of any request for it to be shown. In any case you must take your own Driving Licence which must, of course, be current and unblemished. In the United Kingdom International Driving Licences are available from AA and RAC offices.

Drivers' Age: Drivers must be over 19 years of age.

PRE-EXPEDITION CHECKS

Icelandic terrain is rigorous and you will want to know that your vehicles are in good shape. A thorough technical check-over is essential. Schools may be able to obtain this through their Authority's Technical Services Section. Do allow plenty of time for this, say two months prior to departure, just in case there are any major jobs to be carried out on the vehicle. If any of your members are attending Car Mechanics courses this could be useful to you both at home and in Iceland. Several points concerning Land Rovers need to be borne in mind:

(i)   Continuous dust and water will attack the stub axle inner bearing oil seals. They will certainly need renewal on return and should therefore be in good shape.

(ii)   Land Rovers with replacement radiators frequently stall when crossing rivers. This is because the garage has failed to replace both of the cowls situated on the engine side of the radiator, because there is no apparent reason for the existence of the second radiator cowl under normal circumstances. It is designed to stop the fan spraying water over the engine and ignition when fording, and is **essential** in Iceland.

(iii)   Heavy duty tyres are essential if you plan to leave the main roads.

(iv)   Land Rovers with free-wheel hubs already fixed may expect trouble from them. They seem to cause excessive stress on the axle resulting in periodic 'clunks' and, finally, a broken half-shaft.

(v) A bonnet-mounted spare wheel is a disadvantage when you need to be able to see as much of the track in front of you as possible.

(vi) Under-bonnet sound-damping can be a menace in watery terrains — it holds water thrown up underneath the bonnet, which soaks to the rear end and drips incessantly onto the coil and distributor leads.

(vii)   T.A.C. ignition coils are very susceptible to damp, and frequently misfiring takes place in wet areas. A normal 12-volt coil is recommended.

(viii)   Removal of side steps reduces the risk of fouling underwater obstacles, or other vehicles, on mountain roads.

(ix)   If you have fitted spotlights low down on the vehicle (eg. on the bumper) note that they will quickly fill with water during any protracted river crossings.

(x)   Throttle linkages may tend to stick after about two weeks. Liberal coatings of grease on all moving parts is suggested.

(xii) Liberal greasing is also advisable on the swivel-linkage at the bottom of the transfer lever as this can also gradually lose its free movement and can cause an inadequate engagement of high-gear ratio. Symptoms are bad engagement of high-gear, and jumping out of that gear ratio.

(xiii)   When leaving the vehicle in the hands of the shipping company, remove the fuses from the radio, tape-player etc. Otherwise you may find that your battery is flat after use by warehousemen.

LAND ROVER SPARES

Your attention is drawn to the Rover Company's 'Guide to Land Rover Expeditions'. The following list has been compiled from the experiences of several expeditions to Iceland.

1 Distributor cap	4 spark plug
1 set HD leads with plug caps	1 set distributor points
1 condenser	1 rotor arm

1 coil and coil cap — if screw-in type make sure that it has its brass washer; if a push-fit type it needs a bent retaining pin (easily made from safety pin).

Shock absorber bushes — 6 tapering and 4 flat type. 2 self-locking nuts for bottom of rear shock absorbers.

2 hub oil seals	6 hub oil seals paper gaskets
2 hub oil seals felt washers	2 hub locking plate washers
2 hub split pins	1 water pump
1 water pump gasket	2 fan belts

1 each of all radiator (3) and heater (3) hoses.

1 wiper blade of each type in use	2 brake hoses — front
1 brake hose — rear	1 clutch hose
1 thermostat	2 thermostat gaskets
2 Half shafts (1 long and 1 short)	2 differential gaskets

1 metre thin fence wire
2 front springs — if existing ones look weak and if a large roof rack is being used (the extra weight is taken by front springs on rough ground)
1 each of overhaul kits for: clutch slave cylinder
                              clutch master cylinder
                              brake master
                              brake wheel cylinders — 2 front
                                                     — 2 rear
                              petrol pump
                              carburettor (incl. float)

Exhaust Parts: silencer
               exhaust middle pipe
               exhaust downpipe
               silencer gasket
               exhaust mounting rubbers (2)
               exhaust manifold down studs (3)
               Gungum and firegum
               flexible exhaust pipe and jubilee clips

Gaskets in addition to the above: rocker cover
                                  cylinder head
                                  exhaust manifold
                                  carburettor

1 Four-wheel-drive pivot bolt	1 clutch housing drain plug
1 spare inner tube	1 spare outer tube
1 puncture repair kit	3 tyre levers

2 high-lift jacks — preferably hydraulic and including one bumper jack and a spare for the hydraulic jacks
1 inflatable exhaust jack

4 rubber link mats	1 sledgehammer
1 pick	1 pliers
1 wood saw	1 hacksaw
1 hammer and assorted nails	2 Radweld or Certseal
1 hand drill and assorted bits	1 blowlamp
2 shovels — one standard, one long	1 inspection light

5 litres EP90 with at least one filler bottle
Double the estimated requirement of 20/50 oil

spanners and assorted nuts and bolts
assorted screwdrivers and screws
files and sandpaper
soldering iron and solder (fluxed and ordinary)

gasket cement	Swarfega
brake fluid (2 small tins)	brake bleeding kit
wire	string
evostik	plastic metal
insulating tape	WD40
spare ignition keys	
Parts list	Workshop manual
Spare cash for repairs	

WHAT CAN GO WRONG?

The following examples experienced by one expedition may serve to illustrate the sorts of problem that you are likely to encounter. They are derived from their expedition report and are examples of the type of useful information that could be included in your own expedition report. They had both an old petrol and an old diesel Land Rover.

(a) DIESEL Bolts in front offside steering arm sheared off, on the way to Mývatn. A farmer miraculously found two replacement bolts for us and charged us a nominal sum for two hours work. In Akureyri we replaced the bolts for the correct ones, including plates to prevent further loosening.

(b) PETROL Just as we reached the end of our interior crossing, we noticed a "list" developing in the vehicle, and an increasing tendency to "bottom" on the suspension. The bracket to which the rear offside leaf spring was attached has torn away from the chassis. As we were still 40 miles from Reykjavik, we decided to make two trips in the diesel vehicle so that we could bring the petrol vehicle in empty. A phone call to F.í.B. (The Icelandic A.A.) put us in touch with a workshop in Kópavogur where the repair and welding was done in three days.

(c) (DIESEL) On the way to Reykjavik, whilst being overtaken by a coach, we had been forced to the side of the road, and the exhaust had caught on a rock, fracturing it at the only part we had not replaced in England. An excellent repair was effected with an oil-can and two exhaust bandages. The vehicle was also suffering from steering problems, and a frightening "shaking" of the steering. Three knuckle joints had to be replaced.

(d) (PETROL) On the way east from Vík we developed a "clunk" while travelling in gear. It happened in the middle of a storm, and this meant getting under the vehicle which was anything but pleasant. The tow rope was put on, and we chugged the 10-15 miles to Kirkjubaejarklaustur. Here the garage stayed open an extra hour for us and eventually eliminated that it was a broken half-shaft, unfortunately. The next morning (Saturday and one week from our sailing date) he was able to show us the fault. The crown-wheel and pinion in our rear differential were shattered. Telephone calls to Reykjavik established that we could obtain a reconditioned replacement differential at some cost. It arrived on the Tuesday. Our problem was paying . . .

(e) (DIESEL) Our last problem was saved for the motorway on our way home. At first we thought it was a return of our steering problem but it turned out to be the front nearside tyre which was losing its tread (stripping off). Luckily the bubble, which had spread round one-third of the tyre was spotted in time, and the spare put on. It had been nearly new when we left.

WHEN IN ICELAND . . .:

(a) Tighten everything regularly.

(b) Try to avoid having three people in front. It is far more comfortable for the driver when he can immediately locate all gears without having to disentangle himself from a sleeping passenger. Driving in Iceland is very tiring.

(c) Inexperienced drivers should note that a loaded Land Rover has a tendency to 'wander' on gravel roads and can be dangerous on extreme banks at bends.

(d) Use your gears. Sharp breaking can be dangerous on the frequent loose gravel.

(e) If you get bogged down the Icelandic method is to dig a hole under the bumper into which stones are put and then a length of planking. With jacks on this firm base, the vehicle is raised as high as possible. With a number of jacks the vehicle can be lifted clear of the mud fairly quickly. Mud around the axles is removed with the long-handled shovel and the rubber mats are put under the wheels. The vehicle can now be jumped on to firm ground (low gear, full revs and let the clutch out suddenly).

IF TRAVELLING BY SMYRILL LINE:

There are plenty of seats for deck passengers but keep away from the deck chairs in rough weather; you may be thrown against the bulkhead. Keep your sleeping bags handy. If you have bad weather you will probably not need to feed but for fair weather crossings we suggest you have a large cooked meal before departure and take sandwiches. All the journeys are short. If you have a trailer have someone manhandle it round. To save a long wait when coming off the ferry, be the last vehicle on — like everyone else reading this book!

When disembarking at Torshavn report to the car deck with your green card ready. **ALL** vehicles must be driven off. If stopping-over in Torshavn it is better to camp outside the town at the roadside, **but ask permission first.** Before disembarking at Seyđisfjörđur fill in a customs declaration form in duplicate and send it with the insurance certificate to the smaller of the two yellow huts as soon as someone can get ashore on foot. Then drive ashore for the customs check when possible; your papers will probably have been cleared by then and you can then drive off. The whole procedure can take less than an hour.

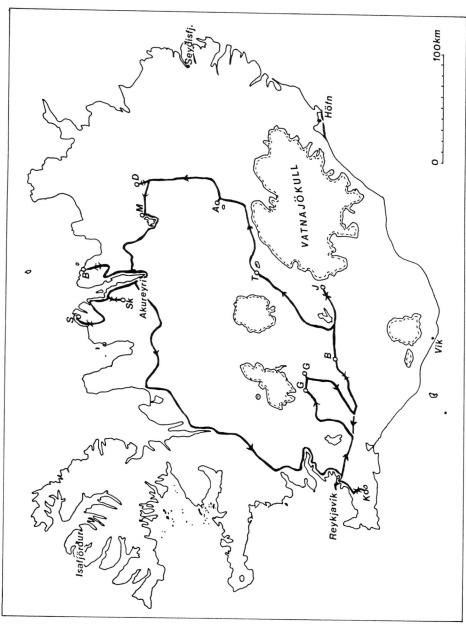

Fig. 17. The route referred to in "Sample Mileages".

If carrying spare fuel cans they must be empty on arrival in Iceland but at Seyðisfjörður the petrol station is 200m. from the dock. There is a campsite but there are also many good spots at the roadside between Seyðisfjörður and Egilsstaðir. Seyðisfjörður to Mývatn is 135 miles and takes 4½ hours by laden Land Rover.

SAMPLE MILEAGES: (Figure 17)

Reykjavík-Krísuvík (R)	50 miles	203 litres*
Reykjavík-Geysir	180 miles	65 litres
Geysir-Gullfoss-Burfell-Jökulheimar-Reykjavík	277 miles	118 litres*
Reykjavík-Jökulheimar-Tungnaá	186 miles	75 litres
Tungnaá-Gaesavötsnleið-Askja-Dettifoss-Mývatn-Akureyri	400 miles	99 litres
Akureyri-Brettingsstaðir-Akureyri	136 miles	63 litres
Akureyri-Skiðadalur-Siglufjörður	213 miles	77 litres
Siglufjörður-Skiðadalur-Akureyri-Reykjavík	388 miles	95 litres

* includes the filling of 8 five-gallon petrol cans. In practice there was no need to have more than 10 gallons in reserve. The figures above are based on refuelling points and are therefore not true consumption figures. The following times may be of interest:

Reykjavík-Jökulheimar	13 hours
Tungnaáfoss-Tungnafell hut	6 hours
Tungnafell-Askja	14 hours
Askja-Dettifoss	5 hours

Miles per Gallon:

The following estimates for Land Rovers may be helpful:

	Petrol:	Diesel:
British Roads	18.50 m.p.g.	29.00 m.p.g.
Icelandic Coast	15.00 m.p.g.	23.00 m.p.g.
Icelandic interior	14.00 m.p.g.	21.50 m.p.g.

ROUTE PLANNING

Note should be taken of the approximate travel speeds suggested in the next section and ample allowance made for stops to eat, sightsee, change wheels etc. Allowance for a spare day on long sections of your route prove valuable should your vehicle suffer a breakdown.

It is very tiring to drive on Icelandic roads and very uncomfortable at times for the passengers in a loaded vehicle. Try not to be too ambitious in your programme. You will probably enjoy a shorter route with ample time to stop, walk, and get to know the country at first hand, far more than a long route where you have to drive for most of the time. Several groups who have used Land Rovers extensively, felt that their dependence on the vehicle to some extent deprived them of that personal contact with the country that is an essential part of any expedition. In other words they drove when really they should have been walking.

Road Conditions

Details of road conditions can be gained from the Icelandic equivalent of the British A.A., Félag Íslenzkra Bifreiðaeigenda (F.Í.B.) whose office is at Nóatúni 17, Reykjavík (Tel: 2-99-99)

In the event of snow conditions it may be possible to obtain a road report from the long-distance bus station on Hringabraut (Tel: 2-23-00). Comments on specific routes appear from time to time in the Iceland Unit Bulletin, "Island". The Gæsavatnaleið is described in Chapter 16.

The 1:750,000 Tourist map is quite good for general motoring but is not very accurate in detail. Several road categories are given on this map: (the speeds are guides only).

Principal Roads: Generally good consisting of hardened grit surface. Potholes may take you by surprise. Tarmac surfaces are found only in main towns and selected stretches out of Reykjavík (eg. Reykjavík-Keflavík, Reykjavík-Hvolsvöllur) but are gradually being extended. Some of the grit roads are first class. (30 mph)

Roads — some rugged and only passable in summer: We would call these 'tracks'. They are often pitted with potholes but small streams are usually bridged. Snow on high passes could occasionally be encountered (eg. Öxnadalsheið, west of Akureyri). You need to develop the Icelanders' panache about road blemishes: "Road? Of course it's a road!". (20 mph)

Mountain Track — normally passable for all vehicles during the summer: The Kjalvegur (Kjölur), between Langjökull and Hofsjökull, falls into this category and is not always passable by all vehicles. The levels of the rivers can vary enormously within a short space of time. The Sandá river, just after Gullfoss has been observed to fluctuate between 0.4m. and 1.5m. within 24 hours. Mud and drifting sand can be other problems. (12 mph or less)

Mountain Track — with unbridged rivers normally only passable for four-wheel drive vehicles during the summer: Four-wheel drive, or split-axle coaches can tackle most of these but some are too narrow or deep in mud or sand. The Sprengisandur route is now quite good but tracks like the Gæsavatnaleið are quite a different proposition. Many of these tracks are difficult to follow owing to the lack of waymarks and the confusion of vehicle tracks that occur in some places. Usual marks are yellow painted stones or posts. Vehicles should travel in groups of two or more, especially if no two-way radio is available. (8 mph or less).

Bridle Path or mountain track: Generally not suitable for any vehicle.

In addition there are many tracks in the interior that are not marked on the maps but which may be used by four-wheel drive vehicles. Lack of traffic here could mean lengthy delays before rescue and travellers in the interior should not consider rescue to be a right. It is troublesome and costly, and the cost will be yours.

Petrol Stations: These are marked on the 1:750,000 Tourist map and on the 1:500,000 Touring Map, but cannot be guaranteed to exist. Similarly you will find that new stations pop up. Only the cheapest grade of petrol is available. Petrol stations are usually open from 7.30am (9.30am on Sundays) to 9.15pm.

Under no circumstances should you at any time use your vehicle to drive off the existing track. The Nature Conservation Act is quite explicit on this. The proliferation of vehicle tracks in the interior has done untold damage to the vegetation and landscape.

98

8 ACCOMMODATION

INTRODUCTION

It is to be assumed that the majority of expeditions will be planning a camp-based expedition. Most school groups will wish to camp, if only on grounds of cost, but research expeditions may find it more appropriate to be hut-based from the point of view of analysis and write-up. We therefore ignore hotels in this chapter and make but brief mention of other forms of accommodation.

Even if your expedition is essentially camp-based we do recommend that you spend your first and last nights in sleeping bag accommodation. On the outward journey this will enable you to adjust to Iceland more readily and give you a firm roof over your head. If the weather is bad your tents will have been spared a drenching and moral will be high as you set out for base camp.

On the return journey a night under cover will allow time to dry out, check equipment, pack freight and, dare we say it, get the expedition report under way.

Accommodation is summarised in Table 2. at the end of the chapter.

SLEEPING BAG ACCOMMODATION

Schools

In Reykjavík the Hvassaleiti Grammar School is given over to sleeping bag accommodation and is recommended for groups. It is modern, spacious and pleasant, and groups may leave food and equipment there under lock and key while they are away in the interior. Whole classrooms with their own attached WC facilities can be allocated to individual groups. Cooking facilities are provided but it is always advisable to take a few extra pots. Although the school is situated to the east of the City Centre it is conveniently close to the No:3 bus route. Tour Operators' coaches will deliver you there on your first day and collect you for the return to Keflavík airport.

In Britain the Iceland Unit acts as general sales agent for the school which can be booked through your Tour Operator.

In other parts of Iceland some school boarding houses become hostels or Edda Hotels (see Table 2). Other schools can sometimes be made available to educational groups but only by special arrangement. The Iceland Unit can advise.

Youth Hostels

Icelandic Youth Hostels are not placed so that you can easily walk between them. In most cases you will need to hitch, drive or use public transport and

HOSTELLING

THE TRUE WAY OF TRAVEL

Y.H. TRAVEL SERVICE
Laufásvegur 41, Box 1045,
121 Reykjavík, Iceland.
Tel.: (91)-24950, Telex: 2228 skjól att. BÍF.

Your travel service waiting to help you making your stay more enjoyable.

for this reason the hosteller in Iceland needs to be very self-sufficient with regard to carrying his own tent, sleeping bag, and cooker. The standard of hostels varies greatly but they are extremely friendly, though often crowded. A leaflet entitled 'Hostelling in Iceland' can be obtained from Icelandair or Tour Operators, and the Iceland Unit can supply details.

It is advisable to book in advance by writing to each hostel, enclosing an International Reply Coupon although in most cases you can book through your Tour Operator and pay in advance.

Youth Hostels are open to anyone although members of the International Youth Hostels Association are entitled to a preferential rate. If you are travelling as a groups only the leader needs to be a member. In Reykjavik the existing hostel on the corner of Laufásvegur and Baldursgata is really too small for groups but a new one is being built adjacent to the camp site and swimming pool on Sundlaugsvegur. In the summer months a school (Miðbaejarskólinn) is opened up alongside Tjörnin, the lake in central Reykjavik. The Akureyri hostel is a good jump-off point for expeditions to the north especially if they have freighted their goods direct to Akureyri. The hostel is in a pleasant locality just 10 minutes walk from the town centre.

Figure 18. shows the location of the principal hostels.

Farmhouses: A number of farms now offer accommodation either within the farmhouses or, as at Húsafell, in chalets adjacent. By and large these are unsuitable for expeditions but could perhaps serve for small field study groups. A leaflet is available through the Iceland Unit.

Abandoned Farmhouses: Although farmhouses may seem abandoned the buildings are usually owned by someone and may even be used by them from time to time in the summer months. Make all possible enquiries. You have no right of entry.

Scout Accommodation

Iceland has had a Scout movement since 1912 and since 1932 has fostered rescue services throughout the country. Scout groups from other countries may be able to obtain accommodation by linking with the Icelandic Scout Association. In any case Scouts who are planning overseas ventures should be in communication with their own national headquarters. The principal camping and outdoor shop in Reykjavik is the Scout shop, Skátabúdin. The Scouts also have a training centre and camp site at Úlfljótsvatn, south of Thingvallavatn.

Huts (Figure 18)

There are various kinds of hut in Iceland. Most belong to a society or a parish for their own specific function but may be used by travellers in an emergency. They are not designed for large group use and by and large are not bookable. Dick Phillips has written a broadsheet on the Huts of South-Central Iceland which is available from the Iceland Unit but this is the only existing regional account. The various types of hut are listed below:

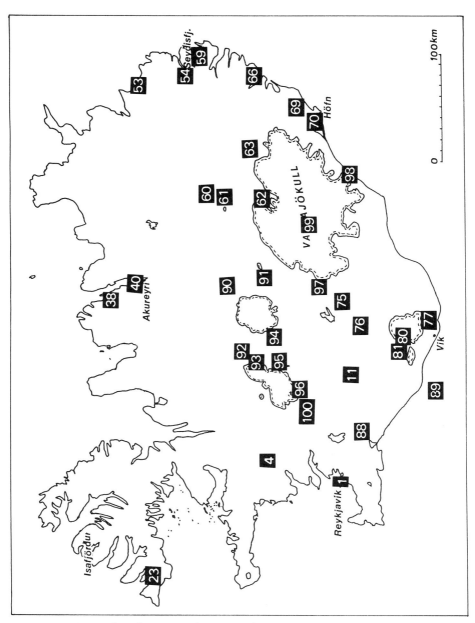

Fig. 18. Youth Hostels and Huts. For key to numbers see text.

Ferðafélag Íslands: There are now 16 huts owned by the Travel Association of Iceland. These huts are for the use of members but are open to others on payment of a modest fee. There is no advance booking but visitors should note that members of the Travel Association have priority. Please leave the hut as you found it and, where there is no warden, place the cash in the box provided. The huts are marked on the 1:750,000 Tourist Map and further details may be obtained from the Unit.

District Travel Associations: Several district associations (eg. Ferðafélag Akureyrar) have their own huts run on a similar basis to those of Ferðafélag Íslands.

Slysarvarnafélag Íslands: The Lifesaving Association is primarily concerned with the preservation of life at sea. The majority of its huts are therefore in coastal situations and are readily discernable by their orange colour and the red cross of the Icelandic flag and the lifeboat symbol of the Association. Some however are situated inland close to the tops of passes for the use of stranded travellers. The huts are for **emergencies only** and any misuse of the huts or their contents is punishable by law. The instructions within read as follows:

(a) This shelter is intended for the exclusive use of shipwrecked mariners and others who have to seek shelter and refuge in bad weather or distress.

(b) The surroundings are remote and difficult to pass for strangers and very misleading. Therefore, if possible, remain where you are until assistance arrives, for you will not have to wait long. Attract attention to your presence by rockets and any kind of light signals by night and smoke signals by daytime. If you must seek inhabited parts, follow the guide posts as best you can. Make a careful study of the map on the spot.

(c) The National Lifesaving Society of Iceland bids welcome all those who stand in need of help and care, and authorise them to make use of the provisions stored in the shelter, as well as such equipment as may be needed. Study the inventory list and instructions for use.

(d) Those requiring comforts are asked to kindly mention this in the guestbook, state all circumstances and say what stores have been used.

(e) The misuse and unnecessary expenditure of the stores belonging to the Association is forbidden, as this may lead to dangerous consequences.

(f) All who come here must treat every piece of inventory stores with care and cleanliness, and not handle anything unnecessarily.

Groups wishing to know of the nearest emergency shelter in their working area may write to the Iceland Unit.

Vegamálaskrifstofan: The Directorate of Roads has several emergency shelters on passes and exposed moors. The conditions applying to these are the same as for those of the Lifesaving Society.

Saeluhús hreppsins: Huts owned by parishes or districts may be used by farmers for sheep round-ups (for themselves, not the sheep!). They may also be used by travellers with permission from the hreppstjóri (sherrif) or

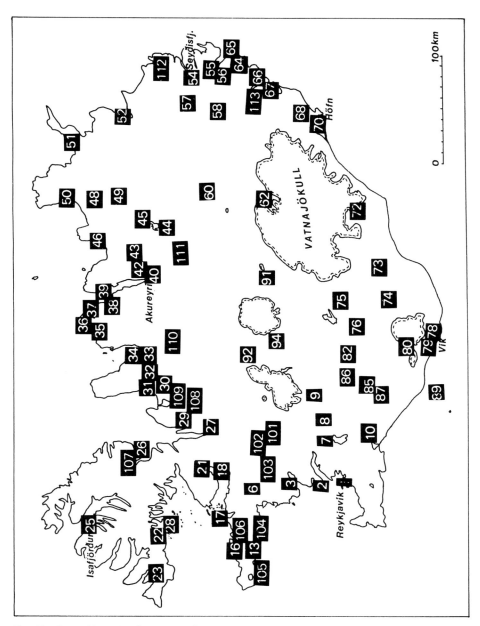

Fig. 19. Camp Sites. For key to numbers see text.

by paying the appropriate fee into the honesty box. These huts should not be used for long periods. They are intended for overnight or emergency use. Should you decide to camp in the vicinity of one of these huts do not camp too near.

CAMPING
Rent-a-Tent
If you do not want to take your own tents to Iceland, perhaps to keep down excess baggage, you can rent a tent from Tjaldaleigan (Appendix G). They have tents of various sizes with built-in groundsheets, also sleeping bags, gas stoves, pots and pans etc. They also do a special hitch hikers package. These can be booked through Tour Operators.

Camp Sites
There are almost unlimited opportunities for camping in Iceland as it is a national pastime. In the towns however tents are usually confined, not unreasonably, to one site. This also applies to areas where people congregate in large numbers as at Mývatn, Thingvellir or Skaftafell.

The comments that follow refer to sites used most frequently by expeditions. Full details of all the sites are given in a leaflet entitled 'Camping' published annually by the Iceland Tourist Board. The locations of most of the sites are shown in Figure 19.

Reykjavik: A good site on Sundlaugarbraut in the north-east part of the city and reached by a No:5 bus from the city centre or from Reykjavik (not Keflavik) airport. Directions from the international airline terminal (Hótel Loftleidir) are given in Chapter 6. The site has hot and cold running water and clean toilets. The site can be crowded and noisy but it does have one great advantage: it is adjacent to the magnificently naturall-heated swimming pool with its warm water and 'hot-pots'. It is also close to the cargo port (Sundahöfn) where your freight will be unloaded.

Akureyri: For many years the site has been in the upper part of the town, behind the church and adjacent to the swimming pool. It is noisy, crowded and being encroached upon by buildings. There is a possibility that it may move to an alternative site.

Mývatn: Situated on the moraine hills to the north of the settlement of Reykjahlíd. The notorious flies come in two batches in the season; to avoid them you need to get as far from the lake as possible. If small groups look around they will find suitable hollows in the area below the airstrip. Toilet and washing facilities, spartan but sufficient. Camping elsewhere in the district is discouraged because the Mývatn district is a Special Protected Area. An alternative area may be found at **Skútustadir** at the southern end of the lake where it is less crowded and probably better if you have a vehicle. Of immediate local interest are the pseudocraters and you are close to the headwaters of the River Laxá of interest to ornithologists and freshwater biologists.

Jökulsárgljúr: Inside the National Park are two camp sites at Ásbyrgi and Vesturdal. This whole area is relatively untouched yet offers scope for a marvellous expedition setting of special interest to geologists, botanists, geomorphologists, and ornithologists.

Skaftafell: Camping within the National Park is restricted to this large well organised site which has excellent facilities. Because of the camping restrictions the Park is not suitable for mobile expeditions but some of the nearby areas are and this is a good base to operate from. Climbing the Öraefajökull is covered in Chapter 15.

Kirkjubaejarklaustur: Alongside the hotel whose facilities (including swimming pool) may be used. Good base for those using the road between here and Landmannalaugar. Geology of the Skaftá lava flows of interest.

Vik: A small, beautifully sheltered site beneath the old cliff line and surrounded by grassy banks to exclude vehicles. A good midway stopping point between Reykjavik and Skaftafell. Close to the Dýrhólaey cliffs.

Skógar: A small primitive site close to the waterfall and not too far from the hotel. Useful base for groups going to Sólheimajökull. The nearby folk museum is fascinating.

Landmannalaugar: The site adjacent to the hut is very stony and useless for pegs and groundsheets. Far better is the first camping plot that you come to when turning into the valley, about 1Km from the hut. Wonderful location.

Gorgeous 80°C water and good base for geological excursions. However, this is a protected area and one in which various research projects are being carried out. Camping in the hills beyond is discouraged and the advice of the wardens should be heeded. The site is open in July and August but may not be accessible at the very beginning of July.

Thingvellir: Now an extremely developed site with cafe, shop and toilets. Main interest geological and related to the rift valley.

Tungnafell: Truly a wilderness location adjacent to two huts which may be used in emergency for a small charge. Accessible from mid-July. Exposed in poor weather. Useful jump-off point for the Gaesavötnsleid. This area however is a sensitive one and one where large groups would be discouraged by the Research Council and Nature Conservation Council from making a base camp there.

Kerlingarfjöll: Visitors should note that the camping site at the ski school is private, as also are the facilities there. Groups should camp either lower down the valley near to the landing strip or about 500m. beyond the ridge on the north-east side. Groups intending to be there for any length of time are advised to inform the ski school.

Camping in the Interior

Never assume that you have the right to camp anywhere you wish even in the wilderness. The land may be grazing land or a nature reserve (see Chapter 2) and it could be as well to check with the Iceland Unit. This applies especially to large groups.

M.H.WEALE

TABLE 2. CAMP SITES, YOUTH HOSTELS and HUTS IN ICELAND

This list is a guide to the principal locations and was accurate at the time of going to press. The list is by no means exhaustive as it does not include the parish huts or those of the National Lifesaving Society for example.

LOCATION	YOUTH HOSTEL	CAMP SITE	SLEEPING BAG	EDDA HOTEL	MOUNTAIN HUT	BEDS (HUTS YH)	ADDITIONAL INFORMATION (see Key)
1. Reykjavík	X	X				53	YH: Laufásv.41
	X					70	Sundlaugsvegur S4
							CS: Sundlaugsv
2. Akranes		X					
3. Borganes		X	X				SB: Hotel Borganes
4. Varmaland	X					82	YH: Stafholtstungur
5. Reykholt				X			
6. Hreidavatn		X					
7. Thingvellir		X					
8. Laugarvatn		X	X	X			SB: Menntaskólinn
9. Geysir		X					
10. Selfoss		X	X				
11. Leirubakki	X					20	YH: Landssveiti
12. Jökulháls			X	X		10	FI
13. Búdir		X					
14. Arnarstapi			X				SB: Félagsheimilid Snaefell
15. Ólafsvík			X				SB: Sjóbúdir
16. Grundarfjördur		X					CS: Kverná
17. Stykkishólmur		X					
18. Búdardalur		X					
19. Svarfhóll			X				
20. Baer			X				
21. Laugar		X	X				SB: Súmarhótelid
22. Vatnasfjördur		X					
23. Patreksfjördur	X	X				40	YH: Breidavík
24. Bildudalur		X					
25. Ísafjördur		X					
26. Drang		X					
27. Stadarskáli		X					
28. Brjánslækur		X					
29. Hvammstangi		X					
30. Stóra Gilja		X					

	C1	C2	C3	C4	C5		
31. Blönduós		X	X				SB: Kvennaskólinn
32. Húnavellir		X	X				
33. Varmahlíd		X	X				
34. Saudakrókur		X					
35. Fljót		X					
36. Siglufjördur		X					
37. Ólafsfjördur		X					
38. Dalvík	X	X				20	YH: Hafnabraut 23
39. Hrísey		X					
40. Akureyri	X	X		X		60	YH: Stórholti 1/Lonsá
							CS: Town centre/ Lonsá
41. Stóru-Tjarnaskóli			X	X			
42. Vaglaskógi		X					
43. Laugaskóli		X	X				SB: Hótel Laugar
44. Skútusstadir		X	X				SB: South end of lake
45. Reykjahlíd		X					CS: Behind Hótel Reynihlíd
							also at Bjarg
46. Húsavík		X	X				
47. Skúlagardur			X				
48. Jökulsárgljúfur 1		X					CS: Ásbyrgi
49. Jökulsárgljúfur 2		X					CS: Vesturdalur
50. Kópasker		X					
51. Thórshöfn		X					
52. Vopnafjördur		X					
53. Húsey	X					20	YH: Hróastunga (28km from bus)
54. Seydisfjördur	X	X				36	YH: Hafaldan
55. Neskaupsstadur		X					
56. Reydarfjördur		X					
57. Egilsstadir		X		X			EH: Eidar — N. of Egilsst
58. Hallormstadir		X	X	X			
59. Mjóifjördur	X					II	YH: Solbrekka
60. Herdubreidarlindir		X	X		X	40	FFA
61. Dreki					X	20	FFA
62. Sigurdurskáli		X			X	60	FFH/FFF/FFV
							CS: Hvannalindir
63. Snaefell					X	30	FFF
64. Breiddalsvík		X	X	X			EH: Stadarborg
65. Stödvarfjördur		X					

	1	2	3	4	5	No.	Notes
66. Berunes	X	X				30	
67. Djúpivógur		X	X				SB: Ask at Hotel
68. Þórisdalur î Lóni		X					
69. Stafafell	X					20	
70. Höfn	X	X	X	X		30	YH: Alaugarey EH: Nesjaskóli CS: Thórisdalur
71. Hrollaugsstaðir			X				
72. Skaftafell		X					
73. Kirkjubaejarkl.		X	X	X			
74. Hrífunes		X					
75. Veiðivötn		X	X			80	FI
76. Landmannalaugar		X	X			110	FI
77. Reynisbrekka	X					14	YH: Mýrdalur (5km from bus)
78. Vík î Mýrdal		X	X				SB: Leikskála
79. Skógarskóli		X	X	X			
80. Thórsmörk		X			X	200	FI (Skagfjörðskáli)
81. Fljótsdalur	X					15	YH: Fljótshlíð (6km from bus)
82. Thjórsárdalur	X						
83. Sandartungu			X				
84. Hvollsvöllur			X				SB: Hlíðarveg 13
85. Leirubakki		X					
86. Flúðir		X	X				SB: Súmarhótelið
87. Hella		X	X				SB: Gisting Mosfells
88. Hvergerði	X					20	YH: Hveramörk 14
89. Vestmannaeyjar	X	X				30	YH: Höfðaveg 25
90. Laugafell					X	15	FFA
91. Tungnafell		X			X	200	FI (2 huts)
92. Hveravellir		X			X	40	FI
93. Thjófadalur					X	12	FI
94. Kerlingafjöll		X			X	40	FI (Ásgardur)
95. Hvítarnes					X	30	FI
96. Hagavatn					X	14	FI
97. Jökulheimar					X		JI only (2 huts)
98. Breiðá					X		JI only
99. Grímsvötn					X		JI only
100. Hlöduvellir					X	15	FI
101. Húsafell		X	X				SB: chalets

103. Bjarnarstadir	X				
103. Hredavatnskáli	X				
104. Gardar	X				
105. Arnarfell	X				
106. Kvenra	X				
107. Laugarhóll	X				
108. Vidigerdi	X				
109. Stóra-Gilsá	X				
110. Steinstadaskóli	X				
111. Hlídarskogur	X				
112. Stapi	X				
113. Eyjólfsstadir	X				

FI   Hut belonging to Ferdafélag Íslands
FFA Hut belong to Ferdafélag Akureyrar
FFV Hut belonging to Ferdafélag Vopnafjördur
FFF Hut belonging to Ferdafélag Fljótsdalshérads
JI   Hut belong to Iceland Glaciological Society

YH:)   (Youth Hostel
CS:)   (Camp site
) Address/directions for (
SB:)   (Sleeping bag accommodation
EH:)   (Edda Hotel

9 EXPEDITION SUPPLIES

GENERAL

Whatever supplies you bring to Iceland must be viewed within the context of your expedition aims. To say that you intend to bring your own food because it is two to three times more expensive in Iceland is an insufficient reason. We should be viewing our arrangements from the point of view that wherever possible we put something back in to the economy of the host country.

In recent years the increase of continental traffic via the Faroese ferry to Seyðisfjörður has caused some concern in Iceland. These entirely self-sufficient groups tour the back country, contribute to the soil erosion of the delicate landscape but put nothing back into the exchequer to compensate. The result in 1983 was a food tax to be levied on entry (Chapter 10). To many this was crippling and especially to young educational groups.

There are of course constraints on expeditions that require the import of supplies:

1. The need to pack all food into man/day units for more efficient use in the field.

2. The need to purchase in bulk lightweight A.F.D. foods that are generally not available in Iceland.

Those groups who can prove themselves to be 'bona fide' research or educational expeditions may be exempted from the tax on productiion of an 'Announcement' from the National Research Council (Chapter 10).

In any case bread, butter, cheese, and milk are very competitively priced and readily available both in Reykjavík and roadside stores out of town. You are not permitted to bring in butter, eggs, or uncooked meat.

The first few hours in another country can always be difficult from a catering point of view either because you have arrived at an ungodly hour, or because the expedition members want to explore the town, or because the hostel is too crowded to cater successfully as a group (Chapter 12). There are several solutions. You can instruct your members to bring with them enough sandwiches etc. to see them through to their first main meal, say on Day 2. You could provide a 'Reykjavík-only' box containing simple cold foods, soups etc. You could give every member a cash allowance and instruct them to eat where and when they wish and we suggest a few suitable expedition-pocket eating houses in the next paragraph and Appendix G.

The same problem may apply on the return to Reykjavík although by then you should have all sorts of odds and ends to finish up. However, expedition members may have had more than their fill of convenience

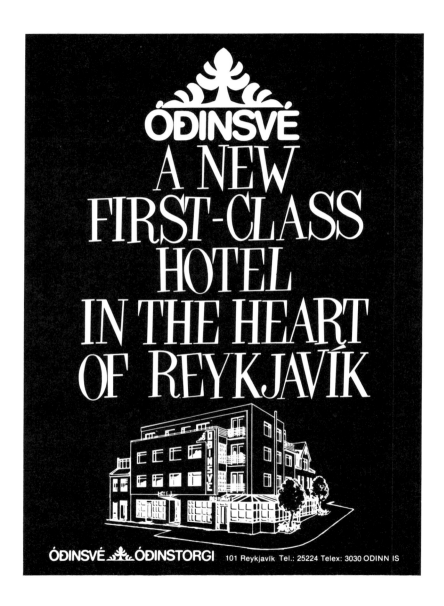

foods by that time and an end-of-expedition 'binge' is called for. For this you could negotiate a special group price at one of the Reykjavík eating houses such as Kokk Husid, Hressingaskálinn (Central), Mula Kaffi (near the camp site on Hallamúli) or Kaffi Vagninn which is on the harbour front. During the summer the University Students Hostel becomes Hotel Gardur. It is on Hringbraut and easily visible from the south end of the lake as you walk from the centre of town or descend from a No:5 bus. If you book in advance you can get reasonably priced meals. Three interesting venues we can recommend are Ódinsvé, Potturin og Pannan, and Ulfar og Ljón.

Don't be too put off by the face value of prices. Even an omelette is well prepared, nourishing and supported with salad and chips. 'Coffee' refers to as many cups as you can drink. At some places the price includes both soup and coffee.

An alternative is to visit one of the Smurbraudstofa where you can order, in advance, open sandwiches of various kinds. These may be whole slices (heilar sneidar), half slices (hálfar snittur) or the smaller 'snittur'. Loads of 'snittur' with roast beef, smoked lamb (hangikjöt), ham (skinka), salmon (lax), shrimps (raekjur), egg, tongue etc. supported by the bottles of wine and cans of beer imported by those of an age to do so (1 litre plus 12 cans per person) can round off an excellent trip and probably extend to a few guests. Doubtless your expedition culinary wizards can add the finishing touches! We particularly recommend Ódinsvé.

ICELANDIC FOODS:

Of Icelandic foods the following are probably suitable for expeditions:

Milk Products:

Nýmjölk	Fresh milk
Surmjölk	Soured milk — good with raisins and sugar.
Rjómi	Cream.
Skýr	Similar to yogurt but thicker; add milk, sugar and, if possible, fresh bilberries — otherwise use jam.
Ostur	Cheese — many varieties, including excellent processed.
Smurostur	Processed cheese — often with shrimps, mushrooms etc.

Fish Products:

Síld	Herring. Comes in a variety of sauces in handy plastic resealable pots.
Þurr saltfisk	Dried saltfish. Soak all day then boil. Keeps.
Steinbitur	Dried dogfish. Good to chew. Cheap.
Hardfisk	Dried cod. Ditto.
Reykturfisk	Smoked fish. If not too hot will last 4-5 days.
Hvalkjöt	Whale meat. Should be fried not boiled.
Hrefnukjöt	Small whale. Especially Eyjafjördur or Ísafjördur.
Fiskibollur	Fish balls. Tinned.
Sardines	Tinned.

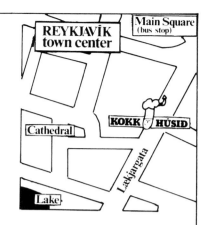
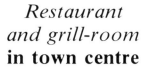

Meat Products:

Hangikjöt	Literally 'hung meat'. Smoked lamb. Expensive but keeps.
Bjúgu	Minced meat in tubular form. Called 'sperðlar' in the North and 'grjúpan' in the south and east. Will last a week in moderate weather.
Slátur	Ready cooked. Two types: 1. 'Bloð' (blood, rye, fat) like salami. 2. 'Lífer' (liver, rye, fat) like black pudding. Keeps four days in stomach lining bag.
Saltkjöt	Salted meat. 1Kg/4 men. Lasts months if lid kept closed. Meat submerged in brine. Add salt from time to time. Bought in barrels from Reykjavík and Akureyri slaughter houses and certain Reykjavík shops.

SHOPS

You will have no difficulty obtaining food around the periphery of Iceland and many petrol stations have food stores attached. Some of the fish and meat items referred to in the previous section will not however be generally available in the self-service type store. The smaller provision shops in Reykjavík will be better.

Farms **may** sell you milk, eggs, butter, cheese or skýr but don't rely on it. Farms are required to buy back a portion of their produce from the cooperative and they will sometimes have spare quantities

TYPES OF FOOD

Food is such an important element in the expedition planning that we must stray briefly into general expedition food planning. However for more detail you should obtain a copy of 'A Handbook for Expeditions' by Tony Land (Butterworths). There is also a very useful article by Ian Milne in 'Polar Expeditions' (Renner). The following is a summary of some key points:

1. **Weight and Bulk:** Tinned foods are utterly impractical except for items such as jam. Use dried foods. As the food must be backpacked or stowed in vehicles it must have low bulk. See Chapter 6. for details of freight. Tea chests are too big for most buses. You could buy some 2-litre cartons of fresh milk in Reykjavík. It will keep for several days.

2. **Nutritional value:** The article by Ian Milne (op cit) is particularly good on this topic. Hard days in the field coupled with poor weather conditions demand a balanced, warming, and appetising diet. Take a supply of apples, cheese, margarine, biscuits, jam, marmalade and even flour. Consider a daily dose of multi-vitamin tablets.

3. **Variety and Palatability:** To keep costs down you will need to buy in bulk and so the menus cannot be too varied. If you develop a 7-day menu this should work quite well. Morale can be uplifted by the occasional appearance of a 'goodies' box containing chocolate, tinned fruit etc.

4. **Packing:** Pack according to the cooking units. Two two-man tents with two primuses makes a convenient unit. Each one can then be issued with the appropriate food pack for each day. To conserve the food and provide for convenient handling and distribution decant as much as possible into polythene bags. Where necessary preserve the cooking instructions as well! Bags may be heat sealed or knotted. Powdered items will need two bags. Involve the whole expedition in the mammoth task of sorting and packing. The concept is akin to packing your own parachute!

WATER SUPPLIES

One of the most important decisions facing an expedition on arrival into its study area is the choice of its base camp site. Many factors affect the choice, such as proximity to the study area, accessibility, flatness, shelter, and size. Somewhere near the top of the list of criteria, however, will appear 'water supply: quality and quantity'. The use of A.F.D. food has lead to an increase in the amount of water needed by an expedition, and the water criterion may over-ride others in some circumstances.

Iceland is noted for its water, either liquid or solid, and you will find little shortage. However, it may not be in a palatable form. We do not suggest that you make a big thing of it but there are three possible problems:

Desert Areas: In the deserts north of the Vatnajökull the icecap produces a rain shadow and the porosity of the lava, lava sand and pumice means that there is very little surface water. You would have to rely on glacial streams, ice or snow patches (see below), springs, or your own water carriers.

Snowy Areas: If you expect to rely on melted snow or ice for your water supply do budget for enough fuel. Twice as much is needed to melt the snow before bringing it up to the boil.

Glacial Outwash: Parties working near glaciers or ice-caps may find that clear water is not available. Thus, any development which enables a party to use water charged with glacial rock flour also allows a leader more freedom in the choice of his camp site; the water criterion becomes less important.

Water charged with rock flour is typically opaque cream or green in colour. It tastes gritty. It is also one of the finest laxatives known to man! The flour is composed of rock particles too small to see, and is in suspension in the water. When faced with the necessity of drinking such water, you are faced with several alternatives:

(a) Storing the water and allowing the suspension to settle out.
(b) Using a flocculation agent to speed up the settling of the water.
(c) Using a centrifuge to spin out the solid matter in the water.
(d) Filtering the water.
(e) Drinking it anyway, and using drugs to cope with the results.

(a) **Storing the water:** This has been tried with some success, although the settling time may be as long as three days. The hurly-burly of base camp life may mean that the settling tanks are upset, or that they are allowed to run dry. The method also implies the ability to store three days' supply of water or even more. Polythene bivvy sacs inside crates or drystone walls may prove suitable rain traps and tanks. Alternatively dig a hole close to an outwash stream and allow the water to filter through by natural seepage. This is one of the most effective natural filters.

(b) **Flocculating agents:** Agents such as Bentonite may prove suitable for inducing flour particles to clump together and settle. However, the operation still takes time, no water is available until the process is complete, and another item is added to the supplies list.

(c) **Centrifuge:** To our knowledge this has never been tried (in the field or anywhere else). Use of a centrifuge implies a power source (ie. a generator) and thus two extra pieces of equipment, and fuel.

(d) **Filtration:** Rock flour particles are sufficiently fine to pass through silk and muslin, so that improvised filters are not usually successful. There are two alternatives. Either purchase a commercially available filter (Portacel Ltd., Cannon Lane, Tonbridge, Kent TN9 1PP) or experiment with darkroom or wine making filters. A Vinbrite Mk.2 filter was successfully tested by the Derbyshire Schools Expedition to Tungnafellsjkull in 1974. They achieved a flow rate of one gallon per pad per 35 minutes. The pad was found to have a $3/32$ in. deposit on it after that time. The water was taken from a turbulent river 800m. from the glacier snout and was not allowed to settle prior to filtration. The pads are not re-usable but are quite compact being 15cm in diameter and 8mm. thick. Had the water been allowed to settle even for as little as an hour or so, flow rate and through-put would have been increased.

(e) **The Medical Solution:** The symptoms produced by consumption of untreated water can be treated by drugs such as 'Lomontil'. But surely drugs only treat symptoms and not the cause of the trouble. Surely dependence upon drugs of any kind when on an expedition should be avoided.

FUEL SUPPLIES
Paraffin
You may find that few people have heard of it. Ask for 'Steinólíu' or 'Ljósólíu' at a garage or ironmongers. It can be bought in plastic containers (1 litre) which have been known to leak. It is better to take along your own 5-gallon containers (empty) on the aircraft. Alternatively, if you need large quantities, a 55-litre drum can be obtained from Olíuverzlun Íslands (BP) at a reasonable cost. The storage depot lies to the north of the Reykjavík camp site. Return the empty drums. Unopened drums may be sold back to the company.

The plastic containers cost up to 50% above the normal price which is charged at the fairly large number of filling stations with a 'steinólíu' pump, but where you need your own container. It has been found in the West Fjords that it is impossible to buy paraffin in quantities less than 200 litres, except in the 1 litre plastic containers but it is still easy in Reykjavík and throughout the south. For a fortnight's supply the price difference is appreciable.

Methylated Spirit
Meths is very expensive in Iceland. The industrial type may be bought at chemists in various sizes of container and at the State Liquor Monopoly (ATVR) store on Snorrabraut. ATVR is the only authority permitted to import meths into Iceland. You are unlikely to obtain a permit to import but if you are successful it can be shipped out provided that it is packed in a separate container to be stored in a separate part of the ship. The flashpoint must be stated (64.6°).

Butane Gas
The two principal types of L.P.G. are:

Primus: The small and large (2202) cylinders are universally available from Shell stations and many stores.

Camping Gaz International: Globetrotter, S200 and 907 rechargeable cartridges can be obtained. Again Shell has the franchise and many stores sell them.

TENTS
This is not the place to discuss or recommend specific tents. Wind and wet are joing to be your main enemies and cheap tents are not worth considering. Essentials include a sewn-in groundsheet and a flysheet that

pins direct to the ground all the way round the tent. A valence on the flysheet would be a great advantage.

If you do not have your own the Icelandic company Tjaldaleigan (Rent-a-Tent) hires 2-, 4-, and 6-man tents at reasonable rates. Also sleeping bags, air/foam mattresses, gas stoves, rucsacs, pots and pans. They also do base camp tents (3.5m x 3m), Bus Packers Kits and Economy Kits for 1, 2, 3, 4, or 5 people. Rates are available from Tour Operators. The two-man tents weigh 6kg and are made of strong sailcloth with a nylon flysheet. They are Icelandic made and not dissimilar to Vango tents. They also have some Lightweight nylon 2-man tents (3.5kg).

If travelling with an Icelandic tour company such as Arena, Guđmundur Jónasson or Úlfar Jacobsen a kitchen wagon and driver, food and cooks, tents and mattresses form part of the package. Rates can be very competitive for groups and details can be obtained through Tour Operators.

CLOTHING This is covered in Chapter 13.

FREIGHT This is covered in Chapters 6 and 13.

PHOTOGRAPHY:

Expedition photography is an art in its own right and this is not the place for a general discourse on the subject other than in the context in Iceland. We can recommend the three articles on photography in Geoff Renner's 'Polar Expeditions'. Photographically Iceland is a photographer's delight because of the clear atmosphere and sharp images.

Ensure that you have a telephoto or zoom lens in addition to your fixed camera lens, and perhaps a wide-angle lens as well to create those important atmospheric shots for the post-expedition report. Little bodies can look very lost in an Icelandic desert landscape! Having said that however it is not necessary to take every conceivable gadget such that you cannot even get off the ground. Be selective and keep it simple.

In Iceland's humid climate great care needs to be taken to keep out condensation (airtight tins and dessicators) and dust, both of which are common problems. Slow film (eg. Kodachrome 25 or 64) is recommended for Iceland and are better for subsequent printing or use in audio-visual presentations. Sharp differences in contrast between basalt landscape, glaring desert surface or ice, make the use of a light meter very necessary for best results. Winter trips will need faster film and Ektachrome 200 or 400 is normally very satisfactory; you can always upgrade the ASA rating if you remember to let the developers know that you have done so. For black and white photography Ilford FP4 or Kodak Panatonic X are best for the bright conditions you will experience.

Even if you are only taking one small camera without sophisticated extras do take cleaning materials with you such as a lens brush and anti-static cloths. A few Kleenex are useful. Icelandic lava surfaces are nasty and your lens runs the risk of being scratched unless you use a UV filter as protection. It will also reduce the excessive sky blue.

If undertaking a winter or icecap expedition beware the fact that most cameras cease to oblige at about -20°C. Batteries need to be removed, kept in a warm place (inside a glove?) and returned to the camera when a shot is needed. In any case your camera will need to be tucked inside your clothing out of Jack Frost's way. Front-zip jacket therefore essential but ensure a sturdy zip. Thin metal ones may break in the cold. Cameras can be 'winterised' to combat this. Your fingers cannot be so treated except by wearing gloves. Mittens are cumbersome but silk gloves rather smart! Winter cold also causes condensation problems when, after a day out in the cold, you return to the warmth of a geothermally heated hut. If you place the camera into a sealed polythene bag the condensation will form on the bag rather than the instrument which can be removed once the termperatures have stabilised.

Whatever you do, have a clear picture of what you want in the way of photography before you depart from home. Is it for the report, lectures, teaching, a personal record, sales, or what? If it is specific then it will need careful thought and the allocation of its supervision to a competent expedition member. An expedition photographer has to opt out of certain chores in order to capture an event and unless specified by the leader this can cause irritation!

If you absolutely cannot wait to see the results of your print film there is now a rapid developing company, Framköllun, in the very centre of town. Here you can actually see your film go in one end and your photographs emerge at the other.

Some expeditions will wish to use 16mm or 35mm film or video equipment. In this case it is useful to know that Iceland has several very professional film companies that are well equipped to assist either in the field or with preliminary groundwork preparation, with preliminary editing of rushes, or transfer of video film. They frequently become involved with visiting film shoots. Saga film, for example, have undertaken filming for the BBC Natural History Unit and a dramatic part of the first programme of David Attenborough's "The Living Planet" series, and have also acted very successfully as agents, at the Icelandic end, for the shooting of one of the sequences for the latest James Bond film.

10 RED TAPE

The title of this chapter is slightly misleading since Iceland is remarkably free of red tape. There are however a number of procedures that you cannot avoid and we hope that this chapter will guide you through. Having said that the rules change every so often so be prepared. If in doubt ask the Iceland Unit.

PERMITS

Fieldwork Permission

The Iceland National Research Council should be aware of the expedition plans. In particular they will want to know the dates, location and numbers in the party. Application for permission may take two forms:

Research Permit for expeditions carrying out any research project of an original nature. Research is defined as 'creative work undertaken on a systematic basis in order to increase the stock of knowledge, including knowledge of man, culture and society, and the use of this stock of knowledge to devise new applications'. Research work would normally be expected to appear in a scientific journal. If one expedition is undertaking research in several field sciences then the leader of each study is required to submit an application for his particular area of responsibility.

Successful applicants will receive a Research Permit which is valid for one calendar year only. On-going research will therfore require re-application on an annual basis.

Educational Permit for expeditions carrying out fieldwork as opposed to research work.

Successful applicants will receive an "Announcement" which is somewhat ambiguously worded in that it says that your expedition "does not warrant a Research Permit". Unless some stipulations have been typed below this statement you can consider yourselves to have been awarded an educational permit. If in doubt contact the Iceland Unit.

Application for both types is made on an official Research Permit Application form available from the Research Council or from the Iceland Unit. Educational Permit applications should be accompanied by a covering letter stating the fact that the application is for education rather than research. Field programmes need to be clearly defined before an application is made and previous discussion with an Icelandic scientist will further your cause. Permission is not normally turned down if the request is sufficiently explicit and the proposals do not conflict with other work in the area. The application will be passed to the appropriate departments for comments before a decision is made and this can take several months before a reply is received. The relevant sections of the Regulations affecting Foreign Scientists and Explorers in Iceland' are given below:

Article 1:   No foreigners are permitted to undertake scientific research work in the field of natural sciences without having first obtained a research permit issued by the Ministry of Culture and Education.

Article 2:   Applications for research permits shall be submitted to the National Research Council.

Article 3:   Each application shall be accompanied by a detailed description of the research programme to be undertaken, specifying among other things the equipment which will be used. In addition to their names the applicants shall provide information on their nationality, educational background, as well as their professional experience and qualifications for carrying out research work similar to that to be undertaken in Iceland. Furthermore, it is desirable that the application be supported by a letter of reference from a well-known scientific institution.

Article 4:   As a rule permits are not granted for research programmes which are currently being carried out by Icelandic scientists, or which they expect to undertake in the near future. **No specimens of birds or eggs may be collected without special permit from the Ministry of Education and Culture.**

Article 5:   Any holder of a research permit shall himself be responsible for obtaining necessary licences for the importation of equipment and other gear. He shall likewise be responsible for the payment of all expenses incurred by the expedition, unless otherwise specifically agreed upon.

Article 6:   **Natural History specimens must not be exported from the country unless permitted by the Icelandic Museum of Natural History.**

Article 7:   Before the members of the expedition leave Iceland they shall submit a preliminary report of their research activities.

Article 8:   When the results of the research programme have been worked out in full, a final report shall be submitted to the National Research Council in three copies. Furthermore, the National Research Council shall be provided with five copies of all articles, books or maps, which are published in connection with the work of the expedition. (This obligation does not apply to those with educational permits but the National Research Council appreciates the receipt of one copy of your report).

NOTE: When permission has been received please be careful to use it in the right way and note that the permit applies **only** to the actual field programme. It does not override any laws pertaining to Iceland. Approval to carry out your plans does not necessarily mean that they are considering your work to be of scientific value. Therefore should you use the approval to support your applications for grant aid? For British expeditions a Royal Geographical Society or Young Explorers' Trust application requires that the permission of the Iceland National Research Council have been sought. The permit is not a 'carte blanche' for duty free imports.

LICENCES

Food Importation: In 1983 a law was passed to levy a tax on imported foodstuffs exceeding 10 kg. per head in weight. This law was designed to catch those European groups arriving by ferry in their own vehicle and bringing all their own food. Such groups were contributing nothing to the Icelandic economy. However, 'bona fide' expeditions who have received a research permit or an "Announcement" from the Iceland National Research Council will, for the time being be exempt from this tax. But please recognise that the research permit is **not** in itself an automatic certificate of exemption, nor does it allow you to import whatever you will. The laws of Iceland must be adhered to (see Customs regulations below).

Groups without permits can expect to be asked to pay the tax on most items in excess of the 10 Kg. limit. This could be as much as 80% of the value of the product in Iceland where prices are already high. The rates do vary according to the product and indeed some items (eg. biscuits and emergency rations) are zero rated.

Fishing Tackle: All angling equipment and waders must be disinfected by immersion in a solution of 4% formalin for a period of ten minutes, well scrubbed in the solution and then washed in clean water. As proof of this the veterinary surgeon should type a declaration on his practice's headed notepaper to the effect that the equipment has been disinfected against all known freshwater fish disease. On arrival in Iceland you may also be required to purchase a further permit for a small sum.

Guns: Only Icelandic citizens are permitted to hold licences for firearms. Expeditions in transit to Greenland will be required to hand over guns when transferring to, say, Akureyri for the flight to Greenland.

Vehicles: Green cards are required for Iceland. Drivers are supposed to have an International Driving Licence in addition to their own licence but this does not seem to be too rigidly adhered to. Drivers must be 22 years or over.

CUSTOMS REGULATIONS

1. The import of butter, drugs (other than for personal medical use), eggs, firearms (handheld mini-flares are not firearms), uncooked meat and poultry is prohibited.

2. Tourists may bring into Iceland 1 litre of wine **or** other drinks up to 21% alcohol, **or** 12 cans of beer, plus 1 litre of liquor up to 47% alcohol. Also 200 cigarettes or equivalent of other tobacco products. Expeditions have been

known to have received supplies of liquor from benevolent firms — this must not be imported into Iceland, even if it is to be consumed solely by the expedition members.

3. The importation and export of Icelandic kronur is controlled. British banks will only receive Icelandic notes of certain values. Check with your local bank. There are no problems in changing travellers' cheques in Iceland and most credit cards are acceptable all over Iceland.

4. 'Bona fide' expeditions may bring in such food and equipment as is proportionate to the length of their stay and the type of activity to be carried out, provided that it does not breach Icelandic law. See the section on the food import tax.

CLEARING CUSTOMS:

The technicalities of customs clearance vary as much as the advice given by different authorities. Those accompanying their equipment by air will have no problems. The problems arise (less so recently) when freight is shipped in advance and needs to be cleared from a warehouse. We recommend that for maximum preparedness you go armed with:

1. Your National Research Council permit or "Announcement".
2. A signed statement on your headed expedition paper saying:
   "We hereby declare that all the imported goods will be used exclusively by the members of this expedition and that the imported equipment and unused provisions will be re-exported on (date)."
3. A duplicate list of equipment and food.
4. The bills of lading from the shipping company.

For details of the process of customs clearance see Chapter 12.

VATNAJÖKULL EXPEDITIONS

Any expedition planning to go onto the Vatnjökull icecap should be in touch with the Iceland Glaciological Society and the director of the Iceland National Life-Saving Society which coordinates rescue services. They will be very helpful with their advice. Rescue itself is not a right and can be expensive. Vatnajökull expeditions are encouraged to be in touch with the Iceland Unit and to try to take advantage of the special winter fares offered by Icelandair to carry out a 'reconnaissance' to see all the relevant Icelandic personnel.

TAXES

Sales Tax

Note that a 24% sales tax is imposed on all that you buy in Iceland and this may not always be apparent on listed prices (eg. for car hire or air photographs).

Diesel Vehicle Tax

Expeditions importing diesel vehicles will find that a tax is imposed according to the vehicle weight and the length of stay. The rates are not exhorbitant but must be budgeted. Details should be obtainable from Travel Operators or the Iceland Unit.

Food Tax: See 'Licences' above.

INSURANCE

Do make sure that you are adequately covered as medical treatment can be very expensive in Iceland. Scandinavian countries have reciprocal agreements but only recently have Britain and Iceland agreed that medical treatment in Iceland should cost a British citizen no more than that for an Icelander who also belongs to a national health service. Ambulance fees will be charged but hospitalization is free for cases of sudden illness.

If using ropes at all then you **must** have mountaineering insurance. Without it the insurance company will not refund any costs. Shop around for quotations but do it in good time so that you do not lose booking deposits in the event of someone dropping out. You will need insurance for medical, repatriation, personal accident, loss of deposits, personal baggage and money, mountain rescue (where appropriate) and, above all else, personal liability. The Iceland Unit can advise on procedures.

The following examples may serve to stress the need for cover and caution by expedition members:

— a fourteen year old boy badly broke his knee cap near Landmannalaugar. As it is four to five hours drive to Reykjavík he had to be lifted out by USAF helicopter. Operated on in Reykjavík and sent home.

— a fifteen year old boy sustained third degree burns on both feet when he slipped into a mud spring. He was fortunate to be treated by a passing doctor, brought to Reykjavík by car, and repatriated.

— a member of an ornithological party fell while bird watching and injured his pelvis. Evacuated by air to Reykjavík and repatriated.

— a fourteen year old boy tried to jump over a hot spring at Deildartunga, slipped and fell in. Two friends tried to help him out and also fell in. A USAF helicopter evacuated the boy while conventional ambulance plane returned the two friends. The boy was in intensive care for 10 days and his mother brought from England. Doctors said that he would require operations and skin grafts for the next two years.

— An Australian girl hitched a lift in a car which went off the road. She broke her leg but was not covered by insurance.

— A well-known British horseman was drowned while attempting to ford a river in spate on horseback.

— Two army officers tried to cross Iceland in the winter. They were experienced and had first class equipment. They got 100 km before abandoning the venture, and all their equipment, because one suffered bad frostbite to his feet.

— A tourist attempted to traverse a glacier in plimsoles. He slipped about 30m. fell 6m. and died within 24 hours.

— Two British students were lost on Vatnajökull, never to be seen again. They were last seen walking side by side pulling a sledge. They had skiis but no crampons.

— A party of cyclists tried to cross Iceland on bicycles but lost one cycle and two tents within the first four days. They had to be collected by lorry at their own, not inconsiderable, expense.

— An expedition using gas stoves in nylon tents suffered a conflagration which left one person badly burned about the arms and neck. Required medical treatment and repatriation.

— A party of young foreigners trying to cross a mountain on the south-west coast at Whit were caught by a sudden snowstorm. Three died.

— Two hikers fell into a stream and were swept away by the current. One went over the Skógarfoss waterfall and was never seen again, although his clothing and rucsac were found.

GENERAL
Visas and Innoculations

None are required by European nationals or nationals of Australia, Bahamas, Barbados, Belize, Bermuda, Botswana, Brazil, Canada, Chile, Dominica, Fiji, Gambia, Grenada, Guyana, Hong Kong, India, Israel, Jamaica, Japan, Republic of Korea, Lesotho, Malaysia, Malawi, Morocco, Mauritius, Mexico, New Zealand, Solomon Islands, Seychelles, Singapore, St. Lucia, Swaziland, Tanzania, Trinidad and Tobago, Tunisia, United States of America. All others require a visa issued by an Icelandic consulate.

If you have returned from certain countries outside Europe within the previous 14 days you should have a smallpox vaccination. We recommend that expedition members have anti-tetanus injections or boosters before leaving home.

Passports

A valid passport is required for travellers coming from any country except Denmark, Faroes, Finland, Norway, and Sweden. A British Visitor's Passport is acceptable.

Embassy Notification

Expeditions are advised to notify their respective embassies as to their intentions while in Iceland. Should anything go wrong during your visit they are more likely to be sympathetic if they already know something about you. In the event of an emergency they will want to know:

1. Where you should be at any given time.
2. How many there are of you.
3. What you are doing.

4. Your mode of transport.

5. The name of every member of the party.

6. The name, address, and telephone number of a home agent who may be contacted in the event of an emergency. This person should be available throughout the expedition and should have the names and addresses of all the expedition members and the full details of the expedition insurance policy.

The leader should call, if possible, or at least leave a message at the embassy on arrival in Iceland to report the arrival of the expedition. He should, **without fail** report the expedition safely out again **before** departure. Again this may be done by leaving a message.

Union of Icelandic Guides

Foreign commercial tour parties are required to employ the services of a professional Icelandic guide. However, 'bona fide' research and educational groups who have the authority of the National Research Council or who have booked their ground travel arrangements directly or indirectly through an accredited Icelandic travel bureau will be exempt from obtaining a guide for themselves. The Unit or Tour Operators can advise.

Young Explorers' Trust Approval and Grant Aid

British youth expeditions are eligible to apply for the Trust's approval or, if considered worthy, financial assistance as well. The awards are not large but the recognition of the Trust is accepted by numerous firms and other bodies to whom you may be applying for assistance of various kinds. Every year outstanding expeditions are recommended to be put forward to the Royal Geographical Society's expedition panel. Applications must be received by 1st December, and the interviews will take place in mid-January. Expeditions will know the results by early February and will receive their grants in early April. The second round of applications is due by 1st May with results/awards in June/July. However most of the award money is allocated at the first round. Full details are available from the Trust's head office at the Royal Geographical Society.

International Relations

It is so easy for one expedition to undo all the goodwill generated by the majority of well-organised parties. In some instances the scar has taken time to heal. For example a group carried out a sociological study in a farming community where little English was spoken. The party walked all over the farmland without permission, making notes and sketches with the mistaken view that their work would contribute to improving the farmers' lot. Another group in North Iceland managed to turn a farmer against all expeditions on account of damage done to a wall and to turf. A boat was borrowed and not paid for, and a group was rescued from the interior without so much as a 'thank you'.

A little thought and manners go a long way.

11 RADIO COMMUNICATIONS

THE PATTERN OF COMMUNICATIONS IN ICELAND

Iceland has a good network of telecommunications for the inhabited areas. Most farms have a telephone, but often the exchange has limited operating hours. The 1:250,000 map of Iceland marks the principal telephone exchanges. They are also shown in the Icelandic telephone directory (Símaskrá).

Beyond populated areas, and in the interior and peripheral fingers of uninhabited land radio provides the only means of communication. Iceland is unusual in that it possesses a chain of coastal radio stations that provide a mobile communications service to the interior of the island in addition to its prime task of marine communications. All stations can be called on a set frequency throughout the daylight hours and the major stations monitor this frequency through 24 hours. Some huts in outlying areas (eg. the Hveravellir meteorological station, Kerlingafjöll ski school) have radios.

A second frequency is allocated for communications between mobile stations and, on a third frequency, it is possible to be connected into the Icelandic telephone service. Most coaches and buses, and many private vehicles have HF/SSB radio telephones. A centre-loaded vertical whip aerial is invariably used.

All this gives an intensive pattern of usage which has to be strictly controlled by the issue of licences.

THE TELEPHONE DIRECTORY

The directory is an invaluable aid to planning. It is arranged with Reykjavík telephone numbers in the front followed by the Reykjavík Yellow Pages. Thereafter the towns and exchanges (Fig. 20) are arranged alphabetically. Right at the back is an alphabetical list of all the farms in Iceland with their telephone exchanges and postal districts. This can be very useful when trying to sort out base camps in advance. The Iceland Unit always keeps the up-to-date directory and so you can always check details with them.

Remember that individuals are listed by their given, first names. Often their professions is listed against their name as well. When seeking names it is often as well to note the person's middle name, if they have one. There may be, for example, a long list of people with the name Jón Magnússon and so it helps to know that the one you seek is Jón S. Magnússon.

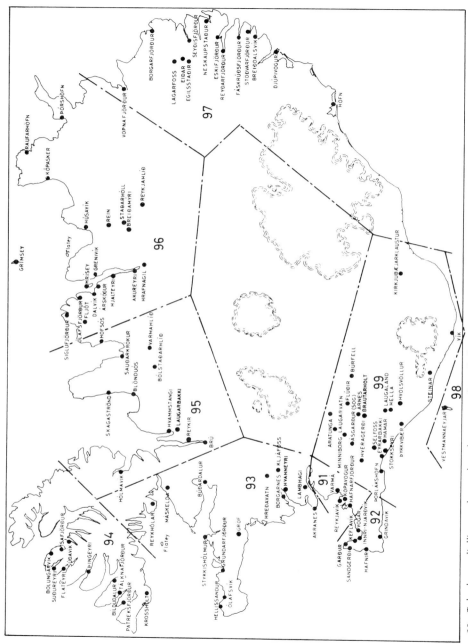

Fig. 20. Telephone dialling codes and exchanges. When dialling from abroad the '9' is not used. c Post & Telegraph Administration.

HOW TO OBTAIN RADIO USE

Casual

(a) Hire of a vehicle, such as a coach, will give you access to a radio.

(b) A nearby farm will have a telephone or a radio for use in an emergency. In rural districts some exchanges are only open at certain times of day but this can be verified in advance by reference to the telephone directory or by writing to the Iceland Unit.

(c) Close proximity to a route with sufficient traffic may allow use of someone else's in an emergency.

In all these cases remember that the use of a radio is not a right. You must offer and expect to pay for the use of it.

Regular

Regular use of a radio implies temporary ownership.

(a) **Hire:** The Post and Telegraph Administration are not able to loan or hire out single sideband tranceivers. Double sideband sets may only be hired in very special circumstances. However, they will fix a radio into your vehicle, and this will not take long. This is not absolutely necessary; all you need is a 12-volt battery. Transmitting only once a day will give you sufficient power for a three week expedition. You will be required to keep a log of your transmission times.

On arrival in Iceland you will need to arrange fixed calling times with the transmitting station at Gufunes. You will be advised to check the signal once in Reykjavik and again on your way out of town just to test that all is well.

At the time of writing, the Iceland Unit has no contacts for radio loan or hire. However we are advised that Pye Telecommunications sometimes loan two-way radios if given ample warning. One expedition successfully appealed for assistance through their local radio station.

(b) **Bringing your own:** All sets must be of the single sideband type. You will need written proof of ownership and date of purchase.

It is advisable to write to the P.T.A. well before your expedition and state clearly your intention over radio use. If you wish to talk direct between two sets then a wave band must be arranged. Documentary proof that you are a 'bona fide' expedition (ie. Research Council approval) may allow a licence fee to be waived, but you should be prepared to pay for a licence. You will be asked to complete a registration form indicating the power, modulation and type of radio.

Licences for CB equipment are not normally issued except under special circumstances and provided that the expedition is approved by the National Research Council.

Expeditions should not hesitate to contact the P.T.A. whether hiring or importing radios. They are most helpful. Do not attempt to import a radio without first contacting them or, like many expeditions, you will find your radio confiscated by customs.

If you bring in an HF/SSB set and intend to obtain service from the coastal stations you should be prepared to name someone domiciled in Iceland who would undertake to be responsible for the payment of your bills.

TECHNICAL NOTES:

A set operating on the marine distress band, Channel 16, is not allowed, and the use of 'personnel locator beacons' is heavily restricted, because of the proximity of the NATO airbase and the risk of unnecessary call out by rescue services.

Licences and a private channel can be provided for the band 154-174 MHz. In this case permission is given for one base station only of a maximum e.r.p. 25 watts.

Almost any receiver is capable of intercepting transmissions of the Icelandic weather forecast, providing it has a battery. The weather forecast is broadcast on 209 kHz in Icelandic plain language at the following times GMT:

0700   0815   1225   1615   2230   0100

The weather forecast is transmitted in morse on 276 kHz in Icelandic plain language and repeated in English, at the following times GMT:

0530   1130   1730   2330

The Directorate approval and subsequent licencing **may** be obtained for the following transceiver description which conforms to the required specification Operating in the band 2.7-3 MHz on fixed channels of which one may be used for communication between mobile users while two other channels are intended for communication between mobile users and fixed stations in the Icelandic telecommunications network. Of these two channels, one is used for calling and short messages, the other, a duplex channel, for connection to the telephone network. A charge is made for each call on the public network.

Channel 1.	2790 kHz	TX/RX for calling.
Channel 2.	2833 kHz	TX/RX for communication with other land mobile stations.
Channel 3.	2854 kHz	TX
	2761 kHz	RX for communication with fixed stations in the land mobile (telephone) network.

including A3h, A3A, and A3J modes, intermodulation not exceeding -30dB, spurious emission not less than 50mW, pass-band not more than 3kHz, and frequency drift not more than 40 Hz within 15 minutes.

In respect of power packs, Nickel Cadnium (TX/RX) and Mercuric Oxide (locator beacons) batteries do not operate effectively at temperatures of -20°C and below.

POINTS TO NOTE

1. Do you really need a radio? Most expeditions do **not** because they are close to direct telephone assistance. If in doubt the Iceland Unit can advise. Even a Vatnajökull expedition rejected the use of radio equipment having regard to weight, bulk and the suitability of the equipment. If you cannot easily transport the set or have it available at all times then it serves little purpose.

2. If you decide to take a radio do not let it induce a false sense of security in relation to matters of safety.

3. Ensure that **all** the necessary parts work before leaving the UK, and that you have sufficient spares.

4. It is vital to pack your radio sets securely. Wooden crates with foam padding and/or polystyrene chips are best and should be suitable for re-use on the return journey.

5. Arrange adequate insurance cover.

6. Bare tracts of lava can absorb radio waves and may reduce the effectiveness over a comparatively short distance. Direct radio communication may not therefore be possible.

7. It is essential to have a trained operator in the field, who has at least a working knowledge of how to repair the set. Take a copy of the blue-print with you. If the P.T.A. has to modify your set it will be needed.

8. Unlicenced radio sets have been known to be confiscated by the Icelandic customs on arrival in Iceland. Be forewarned!

NOTE:

The orange rescue huts around the coast, and at certain strategic passes, are the property of the Iceland National Life-Saving Society. They are NOT for general use except in an emergency as they are primarily for mariners. The radios are tuned to the international distress frequency.

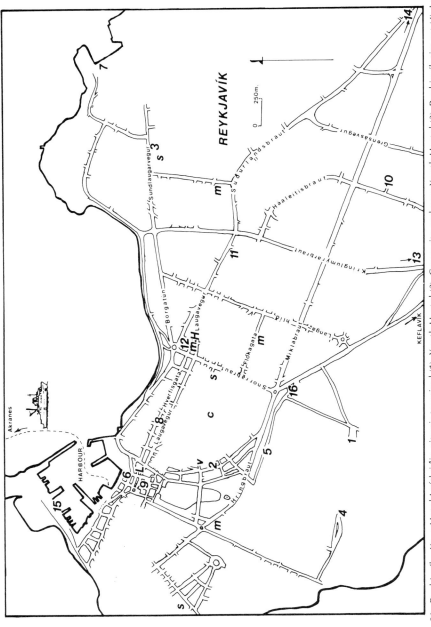

Fig. 21. Reykjavík. Key: Hotel Loftleiðir, city air terminal (1), Youth Hostel (2), Camp site and new Youth Hostel (3), Reykjavík airport (4), Long-distance bus station (5), customs house (6), Sundahöfn (7), National Research Council/Nature Conservation Council (8), Post and Telegraph Administration (9), Hvassaleitiskóli (10), Geodetic Survey (11), Police Station (12), to City Hospital (13), to Árbær museum (14), National Life-Saving Society (15), Tourist Bureau (16), museums (m), swimming pools (s), cathedral (c), Volcano Show (v), city bus terminals (L, H).

136

Much of what is stated below can be quite quickly found out by trial and error and if you like the excitement of sorting it all out yourself then do not bother to read this chapter! It is designed to help the anxious leader with twenty tired youths on his hands.

WHICH AIRPORT?

Although your ticket may tell you that the aircraft will land at Reykjavik this is not so, except on very exceptional occasions. International flights land at Keflavik, 40 km south-west of Reykjavik. Coaches will take you (at cost) to Hótel Loftleidir which acts as the city terminal. You will then have to find your own way to your destination unless your Tour Operator has previously arranged onward transport for you.

DESTINATIONS WITHIN REYKJAVÍK (Figure 21)

City Centre

The bus from Hotel Loftleidir leaves at approximately every 25 minutes to the hour. From the city centre it leaves every 10 minutes to the hour. The bus is run by Landleidir h.f. and not by S.V.R. the city service. The first bus from Reykjavik is 0750.

To obtain a taxi locate the free telephones on the wall directly ahead of you on entering the foyer from the coach. Speak in English and give your name; your first name will do.

Both buses and taxis depart from the opposite side of the building to that at which you arrived from the airport. If in doubt ask at reception.

School Accommodation

Groups using this school accommodation (Chapter 8) will have booked through a Travel Operator and transport to the school will have been booked and paid for in advance. The school is not named on the Reykjavik street map but is located at the end of a very short street called Smáagerdi which runs east off Háaleitisbraut.

Youth Hostel

At the time of writing the Youth Hostel is on the corner of Laufásvegur and Baldursgata and only a short walk from the Hotel. No bus goes there. The simplest direction on foot is to go from the hotel to the main road via the badly tarmaced road (Flugvallabraut) that leads directly towards Miklatorg ('torg' = square). Turn left along the dual carriageway (Hringbraut). After the hospital bear right into Laufásvegur and Baldursgata is the third on the right. You will pass the British Embassy en route, on the corner of

Bragagata. The Hostel opens at 0700 or 0800 but new arrivals are not normally admitted until the warden arrives. However, since late night aircraft are a common feature of travel to Iceland the hostel normally expects arrivals in the middle of the night. But please keep your voices down — do not wake the neighbours; easy to do with a large group.

In the summer the Youth Hostel extends to include a school alongside the Tjörnin, the late in central Reykjavík. It is conceivable that you may have been registered there in which case you must continue on down Laufásvegur. The school is on the left alongside the open space.

A new hostel is under construction adjacent to the municipal camp site and the swimming pool. The directions will then be similar to those for the camp site (see below). It is hoped that the first phase of this construction will be ready for summer 1985.

Camp Site

This is a long way from the Hotel but if you walk along the well-surfaced road, turn right at the main road and first left you will reach Eskitorg. Cross the roundabout into Langahlíd and locate the bus stop for a No:8 or No:9 on the right-hand side of the road. The bus takes a devious route (left, right, right, left); after the last turn left, into Laugarnesvegur, the bus travels about 700m. to a major cross roads. Descend and walk about 500m. along Sundlaugarvegur to the camp site. As the bus crossed the main road, Sundlaugarvegur was on the right, travelling east.

Reykjavík Airport

Internal domestic air services run from Reykjavík Airport. The terminal is visible from Hótel Loftleidir, just across the tarmac runway, but it is not directly accessible. **Either** walk to the main road (Hringabraut), catch a No:6 bus to just short of Melatorg, walk up to Melatorg, turn left into Sudurgata, and catch a No:5 bus to the terminal **or** walk along Hringabraut and opposite the major turning to the right is an unsurfaced road, closed to traffic, that leads almost direct to the Terminal.

Long-Distance Bus Terminal (Umferðamidstöd)

As for Reykjavík airport above, follow Hringbraut and you will see the Terminal on your left.

Conclusion: Make arrangements with the Tour Operator before you depart for a bus to meet you and take your group direct to its destination! In any case it is worth buying a map of Reykjavík in advance from Dick Phillips.

MOVEMENT WITHIN REYKJAVÍK

The city bus service (S.V.R.) is the best way to get around. The No:5 bus service is particularly useful because it links camp site, town centre, and Reykjavík airport. Taxis are expensive. Vans can be hired quite easily to transport goods around from, say, the harbour to the long-distance bus station — dial 2-50-50 for a Sendibil. See chapter 7. for details of the various modes of transport.

LEADER'S CHECK-LIST

When you have settled in to your hostel or camp site you will have to tie up a number of loose ends. The following is a check-list for which one whole day should be allowed:

Customs Clearance

Details of customs regulations are given in Chapter 13. The following is a guide to the mechanics of customs clearance but do be aware that the details may well vary from year to year.

(i) Go to the Customs building in Tryggvagata. The building faces you at the end of Posthússtraeti. Proceed to the fourth floor and turn left to the customs examination section (Tollbúdin Vöruskodun). Follow along the corridor and you will come to an office on the left. Here you will need to fill in a form for each bill of lading. You will also need to show your list of contents and the research permit or 'Announcement' if applicable. Ensure that on your form you write the words 'Leidangurs útbunadur' (expedition equipment) in column 16.

(ii) Go to the warehouses at Sundahöfn. To get there catch a No:5 bus to the camp site. Cross the road and walk up Dalbraut towards the Pepsi kiosk, and then down Sundargardar. The Eimskip warehouses are at the bottom of the slope and are enclosed in a concrete wall with an inverted swastika sign. Present the papers to the clerk and locate your freight.

(iii) Return to the new customs building in Tryggvagata and proceed to the shipping offices on the 5th floor. Present your papers and wait to be called to the cashier, to pay import duties or, more likely, to receive your papers back duly stamped and without charge.

(iv) You may now return to the warehouse at Sundahöfn to claim your equipment, unless in the meantime you have been required to go to the Research Council's offices at Laugavegi 13, to have your papers endorsed by them. If you cannot manage to move the equipment yourself, ring 2-50-50 for a 'Sendibil' to take it to wherever you want it. The cost is not excessive.

Embassy Visit

Report yourself in to your national embassy, leaving full details of your expedition (see Chapter 13). Do not forget to sign out at the end of the trip. For addresses see Appendix G.

Clear Radios

If you have brought in two-way radios these must be cleared with the Post and Telegraph Administration whose offices are in Austurvöllur, the Parliament square. Details are given in Chapter 11.

Purchase Paraffin and additional stores

See Chapter 9. Shopping hours are 0900-1200 and 1300-1800 on weekdays and 0900-1200 on Saturdays although some stay open until 1600. Bakeries and dairies may open earlier. Remember that the first Monday in August is a Bank Holiday.

Change Travellers' Cheques

Banks are open 0915-1600 (1800 on Thursday) but closed on Saturdays and Sundays except 0900-1200 on Saturday when the Útvegsbanki is open for the exchange of travellers' cheques. It is often possible to exchange travellers' cheques at hotels.

Arrange a post-expedition meal: See Chapter 9.

Reserve seats for the Volcano Show: See 'Entertainment' below.

Confirm: (a) your return air flight with Icelandair, and
(b) all onward bookings with the airline and bus operators.

Arrange rentals: (a) vehicle rental, and
(b) tent rental.

Post Letters

The central Post Office and the one at Laugavegur 120 are open from 0800-1700 (Monday), 0900-1700 (Tuesday-Friday), 0900-1200 (Saturday). The Post Office at the Long Distance Bus Station is open 1400-1930 (Monday to Saturday).

Check back-country Roads

This really only applies if the weather is known to have been poor, or you are arriving in the early season (June) when roads into the interior may not yet be open. Obtain advance information from either Ferðafélag Íslands, Öldugata 3 (Tel: 1-17-98), or the Long Distance Bus Station (Tel: 2-23-00) on the Hringbraut.

Purchase maps and air photographs

Maps are available from several Reykjavík bookshops but both maps and air photographs are only available from Landmaelingar Íslands, the Iceland Geodetic Institute, at Laugavegi 178. Details are given in Chapter 4.

Purchase Sweaters

Expedition members in need of a robust and warm sweater can do no better than acquire an Icelandic hand-knitted model. They are very practical for

expedition work. If booking through Tour Operators, some arrange special discount rates with certain Icelandic shops. Some of the shops, if approached by a whole group may do the same. Be sure not to fall into the trap of buying a machine-knitted sweater when you really want the hand-knitted version.

Chemists: Note the late opening times and locations. See "Emergencies" below.

TELEPHONES

There are very few public telephones in Reykjavik. Some may be found in Laekjargata, some cafes and banks. Coins placed in the slot will only go through if the phone is answered. Remember that Icelanders are listed under their first names in the directory — Jóhann Örnolfsson will be found under 'J'. The letters P, Æ and Ö come after Z. To make a collect (reverse charge) call to Britain dial 09. For telegrams dial 06.

LOST PROPERTY

Lost property may be traced by telephoning the following:

Flugleiðir (airline):   2-78-00
Buses: 8-25-33
General: Police headquarters, Hverfisgötu 113 1-02-00

EMERGENCIES

This topic is dealt with in more depth in Chapter 13. but should you require an ambulance while in Reykjavik dial 1-11-00 (Fire: 1-11-66). 24-hour emergency treatment is available at the City Hospital (Borgarspitalinn Slysadeild) (Telephone: 8-12-00). Emergency doctor call outs are on 2-24-11 (0800-1700) and 2-12-30 (1700-0800). There is a duty dentist at Heilsurvern-darstödin, Barónsstigur 47 from 1700-1800 daily. You will need a doctor's prescription for many items that can normally be bought over the counter in Britain. Chemists are open from 0900-1800 on weekdays while two remain open from 1800-2200 on weekdays and 0900-2200 on Saturdays. To locate chemists look up 'Apotek' in the yellow pages of the telephone directory and for late openings look at the list posted in chemists windows. There is a central chemist on the corner of Posthússtraeti and the Austursstraeti pedestrian precinct.

For details of backcountry emergencies see Chapter 13.

ACTIVITIES FOR EXPEDITION MEMBERS

No expedition can survive the effect of too many members sitting around and kicking their heels while awaiting the clearance of freight. General 'looking around' soon wears thin and it is too early to be buying souvenirs. This is a golden opportunity to broaden the expedition experience by

Have you ever tried to swim

in water from the thermal springs?

This is what you are invited to
– hot spring water mixed with crystal-clear drinking water –
the finest possible swimming facilities in excellent pools.

The hours given below
are for the summer a), and winter b); closing
means that admissions cease, but patrons can
remain in the pool for another 30 minutes.
All pools have saunas except Sundhöll.

Sundlaugin in Laugardalur,
outdoor (near Hotel Esja), tel. 34039:
a) Monday through Friday 7:00 to 20:30.
Saturday 7:30 to 17:30.
Sunday 8:00 to 17:30.
b) Monday through Friday 7:00 to 20:00.
Saturday 7:30 to 17:30.
Sunday 8:00 to 15:30.

Sundlaug Vesturbaejar,
outdoor (at Hofsvallagata
in the western sector), tel. 15004:
a) Monday through Friday 7:00 to 20:30.
Saturday 7:30 to 17.30.
Sunday 8:00 to 17:30.
b) Monday through Friday 7:00 to 20:00.
Saturday 7:30 to 17:30.
Sunday 8:00 to 15:30.

Sundhöll Reykjavíkur,
indoor pool (at Barónsstigur
near Hlemmur), tel. 14059:
a) Monday through Friday 7:00 to 20:30.
Saturday 7:30 to 17:30.
Sunday 8:00 to 14:30.
b) Monday through Friday 7:00 to 20:30.
Saturday 7:30 to 17:30.
Sunday 8:00 to 14:30.

Sundlaug Fjölbrautaskólans
in Breidholt, outdoor, tel. 75547:
a) Monday through Friday 7:20 to 20:30.
Saturday 7:30 to 17:30.
Sunday 8:00 to 17:30.
b) Monday through Friday 7:20 to 9:30
and 16:30 to 20:30.
Saturday 7:30 to 17:30.
Sunday 8:00 to 15:30.

REYKJAVÍK
Swimming pools

advising members to investigate some of the historical and cultural elements of Icelandic life. The National Museum and the Árbaer Museum are particularly interesting. The latter has a fascinating collection of old Icelandic houses rebuilt on the museum site. Icelandic art is fostered at The National Art Gallery, Kjarvalsstaðir and the new venture in the very centre of town, Listamiðstöðin hf (The Art Centre). The following is a list of suggestions:

Swimming Pools: There are several excellent pools, and campers will soon discover the one alongside the camp site. Pre-swim hot showers are compulsory but welcome anyway (both to expedition members and to passers by as well, no doubt!) Hairwashing is allowed, but do not use glass shampoo bottles in the shower room. Lockers with keys are available but at Sundhóll the attendant keeps the key and you have a numbered disk. Pools may be reached as follows:

Laugardal	Outdoor. Adjacent to the camp site. Reached by a No:5 bus from the city centre.
Sundhóll	Indoor. On the corner of Barónstigur and Bergthórugata. No:1 bus from the centre in the west end of Njálsgata.
Vesturbaejar	Outdoor. Off Hofsvallagata. No:4 bus from the centre.

Museums and Galleries: The following is a selection only and leaflets are easily available from Icelandair, the Iceland Unit or can be picked up on arrival in Iceland. (The numbers refer to the days of the week/)

National Museum	Suðurgata 41	1-7:	1330-1600
Museum of Natural History	Hverfisgötu 116	2, 4, 6, 7:	1330-1600
Árbaer Open Air Museum	East of R. Ellidaár	2-7:	1330-1800
Kjarvalsstaðir Art Gallery	Miklatún	1-7:	1400-2200
National Art Gallery	Suðurgata 41	1-7:	1330-1600
Ásmundur Sveinsson Gallery	Sigtún	2-7:	1400-1700
Hallgrímskirkja Cathedral	Skólavörðurholt	2-7:	1000-1200
			and 1400-1800

Entertainment

The Volcano Show: Hellusundi 6a. Easy to find if you walk from the centre of town to the road bridge across the lake; turn left and continue up the hill. The Volcano Show will be on your right. This is a 'must' for all. Old and recent films of volcanic activity in Iceland together with some interesting material on, for example, Skaftafell before the road was opened. The auditorium is small and advance booking is recommended (1-32-30/2-25-39/2-99-75). Take a cushion and spare oxygen cylinders; it is hot and stuffy but you'll enjoy it.

Iceland on Film: The Icelandic Opera House, Ingólfsstraeti. Various films and exhibitions. Coffee bar. You will need to check details in Reykjavík but events are daily at 1800 and 2100 except Wednesday.

Light Nights: By the lake, in Tjarnarbío. A solo performance in English by Kristín Magnús who tells traditional Icelandic stories, legends, and sagas every evening from Thursday to Sunday.

Cinemas: There are a number of cinemas ('bío') in Reykjavík whose details are published daily in newspapers. Recently a number of Icelandic productions (eg. 'Atom Stöðin' and 'Hrafninn Flygur') have appeared on the screen and they are recommended even though in Icelandic.

Short Tours

There are a number of regular tours that you can book through your Tour Operator (advisable) or on the spot in Iceland:

Short tours suitable for use while freight is being cleared:

    City Sightseeing
    Krísuvík (hot springs) and Grindavík (fishing village)
    Whaling Station
    Hveragerði (greenhouses)
    Pony Trekking

Árbæjarsafn is an open air museum founded in 1957. The centre of the museum is Árbær farm. Its buildings date from 1900 to 1920, but have retained traditional features from the Icelandic turf farm. At the museum there is also a turf church from the north of Iceland, and several buildings that have been moved from the centre of Reykjavík, the oldest from 1820. Some of the houses are furnished. On display is also a steam locomotive used in the building of Reykjavík harbour.

Open 13.30-18.00 June-July-August every day except Monday. Open on request, September to May. Tel. 84412 (9-10 a.m.)

 ÁRBÆJARSAFN Reykjavík Museum
130 Reykjavík Tel. 84412

Longer tours suitable for whole days, perhaps at the close of your expedition to provide a balanced view of the island:

Westmann Islands: 1973 eruption centre
Skálholt, Gullfoss, Geysir, Thingvellir
South Coast: Vík, Dýrhólaey, Skógar, Sólheimajökull
Thórsmork: glaciers, hot springs
Thjórsárdalur: Hekla ash, Viking farm
Kaldidalur: cold desert, volcanoes, glaciers, Hraunfossar

It is of course possible to incorporate some of these routes into your itinerary to and from your expedition base. Expeditions working in the North, for example, could either drive one way and fly back or go north by the coast road and back through the centre (Kjölur or Sprengisandur routes). Those working in the Central Highlands might go out via Thingvellir, Geysir and Gullfoss and return via Skálholt, Kerid and Hveragerdi.

Ferdafélag Íslands (Touring Club of Iceland) have a number of very reasonably priced tours that may appeal to anyone staying on in Iceland after the main expedition has finished. Details of these are usually available in the Youth Hostel.

13 MOVEMENT IN THE MOUNTAINS AND INTERIOR

INTRODUCTION

This chapter is aimed at a safety awareness among expeditions. Of course the major hazards rarely, if at all, appear in one place so that common sense, coupled with a tendency to err on the side of caution is usually sufficient. It is not possible to lay down hard and fast rules for mountaineering in Iceland, nor is it desirable that anyone should do so. Your approach to the conditions will vary according to the area, your experience, motivation and available equipment. The following notes are intended to give an indication of some of the conditions found in Iceland and to attempt to answer some of the many questions sent to the Iceland Unit.

An equipment check list will be found at the end of the chapter but briefly it may be stated that the equipment required for mountain/desert work in Iceland is similar to that for British mountains and for snow/ice or glacier work is similar to that for alpine climbing.

Mountaineering is a sport which is increasing in popularity in Iceland and with the advent of the Icelandic Alpine Club (ísalp) many areas of the country are being 'opened-up' to ski-mountaineering and conventional alpine-style mountaineering.

WEATHER CONDITIONS

There is an Icelandic saying that if you do not like the weather, wait a minute. The weather is variable and localised. If one can generalise, the atmosphere in the north is relatively stable with finer weather on the whole, although it can be colder. The relative absence of ground vegetation and trees does mean that little protection can be afforded from wind. In the desert areas this produces sand storms that penetrate most tents somehow or other. The bare sand and rock will heat up more quickly and cool down more quickly than over a glacier or icecap; the resultant pressure gradient can cause powerful katabatic winds from the glacier, especially in the morning. Where there is an appreciable difference in altitude between glacier and outwash the downdraught may be so sudden as to flatten tents.

The prevailing wind on the south coast is south-easterly but commonly south-westerly in summer. In view of this the area west and east of the Öraefajökull, for example, may receive quite different weather conditions at the same time owing to the föhn effect across the mountain.

An account of the weather in Iceland is given in the Icelandair leaflet of that title.

MAPS (See Chapter 4)

The 1:750,000 map is quite unsuitable for hiking. The new 1:250,000 series are probably the best at present owing to the fact that the 1:100,000 are rather old and inaccurate — especially along the ice margins — and should be read with an open mind. Roads marked on these maps should be treated with caution but in addition to these there are frequently new routes opened up by farmers, Ferdafélag Íslands, or the Power Authority which will take four-wheel drive vehicles.

The Iceland Unit Bulletin, Island, tries to keep members up to date with significant changes as reported back by expedition leaders at the end of every season.

COMPASS DEVIATION

The compass deviation is about 20° west but this will vary locally on account of fossil magnetism in the basaltic rocks which may give cause to abandon the usual maxim of 'trust the compass'.

TYPES OF TERRAIN

Wet Ground

There is a great deal of wet ground in the valley floors and on the glacial outwash plains (sandar). Lightweight rubber boots are good if you are to be working for any length of time in these conditions. Ordinary boots need to be in good condition and kept dubbined.

The Icelandic method of getting vehicles out of bogs is very efficient. A hole is dug under the bumper and into this is put stones and then a length of planking. With the bumper jacks on this firm base, the vehicle is raised as high as possible. With a number of jacks the vehicle can be lifted clear of the mud fairly quickly. Mud around the axles is removed with a long-handled shovel, and rubber mats (link type) are put under the wheels. The vehicle can now be jumped onto firm ground (low gear, full revs, and let the clutch out suddenly). Inflatable jacks making use of the exhaust are now available and quite good for this purpose. Do not over-inflate!

Lava Desert

This can be very hard on the boots and can be tiring to walk over — especially when pack carrying. The surface will vary from rough lava to sand, and stony areas. Where pumice overlies earlier lava flows, as around Askja, the cavities below may be hidden. Sandy tracts may vary in hardness. Water supplies may be hard to find owing to the permeable nature of the basalt and sand. Sand storms and whirlwinds can be unpleasant, especially for those who wear spectacles.

Snow gaiters or 'stop touts' are useful to keep dust and small stones out of your boots but the tie strings under the boots will not last long before being severed by sharp stones or lava. Take spares.

If you are trying to pioneer a new route with a Land Rover, a steady plod without excessive revs is advised for sand dunes or steep slopes. Do not rush at a slope. Should you run out of power, or your wheels show signs of slipping, stop, roll back down, and try again. You may need to do this several times.

Hot Spring Areas

These are **highly dangerous** areas and carelessness has led to numerous painful accidents (third degree burns, evacuation and repatriation). The casual visitor will not realise that hot springs change their position over time, covering their tracks with a thin layer of mud and minerals overlying boiling mud or sulphur.

Basalt Ridges

The Icelandic maps give very poor definition to the ground detail in upland areas. Only the air photographs give a true indication of the type of country and whether or not it is negotiable. Basalt ridges tend to be very unstable. The rock itself is fractured and loose; scree may only be a thin layer overlying solid rock below. In the northern, heavily glaciated highlands there are numerous sharp ridges that are too narrow to traverse. The problem is heightened by the growth of a thin layer of mossy vegetation which is extremely slippery.

Glaciers

Most glaciers should not be tackled without the right leadership and equipment. Apart from anything else, ordinary insurance will not cover you. Outlet glaciers to the icecaps are known to move in surges that leave the surface highly crevassed (eg. Brúarjökull: 9Km in 1963!). Small cirque glaciers can do the same (eg. Teigardalsjökull: 100m in 1971). Steep slopes and crevasses are not the sole problem; Icelandic glaciers are temperate. That is to say that they are close to their melting point and there is considerable melt water on the glacier surface resulting in:

(a) wet glacier surfaces.

(b) fast-flowing supra-glacial streams that carve deep channels in their lower reaches and frequently disappear down potholes to continue within the glacier. In other words they are not worth falling into.

(c) extensive glacial outwash zones (sandar) that are difficult or impossible to cross because of the innumerable streams.

Above the firn line the snow is often soft, wet, and deep. Progress can be laborious and the use of a Greenland sledge, for example, would be useless. The lower parts of most glaciers are snow-free in summer so that crevasses are visible. Melting creates a rough honeycombed surface that makes walking without crampons quite safe until slopes are encountered. Ice axes, ropes, crampons and prussiks are essential equipment for any glacier — if only for an emergency.

One Icelandic veteran has described the Vatnajökull icecap as 'the white ocean'. It is a serious proposition for anyone and many experienced groups have turned back at an early stage. Rescue from Vatnajökull is exceptionally difficult and advice should be sought before venturing onto the ice. (See Chapter 15)

Groups working on ice should learn how to move on a rope and how to effect crevasse rescues.

Moraines

There are several categories of moraine:

(a) Old stable moraine: a relative term.

(b) Old blocky moraine: boulder hopping can be hazardous owing to the instability.

(c) Recent moraine: generally unstable, hard on the boots and breath.

(d) Ice-cored moraine: a veneer of moraine or volcanic ash overlies an ice core that has become or is in the process of becoming detached from the glacier. This is understandably difficult to walk on and frequently will have a deep, muddy sludge in the hollows that enjoys creeping over your boots and up your legs.

PARTY PROCEDURES ON SNOW OR ICE

This book cannot set out to be a manual for mountaineers and so we refer you to several mountaineering texts in Chapter 18. Suffice to say that if you do not know the procedures then you should not venture onto this type of terrain. The Iceland Unit can supply a broadsheet on party procedures which you may find useful as a summary when training expedition members.

RIVERS:

Iceland has many rivers, most of which are glacial in origin and therefore have certain characteristics:

(a) They are fast and cold.

(b) They are relatively shallow but the floor is difficult to see owing to discolouration by glacial rock flour.

(c) They fluctuate in level and discharge during the day, being lowest in the early morning (c. 3am) and highest in the early afternoon. However, they respond very rapidly to rainfall or melting and this generalisation may be upset.

(d) They may change course quite frequently, notably after a period of high discharge. Rivers may not therefore appear where the maps mark them.

(e) They have beds of boulders and sand. Quicksands are common. Large stones may be constantly on the move.

These facts suggest several precautions for those walking in the interior:

(a) Suitable methods of river crossing should be learned and practiced before departure. Rivers requiring ropes (of which there are many) are serious propositions not to be undertaken lightly.

(b) The extreme cold of glacial water can be fatal. Waterproof clothing will to some extent protect you in the event of brief immersion. The RAF team that crossed Iceland from west to east in 1972 used a specially designed combination rubber suit on account of the large numbers of rivers that they had to cross. For relatively shallow streams, yet too deep for walking boots, snow gaiters are quite effective — so long as you do not stand still!

(c) It is dangerous to cross a glacial river in bare feet. The sensation afterwards may be exhilarating but the cold may make your feet oblivious to sharp projections and you will not have the necessary protection from moving boulders. Many Icelanders wear calf-length rubber boots. Where frequent immersion is likely, as across a sandur plain, the feet will become softened and it is sensible to wear walking boots all the time. Without them, grit may enter the shoes and rub against your heels.

(d) If a river looks too dangerous it may be worth considering camping until early morning to see if the flow abates.

(e) A walking-stick/staff can be a serious handicap if too much weight is applied to it to keep balance. The water may sweep it away suddenly upsetting your balance.

(f) Keep an eye on the weather conditions and try to estimate the response of your area's rivers to rainfall.

(g) Because of constant river bed changes, a single crossing point cannot be relied upon. Use care at all times.

(h) Sandflats bordering rivers may be firm at low water but become soft and liable to quicksand when immersed.

RIVER CROSSINGS (PERSONNEL)

There is no doubt that the crossing of rivers in Iceland can be a very serious undertaking that requires thorough and careful preparation. The following notes have been gleaned from practical experience and also from references such as 'Mountain Leadership' by Eric Langmuir and Bill March's article on 'River Crossings' (Climber and Rambler, May 1977).

ONLY CROSS IF: 1. The alternative is more dangerous.
2. The crossing can be adequately safeguarded.
3. The river is fordable (not swimmable!)

Where to cross

Where possible examine any likely sites from a good vantage point, often on higher ground a little distance from the river. This may also enable the bottom to be seen more easily. It is as well to remember that the force of the current increases at the rate of the square of the velocity (speed). When the velocity is doubled the force is multiplied by a factor of four, if trebled the force is multiplied by a factor of nine. A fast-flowing river therefore must not be underestimated even if it is relatively shallow.

Cross turbulent rivers at the lower end of pools below rapids or waterfalls. In large rivers look for places where the water is flowing through several channels and cross each of these at its widest (shallowest?) part. A smooth firm river bottom is best and one wants to avoid boulders, slabs of rock, sand and mud. Sand (or silt) on the edge of glacier-melt rivers can be quicksand so extra caution is necessary. In general the outside of river bends have deeper water and stronger flow than the inside, so the best place for crossing is between bends where there is more even depth and shallower water. (see Fig. 22)

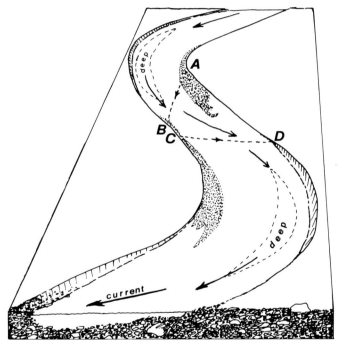

Fig. 22. River Crossings: where to cross.

When to cross

Remember that glacial rivers are deeper from midday to about midnight, therefore it may be worth waiting until early morning before crossing. Small run-off streams rise quickly after rainfall and equally they fall quickly after further time, so a brief pause may save a soaking.

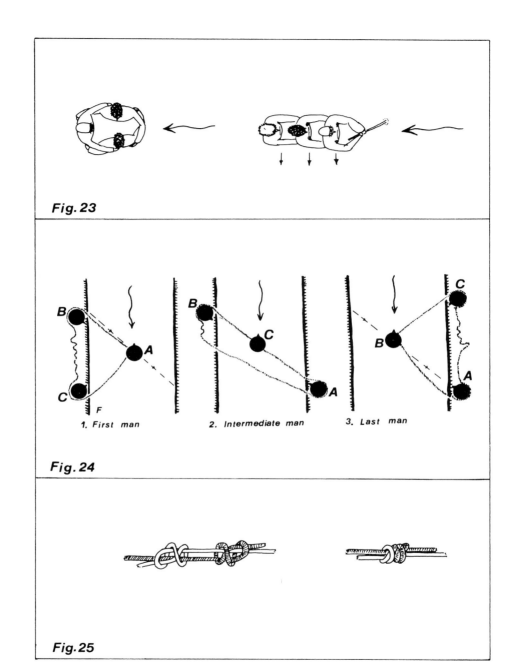

Fig. 23

Fig. 24

1. First man   2. Intermediate man   3. Last man

Fig. 25

Fig. 23. River Crossings: crossing without a rope.
Fig. 24. River Crossings: crossing with a rope.
Fig. 25. Double fisherman's knot.

Clothing

In general wear as little as possible when crossing rivers! But at the same time remember that exposed flesh will chill more quickly than if covered. Close-fitting trousers are ideal if prolonged immersion is likely. Waterproof overtrousers worn next to the skin are useful since they protect the legs and are easily dried after the event. It is essential that boots are always kept on and it is wise to remove socks before entering the water. Snow-gaiters worn against the skin can act in the same way as overtrousers and are particularly useful in shallower rivers. Whatever clothing is used for the crossing, remember that **dry** clothes next to the skin when you reach the other side are essential.

Packs

All members of the crossing party, EXCEPT THE FIRST MAN, should keep their packs on. When crossing the pack should be kept high on the back and it is **imperative that any waist straps are released** so that the pack can be jettisoned instantly in the event of a slip. If the pack has a waterproof extension it is worth extending it and tying it securely so that additional air is trapped within the sack. Any mechanism for increasing the bouyancy of the sac will be beneficial — eg. up-turned billies, inflated polythene bags.

How to Cross

There are numerous methods of crossing rivers but the following ones have been tried and tested in Iceland and have proved quite satisfactory. ALWAYS face upstream because a fierce current will bend the knees.

CROSSING WITHOUT A ROPE

If the river is shallow or if no rope is available then the following methods may be adopted:

Triangle Method: Move in groups of three, facing inwards with arms linked and legs splayed. The downstream man, who is facing upstream ought to be the heaviest/strongest of the team. Move one-at-a-time with the other two giving support to the one who is moving (Fig. 23).

Line Astern Method: Three or more in the party line up one behind the other firmly holding the waist of the person in front. The upstream man moves sideways, then the second, third etc. until all the party are in line again. The upstream man may find a 'third leg' (eg. an ice axe) useful as a support (Fig. 23).

CROSSING WITH A ROPE:

Numerous methods may be adopted but the **Continuous Loop Method** (Fig. 24) is the most satisfactory. The width of channel that can be crossed by this method is determined by the length of rope available. Beware of underwater snags that may trap the rope as this can cause the man to be held under the water.

Firstly, tie the two ends of the rope together with a double-fisherman's knot (Fig. 25). The first man to cross, 'A', ties into a loop in the rope (figure of eight knot on the bight) which is placed high under his arm-pits. He crosses diagonally downstream supporting himself with a 'third-leg' if necessary and is held by 'B' on the upstream rope, who is **not** tied into the rope but allows free movement of the rope through his arms and round his body. Approximately one-river-width downstream is a third person, 'C', who like 'B' is not tied to the rope but allows free movement of rope around his body and through his arms. If 'A' loses his footing whilst crossing then 'B' pays rope out and 'C' draws him into the bank. The upstream man, 'B' must not try to pull the man in as this may result in him being dragged and held under the water.

When 'A' has reached the other side he releases himself from the loop and pays the rope, behind his back, through so that the loop returns to the side from which he has crossed. 'C' then steps into the loop and crosses over to join 'A' who is standing about one-river-width downstream from 'B'. In the event of 'C' slipping 'A' will be in a position to bring him in as long as 'B' pays rope through to him. Additional party members cross in the same way as 'C' and the last man, 'B', crosses supported by 'C' in the upstream position and 'A' in the downstream position, who will bring him into the bank in the event of a slip.

RIVER CROSSING (VEHICLES)

(a) Make a thorough recconnaisance on foot from the bank to decide your precise route.

(b) Remember that smooth flow indicates deep water.

(c) You may not be able to cross straight over but may have to traverse up or down stream travelling from shoal to shoal.

(d) Select a low gear and four-wheel drive and remember that high revs are more important than speed through the water.

(e) If possible, face downstream rather than up to avoid a wave smothering the engine. A flexible extension to elevate the exhaust is a useful fitting.

(f) Should you come to a halt it will probably be for one of two reasons:

(i) the bow-wave has dampened the points etc. In which case you will need to climb out in mid river.

(ii) quicksands. This can be tedious if you have no winch or vehicle to pull you out, therefore:

either stay put and wait for low water and a chance to dig yourself out.

or use two bumper jacks and some rocks to lever yourself out. This may take hours.

or try to get help. Take care. The colleague of an experienced Icelandic mountain driver was drowned trying to do this. The latter saved himself by strapping an empty petrol can to his back before jumping into the river.

SHELTER

Travellers in Iceland should always carry a tent, sleeping bag, cooker and food. Other forms of shelter may be occupied, derelict or non-existent when you arrive. Because of the probability of strong winds, a low mountain tent is most suitable for Iceland. Tents should ideally have a sewn-in groundsheet with a reasonably wide valence around the outside skin. A popular tent is the Vango Force Ten with a ridge pole. The experience of some expeditions suggests that the ridge pole of the Vango weakens the tent and that it should be removed in high winds. One group successfully pitched the tent head-on to the wind; in strong gusts, such as you get off the icecap, the tent proved to be stable enough to fill like a balloon thus separating the flysheet from the inner and preventing leakage. The door zip was held down by attaching a nylon loop and pegging it to the ground. A snow valence reduces the amount of air getting under the flysheet.

You may camp almost anywhere in the interior but **do remember that you are in a fragile environment where conservation of the landscape is paramount. Any damage will be there for all to see for years to come.** Even in the inhabited, or even the uninhabited valleys of the mountain areas you should ask permission before camping on any in-field or out-field land. Grass is an important crop and should not be flattened by tents before the harvest. The following points may be useful (see also Chapter 8):

(a) Streams emerging from glaciers may be charged with rock flour and are therefore non-potable. Look for springs etc. in the mountainside, or snow melt.

(b) Flat, stony areas may be only superficially stony with a layer of smaller material below, BUT take care that the water tables does not rise into your tent after rainfall or prolonged fine weather!

(c) Dry, harmless-looking hollows can fill and empty very rapidly.

(d) Have you camped in an overflow channel? As pointed out earlier on, the rivers can rise rapidly, spilling into new channels.

(e) **Damaged vegetation takes a long time to recover in Iceland owing to the brevity of the summer, the risk of water erosion in spring, and wind erosion after dry spells. Please avoid digging trenches and pits on the sparsely vegetated patches that you may use in the interior. Rubbish should be burned or carried out with you.**

(f) If you are uncertain about obtaining permission to camp in a particular area, the Iceland Unit may be able to advise you.

EMERGENCY SITUATIONS

Your national embassy should be informed of any serious situation so that they can have the facts should any enquiries be made to them. Do this at an early stage. In any case, as mentioned in Chapter 10, they should have the full details of the expedition already.

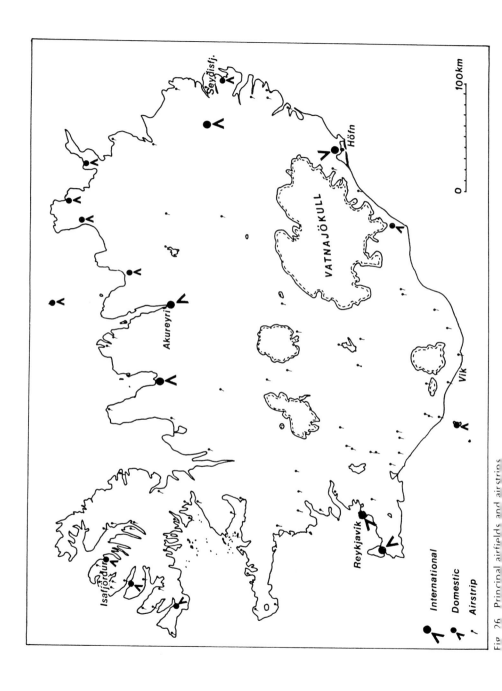

International
Domestic
Airstrip

Fig. 26 Principal airfields and airstrips

Evacuation

Any evacuation will be at considerable cost to your expedition. Be adequately insured. The evacuation procedure for individual groups will depend on their locality, numbers, availability of transport etc. Groups wishing to find out the best procedure for their area should write to the Iceland Unit. Groups working in the Kerlingarfjöll/Hveravellir areas, for example, should know of the following:

Radio: Hveravellir and Kerlingarfjöll Ski School.

Airstrip: Hvervellir and about 2Km downvalley from the Ski School.

Medical Centre: Laugavatn and Laugarás.

Hospital: Selfoss, Reykjavík, Blönduós, Akureyri.

Airfields and Airstrips (Figure 26)

Iceland has six airfields for **international** commercial air traffic (Akureyri, Egilsstaðir, Höfn, Keflavík, Reykjavík, Sauðarkrókur), eleven airfields with no facilities, temporary manning, and use by **domestic** commercial traffic (Fagurhólsmýri, Grímsey, Húsavík, Ísafjörður, Kópasker, Norðfjörður, Patreksfjöður, Raufarhöfn, Thingeyri, Thórshöfn, Vestmannaeyjar). All of these are gravel runways apart from a small section at Ísafjörður. In addition there are 78 **airstrips** for light aircraft wholly unmanned, and equipped only with a windsock and orange cones to demarcate the landing strip. Surfaces may be uncompacted stones, gravel, or sand. The Iceland Unit has notes on the coordinates, length, orientation and surface of these strips. Further information can be obtained from the Directorate of Civil Aviation (Flugmálastjörn). Their offices are in the control tower at Reykjavík airport alongside the Hótel Loftleiðir.

Hospitals and Medical Centres (Figure 27)

Hospitals are to be found in the following towns:

Reykjavík	Akranes	Stykkishólmur
Patreksfjörður	Ísafjörður	Blönduós
Sauðarkrókur	Siglufjörður	Akureyri
Húsavík	Egilsstaðir	Neskaupsstaðir
Vestmannaeyjar	Selfoss	Keflavík

Figure 27. shows the location of the Icelandic medical centres which, as in Britain, deal only with minor injuries and ailments.

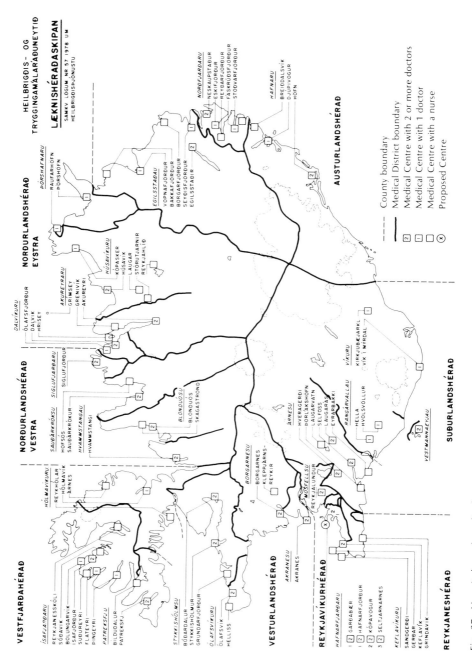

Fig. 27. Hospitals and medical centres.

Remember that although you may be eligible for costs equivalent to those charged to Icelanders, medical treatment can be expensive. So do be adequately insured, especially if mountaineering. See also Chapters 12 and 14. All foreigners staying in Iceland are entitled to free treatment in hospital and casualty wards in the event of sudden illness or aggravation or chronic disease, provided that the patient has not come to Iceland with a view to obtaining treatment, or is not strong enough to return home. Transport has to be paid by the patient. Medical treatment is never wholly free but British nationals, for example, will obtain partial refunds of doctor's, dentist's and chemist's bills on production of their passports.

First Aid

The equipment that you take must be governed by four factors:

1. Whether or not you have a doctor.

2. Space and weight limitations.

3. The degree of dispersal of your field units.

4. The estimated maximum time which will elapse between occurrences of an accident and the arrival of medical assistance (see above).

In Iceland medical assistance will generally be available within 24 hours because you may have relatively speedy access to a farm telephone or a car-borne radio telephone. Even so, at least one member of the party should have a good working knowledge of First Aid, and preferably more than one.

Ailments that are particularly prevalent among Iceland expeditions seem to be:

1. Eye infections and irritations owing to windblown dust.
2. Persistently open cuts.
3. Burns from primuses and hot springs.
4. Blisters caused by grit in the boot.
5. Earache from persistent cold wind.
6. Headache from moving in and out of hot and cold places and from travel generally.
7. Constipation from A.F.D. food.
8. Bites — mainly restricted to midges at Lake Myvatn.

Details of medical kits are discussed in the 'Handbook for Expeditions' and in Robin Illingworth's book on Expedition Medicine. However, from the above, we may conclude the need for:

1. A central base camp kit to cover all eventualities and including local anaesthetic, analgesic, dental dressings, inflatable splints, thermometers, etc.

2. Several field kits containing dressings, antiseptic eye ointment and creams, ear drops, bandages, slings, lint, occlusive dressings, aspirin etc.

3. Personal field kits to include plaster strip, scissors, antiseptic cream, Nivea, fly repellant (where necessary).

4. A thorough pre-expedition dental check-up for all members.

5. Anti-Tetanus injections for all.

6. Adequate insurance (see Chapter 4 and 10).

Rescue Huts

Around the coast is a large number of rescue huts, usually painted orange, that are owned and maintained by Slysarvarnafélag Islands (The National Life-Saving Society of Iceland). These huts are for **emergency use only** and primarily for mariners. Details are given in Chapter 8.

Flies

These are not so prolific as in other countries in the Northlands. They occur around Lake Mývatn in two successive swarms in the summer. They swarm in large numbers at the lake's edge and can be avoided by keeping several hundred metres back! Only one specie bites, and happily this is in the minority.

Clothing colour

Bright orange is the most suitable colour for anoraks and cagoules in Iceland. Blues, greens and browns are very difficult to see against ice or against the basaltic background elsewhere. Should you become lost you will appreciate the need for bright identification.

Flares

It is tempting to take flares but bear in mind that if you had them, how useful would they be in reality? Who would see it and would they act upon it? Most flares are considered as firearms. Homing beacons must be approved by the Iceland Post and Telegraph Administration (see Chapter 11) because of the proximity of the Keflavík NATO airbase and the need for a coordinated approach to marine rescue activities.

EQUIPMENT

Comments on tents appear under the heading of Shelter. Vehicle spares etc. appear in Chapter 7. The following might be used as a guide to the packing of personal equipment for Iceland:

Items of special note

Walking boots: must be sturdy, walked-in, and in good repair. You may need to buy new soles on return. Boots with external stitching may suffer abrasion from lava. The RAF Trans-Iceland Expedition (1972) found the life of boots to depend upon the care with which the foot was placed. The careless 'scuffler' will soon wear his boots out.

Waterproofs:	A good anorak is essential but your enjoyment of the expedition will be improved with the ownership of waterproof overtrousers and cagoule or similar jacket.
Sweaters:	If you are having to buy one, wait until you get to Iceland. Expensive, but a hand-knitted sweater will last you for years.
Insulation:	A lilo or sleeping mat is essential. You will rarely sleep on soft ground. Closed cell mats are best. Lilos rather cold, especially on ice.
Sleeping bag:	Even 'Icelandic Specials' have been reported inadequate at times! A good wall-quilted sack is best.
Cookers:	Paraffin is most suitable (cost, heat). It is cheap and sold in handy containers. Meths is phenomenally expensive. Gaz is available in Globetrotter, S200 and 907 sizes. Also Primus 2202 gas cylinders.
Polythene Bags:	You can never have enough. Airtight tins and silica gel useful for matches, film etc.
Rucksack:	According to preference. Good detachable frame most versatile for expeditions.

Other personal items

2 sets underclothing (string vest or long-johns for Vatnajökull?)
2 warm shirts (long sleeves)
1 light shirt
1 pair warm trousers/breeches
1 pair thinner trousers
3 pairs socks/stockings
1 pair gymshoes/trainers/basketball boots
Swimming trunks
Handkerchiefs
Tracksuits (Trebles as pyjamas, spare sweater, spare trousers)
Woollen gloves/mitts
Balaclava
Toilet kit
Spare laces, polish etc.
Needle and thread
Bivvy bag
Mug, Knife, Fork and Spoon
Torch with spare batteries
Penknife, whistle, compass
Snowgoggles, harness with karabiner, prussiks
Overgloves
Climbing helmet
Ice-axe, campons, dead-man belays, ice-pitons, belay slings, karabiners
Notebook, pencils, ballpoint pen, eraser etc.

Personal First Aid kit, glacier cream, Nivea
Camera, film, binoculars
Patience (plenty of it)

General items of expedition equipment are listed in many expedition reports (reviewable at the Iceland Unit) and in the 'Handbook for Expeditions'.

14 MOUNTAINEERING IN ICELAND

by Roger Smith

INTRODUCTION

This chapter has been compiled by Roger Smith with additional material derived from an article in Icelandic published in **Jökull**. Roger Smith has begun the compilation of 'A Pilot Climbing Guide to Iceland', copies of which may be viewed at the Iceland Unit, the Alpine Club, or the Royal Geographical Society. Figure 31. and Table 3 indicate the zones upon which the guide is based.

Mountaineering in Iceland is largely on the scale of that found in Scotland, together with the Alpine features of glaciers, bergschrunds, crevasses, seracs and moraine. Additionally, the icecaps present a unique challenge for the mountaineer. The climate of Iceland is such that for a larger part of the year the Central Highlands are impenetrable, other than by ski or skidoo, and only peripheral communication and transport are possible. This in turn has a profound influence upon the mountaineering potential of the country which may for convenience be divided into two distinct categories of Ski-touring and Snow and Ice Climbing. These activities can be practiced around the fringes of the country in Winter and Spring and in the Central Highlands during the summer months when there is constant daylight for a significant period. On the whole the rock of the country is so brittle that it does not lend itself to rock climbing. However there is plenty of scope for opening up potential rock climbing areas; not all basalt formations are lethal, indeed some polygonal column formations offer superb routes.

The Iceland Alpine Club (Ísalp) (Appendix G) welcomes contact with foreign mountaineers. They are a small society with no office as such, but they meet every Wednesday (2030 hrs) at Grensásvegi 5. Mountaineering trips are organised once or twice a month to which foreign climbers are welcome. Visiting climbers with slide presentations of their home areas would be welcomed.

Snow, ice and rock climbing courses are run by The New Touring Club (see Appendix G).

SKI-TOURING

There are many areas of Iceland that are suitable for ski-Touring but only the principal ones are included here. They are taken in anti-clockwise order starting in the north of the country.

Trollaskagi, the mountainous peninsula to the west of Akureyri, is provided with a ski-hotel and piste-skiing facilities together with many challenging 'off-piste' routes in Winter and Spring. The mountains Sulur (1114m), Kerling (1538m), and Stryta above the Glerá valley are particularly favourable as are the small glaciers of Glerárdalsjökull (1471m) and

Vindheimajökull (1451m). To the west of the Öxnadalur valley are the three glaciers Thverárjökull (1384m), Tungnahryggsjökull (1387m), which provide ski-traversing potential.

Moving westwards, the north-western fjord peninsula has the small icecap of Drangajökull (925m) which although of low altitude affords some excellent ski-ing opportunities more appropriate in the Spring and Summer months when access is easier.

At the end of the prominent Snaefellsnes peninsula further south is the small glacier peak of Snaefellsjökull (1446m) which provides some excellent ski-traverses in Spring and early summer when the snow level extends towards the lowlands that are well served with roads, making the area justly popular.

The area from Snaefellsnes and southwards towards Reykjavik is popular in Winter and Spring for it is easily reached and has some fine ski-routes over the mountains of low altitude draped in Winter raiment. The ski areas of Bláfjoll and Skálafell have tows and lifts and are readily accessible from the city. The mountains between the two, across Mosfellsheidi and Hengill, provide good country for ski-touring. Further inland Langjökull (1355m) with its outliers Eiriksjökull (1675m) to the north and Thórisjökull (1340m) to the south-west is another area with endless ski-touring potential. The complete traverse, from end to end, although technically not hard, is a long and serious undertaking. Hofsjökull (1765m), a nearly circular glacier of thirty two kilometers diameter, is not as challenging as Langjökull but is more remote. Close to Hofsjökull are the Kerlingarfjöll mountains which present a different proposition. From the outlying hill Ásgardsfjall (919m) the view southwards is breathtaking and beneath it lies a well-provisioned ski-school with a camp site nearby. The lower flanks of the mountain range are provided with tows and other facilities, whilst the mountains Snaekjöllur (1477m) and Ögmundur (1300m) together with their neighbours are readily accessible and provide some excellent traverses in the summer months. The couloir on the north-west flank of Lodmundur (1432m) was descended on ski (Scottish Grade I/II in ascent) in 1975 and was considered to be one of the last problems of the area. This area also has the additional attraction of hot springs in the heart of the mountains.

Moving southwards towards the next peripheral area one passes close to Hekla (1491m) which presents some short ski-routes around the crater rim in spring but does not really warrant a special visit in its own right. At the head of the Thorsmork valley further to the south is the next area of interest. Here the glaciers Eyjafjallajökull (1666m) and Mýrdalsjökull (1480m), offer some of the best ski-ing potential in Iceland and owing to their relative ease of access are notably popular. The traverse of Eyjafjallajökull from Stórumörk, in the west, over Hámandur (1666m) to Fimmvördurháls in the east is a magnificent route as are many of the obvious routes on the western fringes of Mýrdalsjökull. Nearby Tindfjallajökull (1462m) although much smaller offers some ski-traverses in spring and early summer.

Some distance to the east is Vatnajökull, the largest glacier in Europe, which provides some very fine, serious ski-touring routes. Opportunities are legion but the remoteness of the icecap and the extreme nature of the climate up there add to the seriousness of the routes undertaken. This is taken up again in Chapter 15. The mountains on the fringes of the Vatnajökull are more suited to conventional mountaineering but also have some long, technically very demanding ski-ing possibilities. Here the true sport of ski-mountaineering may be practised without hindrance whilst in the vast interior of Vatnajökull cross-country ski-ing may be pursued for mile after mile.

The eastern fjords area of Iceland is not without its ski-ing possibilities but these are only to be snatched by those fortunate enough to be in the right place at the right time.

Cross-country ski-ing in the centre of Iceland is possible but constrained by distance from habitation and by the strong winds that blow across the desert sweeping the snow away to reveal jagged lava fingers. Advance food dumps layed in the autumn or skidoo support would be necessary. The centre is not generally open to vehicles until late June or even July.

SNOW AND ICE CLIMBING

Iceland experiences seasonal climatic changes so that the snow and ice climbing possibilities fall into two seasonal categories. Firstly, winter/spring mountaineering, found principally around the fringes of the country when certain mountains come into condition; and secondly, summer mountaineering, primarily on the icecaps of the interior of the country. In consideration of each type of mountaineering a mixture of Scottish and Alpine grading systems is used.

Winter/Spring Mountaineering

Winter/spring mountaineering is still in its infancy but with the development of 'ísalp' (1977), it has grown in popularity. The areas commonly explored at this time of the year are those nearest to centres of population, especially Reykjavík and Akureyri. However, several British groups have visited the Mývatn area at New Year to undertake snowshoeing expeditions based on the Hótel Reynihlíd. These expeditions have started walking at 0900 hrs in darkness and have returned to base at 1700-1800 hrs depending upon the weather conditions. Snowshoeing conditions cannot be guaranteed in view of wind drift revealing rock and jagged lava. Icelanders never snowshoe — they favour cross country skiing.

The mountainous peninsula to the west of Akureyri, especially the peaks above Öxnadalur, Glerá, and Svarfaðardalur and Skiðadalur, is easily accessible and has an abundance of fine weather climbs to offer. The Akureyri ski-Hotel, at the mouth of the Glerá valley is a satisfactory base for some of the climbs particularly those on Kerling (1538m), Glerárdalsjökull

(1471m) and Vindheimajökull (1451m). The ski-Hotel is not open during the summer months.

Moving westwards the north-western peninsula is not noted for its potential, except for the areas close to Drangajökull (925m) in the north, Lambadalsfjall (957m) and Kaldbakkur (998m) in the central region. The remainder of the area is of lower altitude and does not attract good conditions.

On the Snaefellsnes peninsula there are many fine routes on Helgrindur (986m) most of which have not yet been attempted but are likely to be Difficile (D) to Tres Difficile (TD) in grade. On Snaefellsjökull itself there are a few short, hard (D) ice-routes on the summit blocks but the area has more attractions for ski-ing.

Near to Reykjavík the mountain range sandwiched between Borgarfjörður and Hvalfjörður offers some very fine climbs especially on Skardsheiði (1052m) whose north face has several 700m routes of D to TD standard. Just to the north of Thingvellir is Botnssúlur (1095m) which has numerous routes of Scottish Grade III, IV, and possibly V on it, and when conditions are favourable is a popular climbing area.

In the south of the country suitable conditions can favour winter/spring climbing on Eyjafjallajökull (1666m) and Öraefajökull (2119m), Iceland's highest mountain mass. Both are readily accessible from the coastal road.

Summer Mountaineering

The summer mountaineering potential of Iceland is more of a known quantity since people have been climbing onto icecaps since time immemorial, as reference to the legendary Icelandic sags will bear out. It is on these glaciers and icecaps that attention must focus in order to find out the true wealth of this facet of the sport, for the summer's sun melts much of the winter snow and leaves only ice behind for the short-lived months of summer. A characteristic feature of Iceland's mountains in the summer is their rich colour and the white smears of old snow/ice couloirs that seam their flanks. Couloirs of this nature are abundant and offer straightforward climbing that one might expect of a Scottish Grade I gully — in summer conditions!

Turning our attention to particular areas, in the north of Iceland the mountains of Tröllaskagi, west of Dalvík and Akureyri are of particular merit and contain some excellent routes especially on the fringes of the glaciers Tungnahryggsjökull (1382m), Mýrkarjökull (1387m) and Vindheimajökull (1451m), where ice-tongues present many opportunities in the easier grade brackets (F - PD).

Drangajökull (925m) in the extreme north-west, with its three small nunatuks, Hlódabunga, Reydarbunga, and Hrolleiffsborg, presents little challenge to the mountaineer, but is very remote, making any undertaking all the more serious. Snaefellsjökull (1446m) likewise presents only minor opportunities at this time of year.

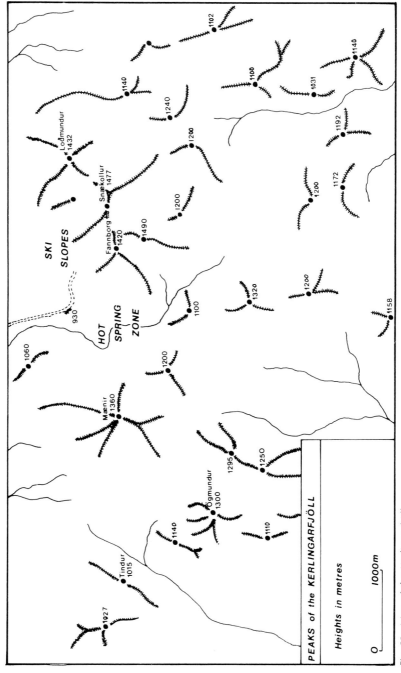

1102

1140

1100 1031

1140

1240

1192

Loðmundur 1432

1200

1200 1172

Snækollur 1477

1200 1200

Fannborg 1420 1490

SKI SLOPES

HOT SPRING ZONE 1100 1320 1200

1158

930

1060 1200

Mænir 1360

1295 1250

Ögmundur 1300

1140 1110

Tindur 1015

1927

PEARS of the KERLINGARFJÖLL

Heights in metres

0   1000m

Fig. 28. Map of the Kerlingarfjöll.

172

In Central Iceland the story is very different, and the area around Langjökull (1355m) well worth a visit. Eiriksjökull (1675m), and outlier to the north-west of the area is a remarkably abrupt and almost circular glacier that has some long, straightforward routes to its summit. Thorisjökull (1340m) and Geitlandsjökull (1400m) are two more outliers, in the south-west, that are well worth climbing. The views onto Langjökull from the latter are just reward for the ascent. The Hagafell-Jarlhettur region on the south-east margin of Langjökull presents some very dramatic rock scenery which contrasts well with the gentler ice slopes hereabouts. For the climber, however, the eastern margin of the Langjökull itself is of more importance. The glaciers that calve icebergs into Hvitarvatn lake are magnificent and give many 3000 ft. routes up to PD (Peu-Difficle) in standard, onto the icecap. The small eastern outlier, Hrútafell (1410m) has six glaciers that tumble from its summit ice-plateau all of which offer superb 2,000 - 3,000 ft. routes up to TD in standard. The tourist hut in Thjófadalir is a good base for this mountain and also for the north-eastern fringe of Langjökull which offers numerous straightforward (Facile) routes onto the nunatuks.

Across the Kjölur plain to the east is Hofsjökull (1755m) a nearly circular icecap with disappointing ice-climbing possibilities. However, to the south of the Kjölur plain are the Kerlingarfjöll mountains (Figure 28). The north faces of the mountains Lodmundur (1432m) (Figure 29), Snaeköllur (1477m), Fannborg (1420m), Maenir (1360m) and Ögmundur (1300m), that overlook the plain, offer climbing of similar scale to the northern corries of the Cairngorms together with the Alpine features of glaciers, bergschrunds, crevasses, seracs and moraine. Numerous climbs of Grade I/II (PD) are to be found in these mountains all about 1000 - 2000 ft. in length. From the summit of Snaeköllur it is reputed that one can seen both the north and south coasts of the country.

About thirty miles east of the Kerlingarfjöll is Tungnafellsjökull (1525m), an outlier of Vatnajökull, which has three glacial tongues that yield routes of Facile (F) to Difficle (D) in grade, about 2,000 ft. in length. The area abounds in climbing possibilities on the mountains that border the Jökuldalur valley mostly in the Grade I/II category. From here approaches can be made onto the Bardarbunga (2000m) area of Vatnajökull across the Vonaskard valley — see later for particulars.

Turning to the south of the country, Hekla (1491m) presents easy (F) snow routes onto its crater rim and is worthy of a visit on the grounds that it is one of the most recent volcanoes to erupt. Eyjafjallajökull (1666m) comes into its own as one of the finest areas for mountaineering in the summer months and the glacier tongue of Gigjökull, on its northern edge presents one of the most attractive ice-climbing areas in Iceland. There are also numerous routes on to the icecap of F — Assez Difficile (AD) grade and the complete traverse from east-west, although long, is worth the effort. There is a hut on Fimmvörðuháls, the pass between Eyjafjallajökull and Myrdalsjökull.

If one travels along the coastal road to the east one is soon confronted with the vast expanse of Vatnajökull whose margin provides some excellent

Fig. 29. Routes on Lödmundur.

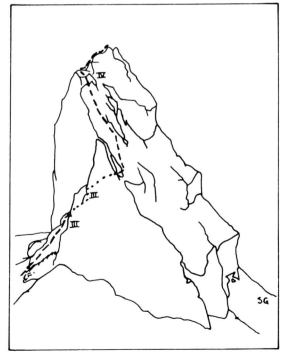

Fig. 30. Púmall.

174

climbing possibilities, comparable in size and grade to many Alpine routes. In the north the first area of interest is Kverkfjöll (1920m) which is an area of former volcanic activity with some residual steam vents. The area is approachable from the Hverdalur valley which is one of the most spectacular hot-spring areas in Iceland. There are numerous long (3,000m) routes of PD grade in this area as well as some rather spectacular ice caves carved by flowing geothermal waters. There is a hut close by. Westwards from here is Barðabunga (2000m) which is best approached from the roadhead and tourist hut, at the mouth of the Jökuldalur valley beneath Tungnafellsjökull. The steep glacial wall hereabouts gives access onto the icecap summit by long and complex routes of about AD standard. South of Barðabunga, on the western edge of Vatnajökull are Hamarinn (1573m) and Kerlingar (1339m) which offer little resistance to the mountaineer willing to attack them from the west after a long approach route over the ashen desert. The ice-cliffs of the Grímsvötn crater, most recently active in June 1983, would be well worth a visit for the mountaineer but involve a 'major' undertaking to even reach the area. Back on the fringe of the icecap just north of the Skaftafell National Park, are the nunataks of Miðfellstindur (1430m) and Hrútafellstindur (1875m) which offer some good, long routes of mixed climbing (approximately AD grade) while the nearby thumb of basalt, Púmall (1297m), is an obvious 'plum'. It was first climbed in 1975 and has been graded III (possibly IV). In the summer of 1984 the Icelandic television filmed a climb of the peak (Figure 30).

Further south on Öraefajökull, which is almost a separate icecap at a higher altitude, are four distinct peaks. At the centre is a high point, Snaebreið (2041m), which although relatively easy in ascent (F) is most rewarding with its panoramic views over sea and ice. Nearby the nunatuks Knappar (2044m), Hvannadalshnúkur (2119m) and Thuríðatindur (1741m) give good ascents and magnificent views. In this area it is the route chosen to reach the icecap that is more demanding than the final slopes to the peak in question. There are numerous possibilities from both east and west, some deliberately avoiding difficulties and some eking them out, but all of them major undertakings of about 5,000 ft. or more in length. Öraefajökull is discussed in more length in the next chapter.

Further east at the head of the Kalfafellsdalur valley, on the true edge of Vatnajökull are more possibilities on the Nunatuks Snaefell (1554m), Karl and Kerling (1140m), Birnudalstindur (1230m) and Kalfafellsfjöll (1460m), all in the easier (F-AD) grades. Close to the eastern end of Vatnajökull are the glacier tongues of Hoffellsjökull and Lambatungujökull around which are further possibilities, especially on Grasgiljatindur (1275m) and Goðaborg (1425m). The ridge traverse on the latter is particularly good at PD grade. In the Lónsöraefi area, just east of Vatnajökull, centred on the small icecap Hofsjökull (1190m), are many shorter climbs of easier (F-PD) grade.

Finally mention must be made of the volcanic plug of Herdubreið (1682m) to the north of Vatnajökull which stands solitarily above the surrounding plain. It has numerous gullies breaking through the rock barrier to the

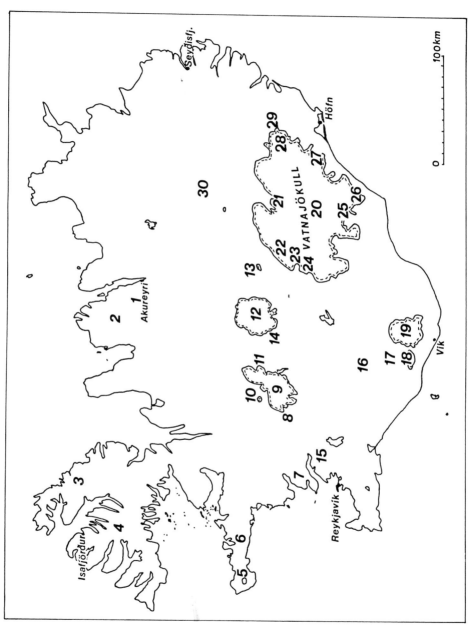

Fig. 31. Key to the mountaineering zones used in the Pilot Guide to Mountaineering in Iceland.

summit snow plateau, many of which yield routes, up to Grade III in standard, when conditions are favourable. The usual ascent is from the oasis at Herdubreiðarlindir following a route to the north and then to the west of the peak. It takes around 18 hours for a round trip. The views from the summit are breathtaking and make the climbing all the more rewarding.

Although the country cannot boast large mountain ranges or north faces of repute, it does have a considerable amount of mountaineering potential. Most mountains have been climbed, and often by more than one route, there remain ample opportunities for new routes.

TABLE 3. SUMMARY OF MOUNTAINEERING IN ICELAND (Figure 31)

No:	Area:	Ski-ing:	Climbing:
1.	Glerá valley	W	W, (S)
2.	Tungnahryggsjökull	W, S	W, S
3.	Drangajökull	(W), S	(S)
4.	Lambadalsfjall	(W)	
5.	Snæfellsjökull	W, (S)	W, (S)
6.	Helgrindur		W
7.	Skarðsheiði		W
8.	Þórisj./Geitlandsjökull	(W), S	(S)
9.	Langjökull	(W), S	S
10.	Eiriksjökull	(W), S	S
11.	Hrútfell		S
12.	Hofsjökull	(S)	
13.	Tungnafellsjökull		S
14.	Kerlingarfjöll	S	S
15.	Botnssúlur	(W)	W
16.	Hekla	(W)	(S)
17.	Tindafjallajökull	W, S	(S)
18.	Eyjafjallajökull	W, S	(W), S
19.	Mýrdalsjökull	(W), S	(W), (S)
20.	Vatnajökull	(W), S	W, S
21.	Kverkfjöll	(S)	S
22.	Barðarbunga		S
23.	Hamarinn		S
24.	Kerlingar		S
25.	Skaftafell		(W), S
26.	Öræfajökull	W, S	(W), S
27.	Kalfafellsdalur		S
28.	Goðaborg	S	S
29.	Lónsöræfi	(W)	S
30.	Herdubreið		S

W = Winter/Spring   S = Summer   (W) or (S) = minor possibilities

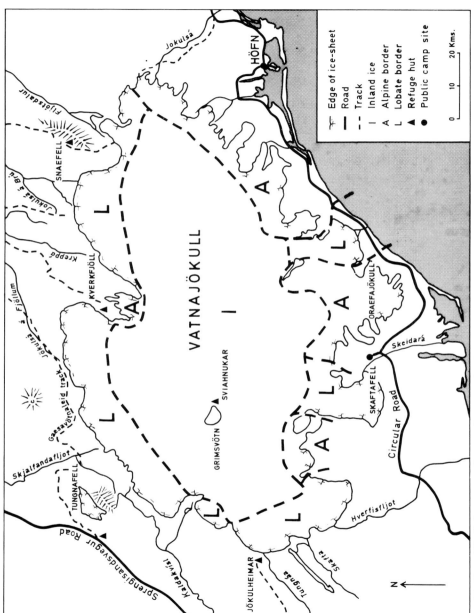

Fig. 32. Vatnajökull: its surroundings and communications.

178

15 VATNAJÖKULL

Dr. I. Y. Ashwell

INTRODUCTION

With an area of 8456 Km^2, Vatnajökull is the largest of the Icelandic icecaps and the largest ice mass in Europe. It has been described by Sigurður Thorarinsson as 'the Kingdom of Vatnajökull' which sums up its pre-eminence well. Since it is so much larger than the other Icelandic icecaps it differs from them in many important ways, most particularly it is large enough to exert considerable control over the climate both over and around its perimeter. Whilst not comparable in severity to the climate over the Greenland icecap under normal conditions, there are some similarities, and Vatnajökull must never be underestimated, because of the possibilities both of rapid change in the weather and of freak outbreaks of exceptionally severe conditions. Those aiming to work and travel on Vatnajökull must be prepared to organise on a scale which is well above that required on any other Icelandic icecap at the same time of year.

PHYSICAL BACKGROUND

Because of its size Vatnajökull straddles several important geological formations. The eastern and south-eastern margins lie on the Tertiary basalt formation, the relic of the now extinct volcanism over a million years old, while the western and north-western half lies on recent lava volcanoes with modern lava-flows which have originated, in some cases, under the ice, and ridges of crumbly yellowish tuff (or 'moberg') forming the margins of the ice. This tuff is the result of eruptions under the ice, which formed also the isolated table-mountains found to the north of Vatnajökull. It seems probable that some of the higher parts of Vatnajökull cover volcanic calderas and table mountains since two of the rather narrow zones of recent and fairly recent volcanism run from north-east to south-west under the ice. The Grímsvötn caldera, with frozen lakes causing the 'jökulhlaups' or glacial floods from under Skeiðarárjökull to the south of the icecap, is part of the most recent volcanic strip (Figure 32).

The relationship of the topography of Vatnajökull to the underlying geology is best seen on the ERTS or LANDSAT satellite photograph from 31st January, 1973, discussed in **Jökull** 23 (1973). This photograph also shows the nature of the surrounding topography, although, being taken in winter, water surfaces do not show up and details are, of course, very small.

In general, there is a marked contrast between the northern and western edges and those of the south and east, due to the fact that the former edges lie on the Central Plateau, with altitudes up to 1000m, the latter reach almost to sea level. The edge of the ice on north and west sides is most often made up of lobes of ice without any great fall, whereas the ice is drained on its south and east sides by true Alpine glaciers falling steeply from the highest levels to nearly sea-level, although Skeiðarárjökull and Breiðamerkurjökull are important exceptions (Figure 33). The central, inland ice, section is undulating rather than flat and the undulations probably reflect the underlying topography. This can be checked by continuing the line of the straight ridges on the ice margin under the ice, when almost always elevated parts will be found, often with marked crevassing. Where nunataks occur, they often have steep, wind-scoured hollows around them as well as crevasses, so that caution is needed in approaching them.

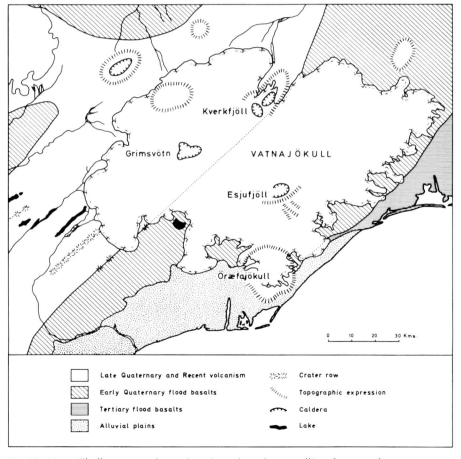

Fig. 33. Vatnajökull: topography and geology (based on satellite photography).

Almost certainly, Vatnajökull has a climatic range quite different from that of its surroundings. The southern half has a very heavy precipitation derived from air coming off the warm Irminger current, probably, on average, more than 4,000 mm per year. There is a climatic divide running NNE to SSW across the highest part of the icecap, and north from this precipitation falls rapidly northwards to values of 400 - 800 mm on the Central Plateau, the driest part of Iceland.

Temperatures can be severe, but in July and August the lower parts of the icecap, and sometimes higher parts as well, can have prolonged period when temperatures are above freezing and surfaces of wet snow make travel difficult. The wind is often the major enemy both on and around the ice, since the southern part of Iceland lies in the path of many low pressure systems moving from the west, and strong, rapidly changing winds bring rapid changes in temperature and visibility. Vatnajökull, as already noted, is large enough to have its own wind circulation, draining from the central area towards the periphery, and round the western half of the icecap margin this drainage clashes with the main westerly atmospheric circulation. With the approach of a depression, therefore, these marginal areas experience exceptionally heavy gusts of wind, apparently falling from the icecap, and severe damage to exposed tents can occur and quite heavy objects can be blown around.

Vatnajökull is also sufficiently large to act as a climatic divide, with good weather on one side, bad on the other. This is particularly marked with the Öraefajökull massif, projecting from the south of the icecap. Although this is comparatively narrow its great helmet (the highest point in Iceland) makes a clear divide in the weather under conditions of average weather. With severe weather, however, this does not apply, and the whole massif can be in cloud for continuous periods of days or even longer than one week. On the inland ice of Vatnajökull there are reports of periods up to two weeks when movement was impossible for man-sledge parties due to high wind and poor visibility. Wind-chill is an ever-present hazard, especially with the high winds and damp conditions, just around freezing point, often experienced, even in summer.

Areas on the opposite side of the icecap to the prevailing wind at any time, can experience föhn-type winds. These can be warm, intermittent, and even gusty. These probably have most effect on the margins, especially on melting conditions, but reports of their occurrence are always useful. Further information about spring weather is given below.

ACCESS TO THE ICE
By larger parties

Any party working on or around Vatnajökull will require to be provisioned and equipped for the period of stay, with adequate reserve, and this implies transport to a road-head by lorry, except in the case of the southern margin, where access to and from the main ring road is often possible from the ice-margin. Two-wheel drive vehicles **can** reach Jökulheimar, although it is always safer to use four-wheel drive because of the frequent occurrence of dust storms in the area and the shifting nature of the track. This is the most favoured approach to the western edge of Vatnajökull, since the main road has been extended to the power station at Sigalda, near where the track branches off to the Veiðivötn and Jökulheimar. The Sprengisandsvegur could also be used in the same way, although the most convenient roadhead is under Tungnafellsjökull, with a fairly long carry to the margin of Vatnajökull. At present it does not appear feasible to transport heavy loads on any of the tracks leading to the north and east of Vatnajökull, although sometimes there are snowmobiles based in the north-west corner of the icecap for tourist trips in the summer.

By smaller parties

As well as the roads mentioned above, parties in small four-wheel drive vehicles can get further afield, although such vehicles should always travel in pairs because of breakdown in a remote area, without radio, could have the most serious consequences. The Gæsavatnaleið, round the north-west corner of Vatnajökull, is not recommended as an approach route (see Chapter 16). However Kverkfjöll can be reached from the north, as can Eyjabakkajökull from Egilsstaðir, although this track is said to be a long and difficult one and two vehicles are essential. Another rather difficult track reaches the eastern tip of Vatnajökull from the valley of the river Jökulsá á Lóni, beginning near the Stafafell farm on the ring road. Local knowledge should be picked up when using this track, since farmers use much of it for reaching a remote valley, Viðidalur, not now inhabited but still farmed. On the south-west side of Vatnajökull a long and possibly difficult track in places reaches the Skaftáreldhraun and Laki craters, from which the 1783 lavas were erupted, and from here the ice of Síðujökull and Skaftárjökull can be reached. This track runs from near Kirkjubæjarklaustur, on the ring road but it may be closed to traffic in the near future in which case information will be available from the Nature Conservation Council (Appendix G).

Access along the South Coast

Although the ring road has opened up access, especially to the Öraefi district, it should be noted that the south coast **air** route now goes straight to Höfn in Hornafjörður, and does not call at Fagurhólsmýri in Öraefi, the district between the Skeiðará and Breiðá rivers. However, a bus service now runs daily between Reykjavík and Höfn and will pick up and deposit passengers at points along the ring road. Large parties should not use this bus on a casual basis, however, as it can sometimes be full, and a number of individuals with large rucsacs stands a risk of being left at the roadside. Times of buses can be found out from the Leiðabók (see Chapter 4).

There are public camp sites at Skaftafell and Höfn. Note, however, that the Skaftafell site is the **only** official camp site in the Skaftafell National Park and that camping is not allowed elsewhere in the Park. The public camp site is very well equipped with showers, washing facilities and a shop. Report to the camp site warden on arrival, small cost on a per tent basis.

For those wanting to take freight along the south coast as far as Höfn, two lorry firms ply this route from Vöruflutningamiðstöðin h.f. in Reykjavík. You may also freight goods in advance from the United Kingdom direct to Höfn (see Chapters 6 and 9).

GLACIAL RIVERS

These are the greatest obstacle in the way of access to the ice, and no plans should be made which involve crossing them in the summer as a matter of course on foot or in a vehicle. If it is necessary to cross one occasionally, say in an emergency, it must be regarded as a major undertaking because such rivers flow in braided courses are constantly changing, and move extremely fast near the ice, with a great volume of water. Ropes and/or poles are essential for foot crossing, which is best carried out about dawn when the river reaches its lowest level. Conversely, a crossing in late afternoon, when flow is greatest, must be avoided if at all possible (see Chapter 13).

Most of the major access routes towards the ice run between the major glacier rivers, thus avoiding a crossing, but if lateral movement round the icecap is necessary, a party on foot should seriously consider getting up on to the ice, especially the lobes, to traverse round the head of any rivers. For a small party with the necessary expertise this is probably the safest course.

Along the southern edge of Vatnajökull all the rivers are bridged where the ring road crosses them, though this is often at some considerable distance from the ice edge. Many of these rivers have occasional 'jökulhlaups' or great floods occurring without much warning, caused by sub-glacial lakes melted by geothermal heat reaching a critical level and melting through tunnels under the ice, or by breaking out of ice-dammed lakes. Rivers carrying volcanic jökulhaup water often smell strongly of sulphur or its compounds. The ring road may be breached under these circumstances, although it was built with jökulhlaups in mind., and can be repaired fairly quickly. The worst of the floods come from the Skeiðará river, which even in its normal state is a considerable river and was the last to be bridged in 1974.

On the west side of Vatnajökull the Skaftá is not bridged north of the coastal plain. The Tungnaá is a very large river and was a major obstacle to reaching the Icelandic Glaciological Society's huts and research area at Jökulheimar until it was bridged at Sigalda, south of Thórisvatn. It should be noted that the Tungnaá also flows between Jökulheimar and the ice edge there, and a traverse has to be made northward some 12 to 15 km to the neighbourhood of the Kerlingar nunataks until a route is found on foot on to the ice. The Kaldakvísl and several of its tributaries which look small on the map are, nevertheless, large rivers. All the rivers flowing from the northern edge of Vatnajökull are large, although it is possible to get from Tungnafellsjökull to

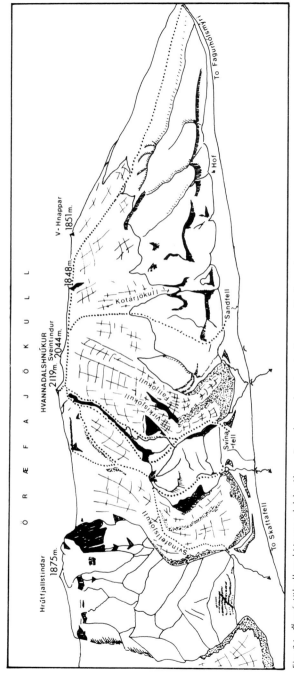

Fig. 34. Öræfajökull and Hvannadalshnúkur. Based on a drawing by Snævarr Guðmundsson.

Labels within the figure:

Ö R Æ F A J Ö K U L L

Hrútfjallstindar
1875 m.

HVANNADALSHNÚKUR
2119 m. Sveintindur
2044 m.

1848 m.

V - Hnappar
1851 m.

Kotárjökull

Hof

Sandfell

Falljökull

Virkisjökull

Svína-
-fell

Svínafellsjökull

To Skaftafell

To Fagurhólsmýri

Barðarbunga, on the north-west corner of Vatnajökull, without crossing a major river.

The safest rule about glacier rivers is to regard map evidence with suspicion. Some river channels shown on the maps do not now exist, but many small-looking streams are quite formidable. Large rivers, especially anything called 'Jökulsá' are always dangerous, but any smaller streams apparently rising from the ice should be closely examined.

GLACIER RECESSION

The state of the ice front has been changing over the last fifty years, generally in the direction of retreat. Old editions of maps will therefore not give a correct picture. Landmaelingar íslands, Icelandic Survey Department, does try to add glacier revisions as new map editions are published, but some map sheets of the more remote areas are not up-to-date. Many glaciers, however, are subject to cyclical rapid advance, or surge, followed by a slow retreat. Skaftárjökull, Tungnaárjökull and Eyjabakkajökull are three known to have a surging regime.

From Breiðamerkurjökull eastwards the fronts of all glaciers tend to be edged with glacier lakes, making access difficult. This is not shown on many maps, but anyone wishing to work along the south-east edge of Vatnajökull should seek up-to-date information about access routes.

ACCESS TO HVANNADALSHNÚKUR

The peak named Hvannadalshnúkur (Figure 34), Iceland's highest mountain (2119m) crowns the crater rim of the Öraefajokull, that southernmost extension of the Vatnajökull. It is an impressive peak for it rises from the sandur plain (100m) to the summit in a horizontal distance of only 10Km. It has been climbed on numerous occasions, especially between Easter and September, the optimum period being late June to mid-August. Climbing outside that period requires a settled weather outlook. Even in the height of summer the weather is unpredictable as it can vary so greatly between one side of the Öraefajökull and the other.

The most usual approaches are from Falljökull and Sandfell on the west side, although the mountain can be climbed from the farm at Kvísker by ascending Rotarfjall. Other 'obvious' lines of approach are generally inaccessible because the rocks are too steep and broken to be safe. Hvannadalshnúkur is well guarded by ice falls (over 1000m) and basalt cliffs.

Given good weather conditions the mountain can be climbed and base regained within 13 hours from Falljökull. The account that follows is adapted from excerpts from the report of the Royal Holloway College ascent from Sandfell in 1976.

"At the end of the first day Camp 1 was placed about 2000 ft. up at three in the afternoon, the winds and rain getting stronger as we climbed. The going was proving quite straightforward. The camp was reasonably sheltered and horizontal, yet strangely enough in spite of the vast amounts of rain the region had had over the past few weeks, many of the nearby streams had run dry and I was forced to walk a mile for water.

"During the night the wind increased and for the first time I was afraid that the tent might rip. By the time that we had prepared our rucksacks in the tent the familiar sound of torrential rain could be heard outside. At 1100 hours it was still raining hard yet the visibility was much better. Two hours later we roped up and strapped on our crampons. Having reached the ice border we started up the steep ice slope following a bearing to a point on the plateau. The visibility was rapidly detiorating and we were in whiteout. Suddenly in front of me loomed a huge black nunatak. The compass said that I should go to the right of it, yet something else, perhaps not an entirely wise judgement, told me to go to the left, which I did. All at once, whilst staring into the uninterrupted whiteness beyond, the fog cleared sufficiently for me to make out what had been to the right. I was looking into a cataclysmic ice-fall, huge in size, terrifying in nature, some 30 yds beyond. Had I in fact gone right, I would have led us down into it, probably not seeing the crevasses until too late. We decided it wisest to camp on the nunatak as best we could be clearing some bigger rocks to form a site which became Camp 2.

"That night was the most miserable night so far. The cold reached me from below until I put on my duvet for extra warmth and comfort. Getting out in the morning required vast amounts of willpower but the weather had cleared and we were away in record time. Travelling light, leaving the tent pinned down with boulders, we set out for the summit. After $2^1/_2$ exhausting hours without rest we had reached the plateau. We rested below the vertical rock band of the east face, the summit towering 1000 ft. vertically above us, and even as we relaxed, rockfalls poured off the face every five minutes or so.

"We decided to attempt the N.E. face by first crossing a large bergschrund consisting of a delicate snowbridge leading on to a 15 ft. section of vertical ice. Mike slipped here and fell six feet, spiking his leg with a crampon in the process. The snow that we had seen in photographs had peeled away revealing ice that was getting steeper and steeper. Clearly we were neither experienced enough equipped sufficiently to get over the next section and the afternoon sun had increased the chances of the whole lot suddenly avalanching. But before I had a chance to voice my disappointment our most vital items of ice-climbing gear slipped into a deep crevasse 25 ft. away. There was no option but to return.

"Very soon we found a way round and on to the west face and within an hour had gained the summit ridge. To the north the mountains of Esjufjöll were visible through thin cloud, which gave the impression that we were a great deal higher than 7000 ft.

"After 45 minutes we started down again. Suddenly my leg plummeted through the snow, leaving me lying on my right side. I could feel my leg dangling in a complete void. With the security of a tight belay I could roll safely out and view what was only a 12 ft. deep crevasse; nothing serious but a sobering reminder that even though we had reached the summit the dangers were still present. By 2115 we were back at Camp 2 after a perfect yet exhausting day."

CONDITIONS ON THE ICE
Normal summer conditions
After early June it is normally a short day's drive from Reykjavík to Jökulheimar, although the odd freak blizzard can cause hold-ups, and dust-storms and sand-drifts in the section between Sigalda and Jökulheimar will delay two-wheel drive vehicles. Glacier rivers will be high at this time of the year which may hinder access to the ice, while the lower reaches of the ice will be rapidly losing the winter snow cover. The snow line moves upwards progressively through the summer and there is usually a belt of exposed and rapidly-melting ice perhaps 2-4 Km broad round the periphery of the ice in some places during August. Crevasses are quite common on both lobes and outlet glaciers, but the scale of crevassing is, of course, much more extensive on the latter because of their rapid fall in altitude. On the exposed ice the crevasses may be large but are easily visible, on the snow they are more of a problem, but are usually only evident on the inland ice where it is moving over a submerged ridge, and their existance can often be estimated from an inspection of one of the smaller-scale maps showing the ridges round the ice margin and their probably trend under the ice.

The main feature of even the summer weather is its changeability. The odd fine day does occur, with clear skies and warm sunshine, but with a chilly breeze always tending to drift down from the centre of the ice. Cloud will appear quickly over the western horizon and thicken in a few hours to fine snow, strong winds and zero visibility, perhaps for a period of several days. Movement is usually impossible during these conditions, and small tents tend to be snowed over. Temperatures are sometimes variable, and during warmer periods melting snow and condensed moisture will run down and freeze on the skirts of the tents, which are then difficult to strike for this reason.

It is extremely difficult to plan movement to fit in with restricted time. Even allowing one day's travel in two is sometimes risky, and parties have been immobolised for more than a week. Always, therefore, give yourself plenty of time if you are travelling across the ice to some specific goal. There is a refuge hut above the Grímsvötn lakes in the middle of the ice, but this is the property of the Icelandic Glaciological Society and is used in their scientific investigations. Exploring parties should avoid using the hut on a casual basis, certainly for sleeping in, although it is always there in case of an emergency. Camping near the hut provides some central location on the ice, from which other objectives can be reached. It must be emphasised that careless use of the hut by one party can damage the prospects of use by many other people, since repairs and replacements in this remote location are exceptionally difficult. Always clear up if you go into the hut, and make sure the door is closed when you leave.

Most of the work on the ice by Icelanders is done in early summer or early autumn, not in late July or August, because then the surfaces are very bad for travel. Even on the snow there may be periods of many days when the snow is too soft for travel either on foot or with sledges, and the only answer is to travel as much as possible in the very early morning, though sometimes even then the snow is soft. The use of ski and lightweight sledges is one solution to this problem for parties with the required training.

Extreme Conditions

In April and May a party tried to cross Vatnajökull from Jökulheimar to Höfn. Unfortunately the weather conditions turned out to be exceptional even for that time of year.

The five-man team was equipped with a sledge, two Black's 'Mountain' tents, paraffin stoves, 'Borg' cold weather jackets and trousers and rubberfoam cell boots. They left Reykjavík on the 28th April, having been held up for six days with delays over freight. Guðmundur Jónasson had provided a lorry and two skidoos for the transport, which had only been estimated for one day. Two other skidoos also joined the party, but the journey, in fact took four days to Jökulheimar, although no extra charge was made. What follows is excerpted and edited from the party leader's report:

"We left the hut at Jökulheimar at 6.00 a.m. on a beautiful, clear, although cold and crisp morning, taking three hours to reach the limits of the Vatnajökull just south of the Kerlingar (Note: the Tungnaá river was frozen at this time of year). We climbed slowly up on to the slopes of the glacier and the higher we climbed the stronger became the wind causing heavy drifting of snow. Mid-afternoon brought about dark skies and heavy snowfall, but visibility was still fair. At 7.00 p.m. we had covered a good twenty miles up to the ice field but now the winds were fierce and the snowfall very heavy. Camp was made and a large snow wall was erected around the tents pitched close together. While the meal was being cooked the temperature dropped by 15° and the conditions became calm. We were able to get a good view of the regions to the west of the glacier for about half-an-hour, the last time we saw the mountains. The temperature began to drop again and snow to fall. By 9.00 a.m. white-out conditions prevailed and the winds were gusting to 35 m.p.h., hitting the tents like a sledge-hammer. The tents were soon snow-covered, being buried completely every two to three hours, with consequent breathing problems for the occupants, and these problems were even worse when one had to venture outside, roped to those in the tent because the visibility was nil and even the other tent six feet away was invisible. On stepping out from the comparatively warm tent, the warmth caused by the great effort in dressing and digging out from the tent, clothing froze instantly and the face was frosted. Though in retrospect amusing, the most uncomfortable part was that the need to pass water occurred every $2^1/_2$ to 3 hours, almost immediate and without warning. The problem was that it took so long to dress and to dig out, and the necessary clothing was so bulky, that it was a race against time, sometimes not won.

"As we found ourselves able to withstand these conditions for some time, and as the weather was slightly worsening, we set about a routine of sleeping when we could, eating, and digging out the tents from the snow every three hours, to coincide with the need to pass water. During the period of sleep after three days, the two-man tent began to collapse, seriously hampering movement and breathing for those inside. There was by now little to distinguish night and day and a short time later the tent collapsed with the ridge pole and 'A' frames bent and twisted, and even the seams opening, and large tears appeared in the canvas, so that evacuation was necessary.

"As the damaged tent required considerable repairs we had to decide whether to cram five men into a two-man tent or break the major rules of the mountain code and move camp. One member had become seriously ill due to dehydration and stomach trouble. It is always a major problem when travelling on snow that there is no running water, and this was made worse for us by the force and continuity of the wind which made it impossible to light a match outside the tent, while inside there was a high risk of fire due to the restricted space and shortage of air for combustion due to the snow cover. Liquid gas stoves would have been useless in these low temperatures below -15°F. We could thus not melt snow and had to eat it, causing excessive dehydration since it was impossible to obtain enough liquids for the body to function normally, and eating too much snow would cause dangerous falls in body temperature. Prolonged shortage of liquids began to cause serious liver complaints evident in tests of urine. We were also forced by the shortage of water to eat only the emergency rations, since the normal rations were dehydrated or highly concentrated and were either inedible due to dryness or would cause severe burning of the mouth and digestive tract due to the high concentration. The dangers of exposed flesh freezing increased as windchill equivalents of -63°F to -72°F occurred at night and because there was little moisture near the skin surface.

"Because of these problems and since we had lost a large amount of equipment, irretrievably buried deep in the snow, and because we had grave doubts about survival in another such storm so far on the glacier, all agreed that we should take the risk and break camp, and it then took several hours for the team to get ready to break camp without delay and serious discomfort. Dressing was difficult since everything was frozen, and while one man dressed, the others worked at softening boots, gaiters and outer clothing, even if it meant chewing them.

"When everyone was ready we quickly began to strike the tents, two men working on each, with the fifth loading the sledge. It was only possible to work for five minutes at a time with backs to the wind and drift, since facing it was like standing in a cold shower facing the water and ice forming over our mouths and nostrils in the freezing vapour was hindering breathing.

"With everything packed we roped on short lines to the sledge and set off into the wind on what we thought and hoped was the way to Jökulheimar, trying not to allow the wind to sway our line of downhill travel. As the slope became steeper the sledge began to over-run and pull us in the wrong direction. Finally, utterly exhausted, we arrived at a flat plain which we thought must be the frozen river Tungnaá which runs to the east of Jökulheimar and camped. With outside temperatures now colder than ever and the morale of the team dangerously low we attempted to get some sleep, taking it in turns to dig out the tent and check on the physical condition of the others. This was the first time that anybody had really felt the cold and it was difficult to stop shivering, to conserve energy. The following two days were difficult ones personally for the team members, but early one morning the wind stopped and I ventured out. Although I froze instantly I could see the sun trying to peer through the drift at a higher level and that we had been camped on the surface of a frozen lake. From the top of a hill some distance away I was able to catch a glimpse of the Jökulheimar huts some $5^1/_2$ km. away to the North-west.

"This news brought back life to the team and we quickly broke camp and headed towards the huts. The going became progressively more difficult as we had to cross difficult snowdrifts and the weather was deteriorating again. After five hours we were in a dense snow blizzard with the wind blowing from our left. Once again we took the risk and abandoned everything except the tent, sleeping bags and emergency rations, even leaving the sledge to make a final bid for the hut. Completely exhausted, we began to forget that we were a team and must rely on one another for survival, occasionally losing sight of the others in the blizzard. Suddenly we walked out of the blizzard as into a forest clearing and were standing only 20 feet from the hut.

"We must have slept for many hours before we even attempted to take off our protective clothing. As we began to function normally again we began to realise the extent of our 'injuries' and in the increasing warmth of the paraffin stoves began to peel off frozen clothing, tearing out skin hair and sores on face and hands. One member had slightly frostbitten fingers, but our main worry was the youngest member who had for some time been complaining about the lack of feeling both his feet, and removal of his boots showed that all ten toes were black and swollen. It was clear that if there was no improvement in three days the toes must be amputated."

Postscript

The party spent the next week at Jökulheimar, gradually collecting the sledge and equipment, recuperating, and doing what repairs were possible. On the eighth morning, which was bitterly cold but clear the party left the hut to try to reach Reykjavik across the centre of Iceland. The sledge and all inessential gear were left at the hut, and each member carried about 80-lbs of essentials.

Having expected to cross to the east side of the icecap, the party had only the 1:250,000 maps of this western area, and these show very little detail. The problems were compounded by the deep snow cover of the area which they had to cross. They headed round the northern end of Thórisvatn, having to cross a very rugged area with the deep rift of Heljargjá, which was reached at a very difficult place where one member, already injured, had a fall. It thus took three days to reach a small dam on the Thórisós river, flowing into the northern part of Thórisvatn, and on this dam was a small hut which just held the party. Examination of the youngest member's feet showed the toes to be in a critical state so the leader and one other set off for the power station site at Sigalda, which they were able to reach after numerous changes of route, and get assistance, which only became effective when a Bombardier snowmobile was called in with an expert driver who rescued the remainder of the party. A radio distress beacon had been left with this group, to be used if no rescuers appeared after three days, but fortunately it did not have to be used. If the two who set out for Siglda had not arrived, and the beacon had been used, the two would probably have not been found as their route had changed so much from that known to the other party.

COMMENT

This description gives some idea of extreme conditions to be experienced on Vatnajökull in what we consider to be spring. It is clear that only a party with equipment suited to travel in the Antarctic winter/spring period could have dealt with the conditions experienced. In particular, some kind of pyramid tent would have made life on the icecap more bearable, since its stability and height would allow better ventilation and more space for cooking inside. However, it is all too easy to make such suggestions with hindsight.

As a general rule we do not recommend the use of beacons without prior consultation with the Icelandid authorities and the NATO airbase at Keflavík. Given that you have a beacon you have to ask the question "Even if I did use it, who would be able to pick me up, and who would pay for the rescue?" It is unreasonable to expect people to turn out on to Vatnajökull to rescue you.

You need the permission of the Glaciological Society to use any of their huts but if you do use one in an emergency do treat it with respect, clean up afterwards and notify the Society of any deficiencies as a result of your visit.

WORK ON VATNAJÖKULL

The Icelanders are doing a great deal of scientific work in traverses across the ice with tracked vehicles, and it is recommended that young exploring parties can most usefully work round the margins of the ice. Survey of glacier positions, examination of river processes, geomorphological studies of ice-margin features, and meteorological observations are all useful topics for which there is a need. These are covered in Chapter 1.

The Gæsavatnaleið

1 : 750.000

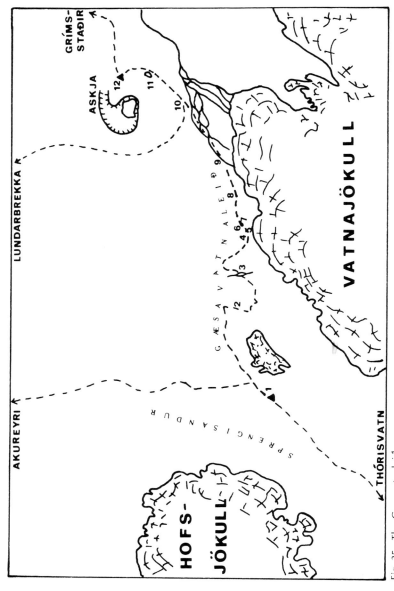

Fig. 35. The Gæsavatnaleið

16 THE GÆSAVATNALEIÐ

Patrick Molony

INTRODUCTION

Most of the main mountain routes have been previously described by Sigurjón Rist in the handbook "Iceland in a Nutshell" which is currently out of print. These include:

    Sprengisandsvegur
    Fjallabaksvegur Nyðri
    Kjalvegur
    Kaldidalsvegur
    Stórisandur and Arnarvatnsheiði

The route described here (Fig. 35), and in Desmond Bagley's novel "Running Blind", is one for which the Unit receives numerous requests for details. It crosses the north side of the Vatnajökull icecap from the hut at Tómasarhagi (Nýidalur/Jökuldalir) to the Dyngjufjöll mountains (Askja). It also illustrates the general problems of interior driving.

At the outset we must stress two things:

1. This is **not** a route to be taken lightly.

2. **Conservation of landscape must take priority over any other decisions. This is an environmentally sensitive area where the track should be adhered to strictly and all attempts made to cover up for man's intrusion.**

SOME PRACTICALITIES

The Gæsavötn route is a situation where man and machine are pitted against nature, and where nature throws almost everything into the attack. Tracks ahead may prove that other people have been before but this stubborn assumption, that one may follow where others have been, could prove fatal to an expedition if the weather turned nasty or there was any mechanical failure. Luck may well be on your side but it is not advisable to drive the route without serious planning beforehand. One **must** travel in convoy in case of breakdown and one ought to have an Icelandic two-way radio in one of the vehicles. Both of these conditions may prove difficult for the average expedition using only one vehicle brought from home and without any radio. You must find other parties crossing when you are and join up with them; they may of course be looking for other vehicles to accompany them anyway. You can do this beforehand — arranging to meet them, say, at the hut at Tómasahagi (1) on a particular day, or you can merely camp at the start of the crossing and wait for people to join you. As for the radio link it becomes less essential the more vehicles you have, but as a precaution in case of emergency it is worthwhile to have one if possible (see Chapter 11).

Naturally it goes without saying that only four-wheel drive vehicles can make this journey; and a long wheel-base Land Rover is not the best machine as it is less manoeuvrable than the short wheel-base and the length between wheels means that it can catch on many rock projections that the short wheel-base will ride over. Icelandic mountain buses can make the journey but they have a very high ground clearance, and are fitted with a long winch on the front. This attachment could also be recommended for an expedition vehicle as it comes in very handy for self-recovery.

This route is a good illustration of the Rover recommendation that a long wheel-base Land Rover should carry a maximum of three people! Equipment could be put onto a trailer but other groups found considerable difficulty with manoeuvring over rough terrain, crossing the swift rivers and the sometimes soft snow. In the latter case the trailer tended to drag the vehicle into the snow. In general, trailers are not recommended on the interior routes of Iceland.

THE ROUTE

The journey takes about fifteen hours from the hut at Tómasarhagi (1) to Askja which includes numerous halts for route finding and one or two major stoppages — $1^1/_2$ hours for a meal and $3/_4$ hour for repairs to vehicles. Much of the route is well marked track with poles or painted rocks to guide you, but at some points one must search out the way with great care and often plan forward for a considerable distance before you actually drive it. As the driver you will like to know exactly where you are heading and what you are being expected to do with the vehicle. Often a guide in front signalling you on is a great psychological help if nothing else.

The first part of the route from Tómasarhagi gives no indication of what lies beyond. The track veers to the right (east) from the main Sprengisandur route and rises gently through some grassy vegetation. In some places the main track is rather bad and people have made their own in the mud and vegetation on each side. After this first gentle ascent the land levels out and vegetation dwindles as the volcanic desert asserts itself. The track is relatively good at this point and one can speed along. But, beware! As the track gently undulates it also has the habit of having small kinks in it just out of sight in small dips, or the odd large boulder lying in the path. If you do not concentrate all the time you may drive off the track into the dust — or worse.

There are nine river crossings in this section of the track. It is most advisable to plan your journey so that these are encountered early in the morning, say 6-8 am for as they are all meltwater streams from the Vatnajökull or Tungnafellsjökull the water level rises considerably after the heat of the day and after rain. Each crossing presents its own problems and it is best to treat every river with great respect and to plan fully the route across before you attempt it. In some one can see the entry and exit points quite clearly, in others you may have to island-hop and do some manoeuvring in mid stream. Naturally, the rivers change their courses from day to day and year to year and it is pointless to explain exactly how each is crossed. One must work the crossing out when you have seen the lie of the land. We crossed always in second gear, low ratio moving gently but firmly without creating too much wake and keeping the revs up. If possible it is best to keep the car pointing up stream on some diagonal line so that water is not forced up the exhaust system. However, some prefer to travel downstream to reduce the wave into the electrics. Also, why fight the current if it can help you. It is also suggested that the fan belt be removed when crossing rivers of more than one foot in depth; this will prevent damage to electrics, and the embarrassment of a real stoppage in mid-river.

The track between each river remains relatively good and there is the long section between the fifth and sixth river when you cross a large, flat, desert area marked on the map as Langadrag (2). After the last river you come to Gæsavötn, a small oasis (3) in the desert. From here the track climbs and the nature of the scenery changes. The undulating desert gives way to rugged volcanic rock outcrops, and the track's surface varies from hard rock to thick sand in the hollows and on some slopes. In some places slopes can be very steep and route finding begins to become a priority. There are a few stakes marking somebody's efforts many years ago on the route, and there is also a series of yellow painted rocks that appear with some irregularity. But in many places one must send out scouts to check on which of the bewildering array of tyre marks is the best route for you to follow. One seems to climb for hours up over this mountain mass until the highest point is reached at Trölladynguháls,(4). Here they have either had a cairn-builders convention, or it is custom to construct your own mammoth cairn as you pass. It really is the end of the world here, and the whole place looks like a demolition site — great piles of volcanic boulders everywhere. Slow progress brings you to the edge of the Vatnajökull (5).

A sobering discovery is the sudden realisation that the rock over which you are driving is not as solid as you thought. The lava buckled and weaved as it cooled and pockets of gas were encased in the solidifying mass. Many of these domes have now collapsed but others you drive across oblivious of the fact that the rock may be only inches thick. Near the ice you actually drive over one dome which has fallen in for about a square foot in the middle.

Turning away left (north) and downhill from the icecap one soon reaches the first snow patch which you have to descend (6). Now the best time to cross the snow is late at night when it is coldest so that the snow surface is relatively hard. As it is you must disgorge your passengers and some of the equipment, check your entry point and plan a straight course to a suitable exit. Your team should position themselves on the snow near the entry point ready to push the vehicle if it shows signs of digging in. A series of vehicles cannot take the same tracks each time, so a plan of routes must be worked out first. If the first person takes a very diagonal course it may be difficult for the other vehicles to cross his route. The steep, muddy descent onto the snow must be taken quite fast to gain momentum which you hope

M.H.WEALE

will carry the vehicles across. Your passengers should try to keep up with the vehicle in case it slows down when their pushing should keep you going. If you do stop you must immediately attempt to dig the vehicle out by laying down mud and rocks in the tracks and in the front of the vehicle for it to get some grip when the passengers begin to push you on. One must check very carefully one's exit point for as the snow slopes downwards the lower edge is normally quite thin and weak with pools of water and run-off in evidence. These must be avoided. If you do bog down on this material it may be possible to tow the vehicle out (assuming one vehicle is safely on the far side already). A winch self-recovery is most useful here and if the wire is long enough it could be used to pull yourself across the whole snow patch.

There are two snow patches to cross and they are only passable in the downwards (easterly) direction (unless you have a long winch). So if you cannot cross the second you may be stuck. Check carefully therefore before you cross the first that you will make it. Before the snow you can always retrace your steps back through the nine rivers to Tómasarhagi. After the first snow crossing the only way that you can go is ON. In fact another party did not cross the second snowfield. Having been stuck for a few hours while they built a road across the first snowfield they did not relish another epic, for they arrived at the second patch by mid-afternoon. After a very careful recce they found it was possible to avoid the snow completely by travelling right around its north side and then joining up with the 'main route' on the other side. It was longish but safe — just difficult to drive and plan.

After the second snow crossing the track winds on generally losing height. Scouts are needed, as there are few poles and yellow painted rocks to help you to find the way. There are some very difficult rock platforms to ascend and descend — very rough and very steep. Also there are a lot of deep, dusty areas which you can become bogged down in. The track winds down over a series of rock platforms and then breaks out onto a less rugged area. Large boulders strew the area and progress can be very slow. A huge crater, Urðuháls (8), is passed on the left-hand side and it is well worth stopping to examine it. If one has crossed the snow patches at, say, 3 am, the crater is reached at about 6 am, and one can watch the light gently brighten over the whole landscape that includes the expanse of the Dyngjujökull. A very rough descent over boulders and one passes onto a rock terrace which slopes down to the glacial outwash plain (9) which stretches out towards Askja. This flat desert is the third area of the journey which requires great care. It can be impassable either because it is too wet and water-covered, or because it is too dry and one merely sinks into the sand. If you can cross, it is only 20 miles of flat wasteland which takes two hours. The first sign of 'civilisation' reappear as the track joins the route heading north to Lundarbrekka (10) — a small signpost leaning against a rock pointing in the three directions. From here on the track is much drier and subject to sandstorms and drifting. Dyngjuvatn (11), a small lake is passed on the left, and the track heads towards the base of Askja. It passes onto light-coloured pumice, which was ejected from the 1875 eruption of Viti, and winds up to the Dreki hut at the mouth of Drekagil (12). This triangular-shaped hut is a most welcome sight and is well used by people who come down from the north to visit Askja. The trek up to the crater is rewarded with a moonscape view and a bath in Viti, the hot water of the 1875 explosion crater.

The total mileage between Tómasarhagi and Askja, of course, depends on how long you spend on the route and whether you make any lengthy detours. It is about 80 miles (120 Km) — not far, you say — but the most taxing journey the author has ever had the pleasure (or misfortune) of making.

17 AFTER THE EXPEDITION

POST-EXPEDITION QUESTIONNAIRE

When you consider that the contents of this Handbook represent the accumulated experience of numerous individuals over the years you will appreciate that **your experience** will add to the stock of knowledge. The information contained within these covers must already be out of date, so please help us to update it. For this purpose a tear-out questionnaire is included at the back of the book.

Any information will be gratefully received and will be used both in the Iceland Unit Bulletin, ÍSLAND, and entered into the computer record of this book.

YOUR EXPEDITION REPORT

Do write one, however brief. You have no idea how useful reports can be. Over the years we have come to recognise what makes for a good report and feel that an expedition report should serve the following purposes, and in the order listed:

1. To indicate the work that you set out to do and to record your results for the benefit of future expeditions.

2. To record your experiences, difficulties etc. for the benefit of future expeditions.

3. To prove a lasting record for the expedition members.

4. To indicate your achievements to your sponsors, and to thank them.

In our experience too great an emphasis is placed on items 3 and 4 and too little on items 1 and 2. We hope that the following notes may be a helpful guide. Your outline plan for the report really needs to be thought about **before** departure and various sections allocated to different individuals.

Title
The expedition and its report should ideally have short, distinctive titles by which they are invariably known — this avoids confusion.

Date and Location
These should be accurately stated — and a map of the area(s) and route(s) **studied in detail** (not those just briefly visited) should be included, with an inset diagram to show the exact position in Iceland. Absence of a map can cause innumerable problems for a country where many names are repeated (eg. Snaefell).

Index
A list of contents is invaluable to future leaders. Quite apart from the usefulness of a list the exercise in titling and subtitling your report is worthwhile from the point of view of clarity and rapid reference.

Personnel

Expedition members should be listed, with a statement of their academic status, their qualifications and their field experience. A name and address for all correspondence relating to the expedition and its report for the next few years should be quoted.

Expedition Aims and Achievements

A reasonably detailed and honest statement should appear. In the case of more or less progress than was foreseen being made, a note should be made of the unforseen difficulties etc. for the benefit of those who may follow on after you.

Account of the Expedition

Be careful not to swamp the important facts (which should appear in other sections of the report) in a sea of descriptive material. The account of the expedition should be kept quite distinct from fieldwork reports and useful notes.

Account of Fieldwork

What was the original intention? Did you have to modify this in the field? If so, why? What area was chosen for study, and how or why? Outline the methods used, any difficulties or innovations. Outline sampling, observing and recording techniques. Present a summary of your results, and any detailed results you think to be important in themselves or as illustrating a worthwhile technique. Aim to include field observations first and foremost — it is usually wise to avoid any large-scale interpretation; better to allow readers with a wider knowledge of the area and subject to draw conclusions by providing them with a wealth of accurate and relevant details. Drawing conclusions is a useful exercise for the expedition — but for the purposes of the report, these should be relegated to an unpretentious paragraph near the end.

Practical Information

Do not attempt to write a guide to Iceland, or even to your corner of it. There is already plenty of literature available, and any expedition ought to have dug it out in advance. It would be useful to list books, information sources, expedition reports etc. which you found most useful for the benefit of future workers. In short, any facts which do not appear in this book would be very helpful to others!

We might emphasise the need for notes on the following:

(a) Obscure transport services (such as local ferries, bus routes etc)

(b) Food and service costs.

(c) Unforseen practical difficulties of which advance information would have been welcome.

(c) The state of lesser-known roads, mountain routes and passes.

(e) The state of settlement in your area — which farms are still occupied and which tracks still passable?

(f) The existence of refuge huts, footbridges, petrol stations etc.

(g) Any problems relating to water supply.

(h) Facilities for emergency evacuation from your area (telephone, doctor, airstrip, hospital etc.)

One expedition had a useful section in their report entitled 'Hints and Wrinkles'.

Stores and Equipment

Long lists of these **can** be superfluous but also very useful indeed. Be selective and comment only on those items which require comment in the light of your experiences in Iceland. Add notes on their packing, how suitable you found them, experiences with Icelandic customs procedures etc. If anything you took seemed unnecessary, or if you failed to take anything you wished that you had taken, mention this.

Suggestions for Further Work

There is a great deal to be said for successive expeditions working within the same general area, building up a body of results and ideas which may in time lead to even more useful results. If your own expedition followed others in the same or neighbouring areas, make some attempt to make the results comparable (eg. by adopting comparable techniques of recording etc.) If you feel able, suggest further specific areas and projects which might usefully be considered by future expeditions.

Bibliography

Omit the obvious, and well-known books on Iceland as a whole; otherwise, mention any useful references to previous expeditions, previous detailed results from the area, parallel problems in other areas, field techniques etc.

Finally

State where copies of the report are to be lodged for future reference by expedition leaders. The following ought to receive copies:

> The Royal Geographical Society
> The Scott Polar Research Institute
> The Iceland Unit (2 copies)
> The Iceland National Research Council (If research — 5 copies)

PS: Do spell Icelandic names correctly! Any fool can mispell but it is not very polite to the host country, especially if repeatedly incorrect. This applies particularly to personal names.

THE ANNUAL 'ÞING'

If you attended last year's annual Iceland Unit gathering (see Chapter 7) you will know how useful the presence of previous expeditions can be. Do come along next year and share your experiences. It is always on a Saturday and usually in early February.

PHOTOGRAPHIC PROCESSING

If, as has happened before, a strike has held up Kodak processing try one of the European laboratories. It costs no more than the postage. We have found the Belgian laboratory very good and very efficient:

> N.V. Kodak S.A.,
> Steenstraat 20,
> 1800,
> Koningslo-Vilvoorde,
> BELGIUM.

To do this write your name and address as usual on the yellow mailer. Place the film(s) and yellow mailer(s) inside a plain envelope/package, otherwise it will be delivered to Hemel Hempstead. Complete a Customs Declaration Certificate C1 for each package. For 'Description' write "Exposed unprocessed safety film — no commercial value". The certificates are supplied by the Post Office.

18 BIBLIOGRAPHY

Over the years much bibliographical material has been gathered together by Paul Sowan, one time secretary of the former Anglo-Icelandic Field Research Group. It is to his endeavours that we must owe the basis for the list that follows. The Iceland Unit holds a certain amount of material in its own library but has the references to several thousand books and articles on Iceland. Visitors may use the library, correspondents may request bibliographic material provided the request is specific enough for us to readily extract it. The material is indexed by subject heading but information referring to either author or area within Iceland may be extracted quite easily. The key to the Iceland Unit's Punch Card Filing System is shown in Figure 36.

The student of literature about Iceland may well raise an eyebrow at the type or even the age of some of the references but we have inevitably restricted the material to some of the more useful or more readily available texts or articles. We have tried to keep in mind the needs of expeditions and have also tried to take a middle path between the highly scientific and the touristic in the belief that the research student will either have access to a reference system or will contact the Iceland Unit anyhow. You can keep up to date with Icelandic bibliographic material by subscribing to ÍSLAND, the bulletin of the Iceland Unit. **You too can help us to keep the list up-to-date by notifying us of any new literature that you come across.**

The bibliography falls into 5 sections:
A. General books about Iceland
B. Expedition planning
C. The field sciences (as in Chapter 1)
D. Conservation
E. The regions of Iceland (as in Chapter 3)

A. **GENERAL BOOKS ABOUT ICELAND**
Land and People:
ASHWELL I. Y. (1973) Saga of the cod war. Geographical Magazine No. 45 vol. 8., p. 550, 553-4, 556.
BARÐARSON H. R. (1982): Iceland: a portrait of its land and people. Reykjavík: Hjálmur R. Barðarson.
BARÐARSON H. R. (1971): Ice and Fire: contrasts of Icelandic nature. Reykjavík: Hjálmur R. Barðarson.
GÍSLASON G. P. (1974) The problem of being an Icelander, past, present and future. Reykjavík: Almenna Bókafélagið.
HORTON J. C. (1983): Iceland. World Bibliographical Series Vol. 37. Oxford: Clio Press.
MAGNÚSSON M. and PÁLSSON H. (1960): Njáls Saga. London: Penguin.
MAGNÚSSON M. and PÁLSSON H. (1969): Laxdaela Saga. London: Penguin.
MAGNÚSSON S. A. (1984): Northern Sphinx: Iceland and the Icelanders from the settlement to the present. Reykjavík: Snaebjörn Jónsson.

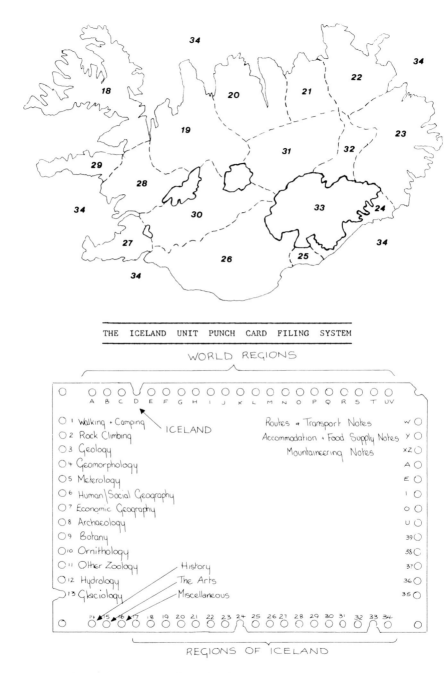

Fig. 36.   The Iceland Unit punch card index system.

O'DELL A. C. (1957): Iceland. In O'Dell A. C. "The Scandinavian World". London: Longmans.

SIMPSON, J. (1967) Everyday life in the viking age. London: Batsford.

SPARRING A. (1972) Iceland, Europe and Nato. World Today.

THORARINSSON S. (1956): The thousand year struggle against ice and fire. Reykjavík: Bókautgafa Menningarsjóds.

THORARINSSON S. (1960): Iceland. In Somme A. "The Geography of Norden". London: Heinemann.

THORLAKSSON, G.: A brief Geography of Iceland. Reykjavík: Icelandair.

TOMASSON R. F. (1980): Iceland: the first new society. Minneapolis: University of Minnesota Press.

VON LINDEN F-K and WEYER H. (1974): Iceland. Reykjavík: Almenna Bókafélagid.

Fiction:

BAGLEY, D. (1971): Running Blind. London: Collins.

FALKIRK R. (1971): The Chill Factor. London: Joseph.

FLEURON S. (1933): The wild horses of Iceland. London: Eyre and Spottiswoode.

HAYES J. (1981): Island on fire. London: Sphere.

LAXNES H. (1936): Salka Valka. London: Allen and Unwin.

LAXNES H. (1946): Independent people. London: Allen and Unwin.

LAXNES H. (1961): The atom station. London: Methuen.

SIMPSON J. (1972): Icelandic folktales and legends. London: Batsford.

VERNE Jules (1965): Journey to the centre of the earth. London: Arno Publications.

B. EXPEDITION PLANNING
General:
ILLINGWORTH R. Expedition medicine: a planning guide. Ambleside: Brathay Exploration Group.

LAND Tony (1978): The Expedition Handbook. London: Butterworths.

LANGMUIR E. (1969): Mountain Leadership. Edinburgh: Scottish Council of Physical Recreation.

RENNER G. (1984): Polar Expeditions. London: Royal Geographical Society.

Iceland:
HÁLFDÁNARSON Ö. (Ed) (1975): Iceland Road Guide. Reykjavík: Örn and Örlygur.

KIDSON P. (1974): Iceland in a Nutshell. Reykjavík: Iceland Travel Books. (out of print)

NAGEL (1982): Nagel's encyclopaedia guide: Iceland. Geneva: Nagel.

PHILPOTTS D. (1985): A visitor's guide to Iceland. Ashbourne: Moorland Publishing. (in preparation)

THORARINSSON S. (1980): Pú stódst á tindi (mountaineering in Iceland). Jökull, vol. 30, p. 81-87. (The Iceland Unit has a translation of this article).

WILLIAMS D. (1985): Iceland: the visitor's guide. London: Stacey International.

Language:
GLENDENING P. J. T. (1961): Teach Yourself Icelandic. London: English Universities Press.

JÓNSSON S. (1927): A Primer of modern Icelandic. Oxford, England: Oxford University Press.

PÁLSSON E. (1977): Icelandic in easy stages. vol 1 and 2. Reykjavík: Mímir.

TAYLOR A. R. (1972): English-Icelandic, Icelandic-English Pocket Dictionary. Reykjavík: Ordabókaútgáfan.

C. CONSERVATION:
BRADLEY C. (1983): Conservation in Iceland: a report on the initiation of practical conservation projects with volunteers. Conservation Volunteers/Icelandic Nature Conservation Council.

KJARAN B. (1969): The National Parks of Iceland. Reykjavík: Örn & Örlygur.

NÁTTÚRUVERNDARRÁD (1981): Náttúruminjaskrá: pridja útgáfa 1981. (Icelandic sites of conservation interest. Reykjavík: Náttúruverndarrád.

D. THE FIELD SCIENCES:
NB: See also the regional bibliographies in Section E.

Botany:
BELLAMY D. (1976): Some like it hot. In "Bellamy's Europe" London: British Broadcasting Corporation.

BJARNASON A. H. (1983): íslenzk flóra með litmyndum. Reykjavík: Iðunn.

CRAWFORD R. M. M. and BALFOUR J. (1983): Female predominant sex ratios and physiological differentiation in arctic willows. Journal of Ecology vol 71 no. 1 p. 149-60.

DAVIÐSSON I. (1967): Immigration and naturalisation of flowering plants in Iceland. Greinar, vol. 4, no. 3, 32p.

EINARSSON E.: The flora and vegetation of Iceland. Reykjavík: Icelandair.

FRIÐRIKSSON S. (1969): The effects of sea ice on flora, fauna and agriculture. Jökull Vol. 19, p. 146-57.

FRIÐRIKSSON S. (1975): Surtsey. Evolution of life of a volcanic island. London: Butterworths.

JOHNSON T. W. (1971): Aquatic fungi of Iceland: pythium. Mycologia Vol. 63, no. 3, p. 517-36.

LOVE A. (1970): íslenzk Ferðaflóra. Reykjavík: Almenna Bókafélagið.

STEINDÓRSSON S. (1962): On the age and immigration of the Icelandic flora. Reykjavík: Vísindafélag íslendinga, vol. XXXV.

STEINDÓRSSON S. (1964-68): Um hálendisgróður íslands (On the vegetation of the Central Highlands) Several articles in Flóra.

STEFÁNSSON S. (1948): Flóra íslands. Reykjavík: Bókaútgáfan Norðri.

WOLSELEY P. (1979): A field key to the flowering plants of Iceland. Sandwick, Shetland: Thule Press.

Freshwater Biology:
JÓNASSON P. M. (1979): Ecology of eutrophic, subarctic Lake Mývatn and the River Laxá. Oikos 32. 1-2, p. 1-308. **Also** as "Lake Mývatn". Copenhagen: The Icelandic Literature Society in Copenhagen.

Entomology:
BENGTSON S-A (1983): Geography of leg colour dimorphism in the carabid beetle (Nebria gyllenhali) in Iceland and the Faeroe Islands. Entomologica Scandinavica 14. p. 57-66.

PRYS-JONES O. E., ÓLAFSSON, E., and KRISTJÁNSSON K. (1981): The Icelandic bumble bee fauna (Bombus Latr. Apidae) and its distributional ecology. Journal of Agricultural Research 20 (3) p. 189-97.

ROYAL ENTOMOLOGICAL SOCIETY: Handbooks for the identification of British Insects: coleoptera, diptera and hymenoptera.

Geology:
AUBOUIN J. (Ed.) (1980): Geology of the European Countries. Volume 2. London: Graham and Trotman.

EINARSSON P. and BJÖRNSSON S. (1979): Earthquakes in Iceland. Jökull 29, 37-43.

FRIÐLEIFSSON I. B. (1979): Geothermal Activity in Iceland. Jökull 29, 47-56.

FRIÐLEIFSSON I. B. et al (1982): Iceland research drilling project. Jour. Geophys. Res., vol. 87, no. B8, p. 6359-6667. (28 papers).

GRUM R. and ESCRITT E. A. (1985): Iceland. A field Geology. London: Iceland Information Centre. (in preparation).

JACOBY W. R. et al (1980): Iceland: evolution, active tectonics and structure. Journal of Geophysics, vol. 37, no. 1-3, p. 1-220 (26 articles).

PREUSSER H. (1976): The Landscapes of Iceland: Types and Regions. The Hague: Dr. W. Junk.

SAEMUNDSSON K. (1979): Outline of the Geology of Iceland. Jökull, vol. 29, p. 7-28.

THORARINSSON, S. (1959): On the Geology and Geophysics of Iceland. Geografiska Annaler Vol. 41, No. 2-3, p. 135-69.

THORARINSSON S.: On the geology of Iceland. Reykjavík: Icelandair.

THORARINSSON S. (1967): Some problems of volcanism in Iceland. Geol. Rundschau. vol. 57 p. 1-20.

THORARINSSON S. and SAEMUNDSSON K. (1979): Volcanic activity in historical time. Jökull 29, 29-32.

THORARINSSON S. (1979): Tephrachronology and its application in Iceland. Jökull 29, 33-36.

WARD P. L. (1971): New interpretation of the geology of Iceland. Bull. Geological Society of America. p. 2991-3012.

WILLIAMS S. et al. (1983): Geomorphic classification of Icelandic volcanoes. Jökull, vol. 33, p. 19-24.

Geomorphology:

HOPPE G. (1968): Grímsey and the maximum extent of the last glaciation in Iceland. Geografiska Annaler Vol. 50A, p. 16-24.

HOPPE G. (1983): The extent of the last inland icesheet of Iceland. Jökull vol. 31, p. 3-11.

PREUSSER H. (1976): Viz supra.

PRICE R. J. (1973): Glacial and fluvioglacial landforms. Edinburgh: Oliver and Boyd.

SUGDEN D. E. and JOHN B. S. (1976): Glaciers and landscape — a geomorphological approach. London: Edward Arnold.

TÓMASSON H. et al (1981): Comparison of sediment load transport in the Skeidara jokulhlaups in 1972 and 1976. Jökull Vol. 30, p. 21-33.

WHALLEY W. B. et al. (1983): The magnitude and frequency of large rockslides in Iceland in the postglacial. Geografiska Annaler, vol. 65 A, no. 1-2, p. 99-110.

Glaciology:

BJÖRNSSON H. (1979): Glaciers in Iceland. Jökull vol. 29, p. 74-80.

CROOT D. G. and ESCRITT E. A. (1976): Scourge of Surging Glaciers. Geographical Magazine vol. 48, no. 6, p. 328-34.

ESCRITT E. A. (1974): North Iceland Glacier Inventory: manual for field survey parties. London: Young Explorers' Trust.

RURIKSSON B. (1983): The power of ice. Geographical Magazine Vol. 55, no. 8, p. 412-7.

Human Geography and Population:

ASHWELL I. Y. (1963): Recent changes in the pattern of farming in Iceland. Canadian Geographer, vol. 7, no. 4, p. 174-80.

JACKSON E. L. (1982): The Laki eruption of 1783: impacts on population and settlement in Iceland. Geography, vol. 67, no. 1, p. 42-50.

STONE K. H. (1971): Isolations and retreat of settlement in Iceland. Scottish Geographical Magazine Vol. 87, no. 1, p. 3-13.

SVEINBJARNARDÓTTIR G. (1982): Farm abandonment in Eyjafjallasveit, South Iceland. Nottingham: Working Paper Series No: 14. Nottingham University Department of Geography.

THORARINSSON S. (1961): Population changes in Iceland. Geographical Review vol. 51, no. 4, p. 519-33.

WHEELER P. T. et al. (1984): Vestfirðir Studies: Farming, fishing and settlement in north-western Iceland, 1979. Regional Studies No:23. Nottingham University Department of Geography. Nottingham: Geographical Field Studies Group.

Hydrology:

GUÐMUNDSSON G. and SIGBJARNARSSON G. (1972): Analysis of glacier runoff and meteorological observations. Journal of Glaciology, V.11, p. 303-318.

KJARTANSSON G. (1967): The Steinshóltshlaup, central south Iceland on January 15th, 1967. Jökull Vol. 3, p. 249-62.

ÖSTREM G. (1964): A method for measuring water discharge in turbulent streams. Geographical Bulletin No. 21 p. 21-43.

RIST S. (1967): Jökulhlaups from the ice cover of Mýrdalsjökull on June 25th, 1955, and January 20th, 1956. Jökull Vol. 3, p. 243-48.

RIST S. (1983): Floods and flood danger in Iceland. Jökull 33 p. 119-132.

Meteorology:

ASHWELL I. Y. (1958): Meteorological factors in the central desert of Iceland. Meteorological Magazine Vol. 87, no. 1038, p. 353-64.

ASHWELL I. Y. (1959): A rapid variation of air and crustal temperatures on Langjökull. Geografiska Annaler Vol. 41, no. 1, p. 67-73.
ASHWELL I. Y. (1966): Glacial control of wind and soil erosion in Iceland. Annals of the Association of American Geographers, vol. 56, no. 3, p. 529-40.
ASHWELL I. Y. (1980): The influence of Vatnajökull, Iceland, on regional air circulation and soil erosion. Discussion Papers in Geography no. 11. Salford, England: University of Salford, Dept. of Geography.
BERGTHÓRSSON P.: The Weather in Iceland. Reykjavík: Icelandair.
ESCRITT E. A. and GEORGE J. (1984): Meteorological projects in the glacier environment, in Renner G. "Polar Expeditions" p. 160-65. London: Royal Geographical Society.
EYTHÓRSSON J. and SIGTRYGGSON H. (1971): The climate and weather of Iceland. Zoology of Iceland, vol 1., pt. 3. Copenhagen: Reykjavík: Munksgaard.
GUÐMUNDSSON G. and SIGBJARNARSSON G. (1972): Analysis of glacier runoff and meteorological observations. Journal of Glaciology, vol. 63, p. 303-18.
LISTER H. (1959): Micro-meteorology over dirt coned ice. Jökull Vol. 2, p. 1-5.
SCHELL I. I. (1961): The ice off Iceland and the climates during the last 1200 years. Geografiska Annaler, vol. 43, no. 3-4, p. 354-62.
SíMONARSON L. (1979): On climatic changes in Iceland. Jökull 29, p. 44-46.
THORARINSSON S. (1956): The thousand years struggle against ice and fire. Reykjavík: Bókaútgáfa Menningarsjóds.

Ornithology:
BENGTSON S-A (1970): Densities of passerine bird communities in Iceland. Bird Study, vol. 17, no. 3, p. 260-68.
BENGTSON S-A and OWEN D. F. (1972): Polymorphism in the arctic skua Stercorarius parasiticus in Iceland. Ibis, vol. 115, no. 1, p. 87-92.
BRUUN B. (1970): The Hamlyn Guide to the birds of Britain and Europe. London: Hamlyn.
BULSTRODE C. J. K. et al. (1973): Breeding of whooper swans in Iceland. Bird Study, vol. 20, no. 1, p. 37-40.
GARÐARSSON A. (1970): Selection of food by Icelandic ptarmigan. In Watson A. "Animal populations in relation to their food resources." Oxford, England: Blackwell.
GRANT P. R. (1971): Interactive behaviour of puffins and skuas. Behaviour. Vol. 40, no. 3-4, p. 263-81.
GRANT P. R. and NETTLESHIP A. (1971): Nesting habitat selection by puffins in Iceland. Ornis Scandinavica, vol. 2, no. 2, p. 81-7.
HEINZEL H. et al. (1972): The Birds of Britain and Europe. London: Collins.
PETERSEN Æ.: Bird Life in Iceland. Reykjavík: Icelandair.
PETERSEN Æ. (1980): Population study of black guillemots (Cepphus grylle) in Iceland. Nord Ecol Newsletter 12 p. 16-17.
SCOTT P. and FISHER J. (1953): A thousand geese. London: Collins.
YEATES G. K. (1951): Land of the Loon. Country Life Ltd.

Pedology:
ASHWELL I. Y. (1966): Glacial control of wind and soil erosion in Iceland. Annals of the Association of American Geographers, vol. 56 (3) p. 529-40.
JÓHANNESSON B. (1960): The soils of Iceland. Reykjavík: University Research Institute.

Spelaeology:
MILLS M. T. (1970): A bibliographic history of Icelandic lava cave exploration. Trans. Cave Research Group of Great Britain, vol. 13 (4), p. 229-34.
WOOD C. (1971): The nature and origin of Raufarhólshellir. Trans. Cave Research Group of Great Britain, vol. 13 (4), p. 245-56.

Zoology:
VARIOUS (1937—): The zoology of Iceland. Copenhagen: Munksgard.

E. REGIONS OF ICELAND

I.1. South-west Iceland:

ASHWELL I. Y. (1976): Morphology of upper Lundarreykjadalur, western Iceland. Jökull, vol. 26, p. 1-7.

ASHWELL I. Y. (1975): Glacial and late glacial processes in western Iceland. Geografiska Annaler vol. 57 A, no. 3-4, p. 225-245.

EINARSSON T. (1965): On the geology of Stapafell-Sulur and the surrounding area. Greinar, vol. 4, no. 1, p. 49-76.

FRIÐRIKSSON S. (1975): Vegetation of the southern coast of Iceland. In "Surtsey- evolution of life on volcanic island". London: Butterworths.

JONES J. G. (1968): Intraglacial volcanoes of the Laugarvatn region, south-west Iceland. Quart. Jour. Geol. Soc. London, vol. 124, no. 3, p. 197-211.

SAEMUNDSSON K. (1970): Interglacial lava flows in the lowlands of southern Iceland and the problem of two-tiered columnar jointing. Jökull 20 p. 62-77.

TÓMASSON H. et al (1974): Þórlakshöfn: geological report. Reykjavík: Orkustofnun.

WOOD C. (1975): A preliminary investigation of lava caves of the Gullborgahraun, West Iceland. Journal Shepton Mallet Caving Club vol. 5., no. 9 p. 25-34.

II.1. Austur-Skaftafellssýsla:

COLLIER R. V. and STOTT M. (1976): Review of ornithological studies in south-east Iceland, 1973-75. Ambleside, England: Brathay Exploration Group.

COLLIER R. V. (1980): The fauna of the Skaftafell National Park, south-east Iceland. Field Studies Report no. 34. Ambleside, England: Brathay Exploration Group.

KING C. A. M. (1966): The coast of south-east Iceland near Ingólfshöfði. Geographical Journal, vol. 122, No. 2, p. 241-46.

PRICE R. J. (1983): Changes of the proglacial area of Breiðamerkurjökull, south-eastern Iceland. Jökull, vol. 32, p. 29-35 (see also numerous references in PRICE (1969) "Glacial and fluvioglacial landsforms" Edinburgh: Oliver & Boyd.

II.2. Vesturskaftafellssýsla:

CARSWELL D. A. (1983): The volcanic rocks of the Sólheimajökull area, southern Iceland. Jökull, vol. 33, p. 61-71.

JACKSON E. L. and RINNE L. (1973): Changes in the pattern of farms in Vestur-Skaftafellssýsla. Report of the Toronto University Geographical Society Expedition.

SVEINBJARNARDÓTTIR G. (1982): Farm abandonment in Eyjafjallasveit, southern Iceland. Working Paper Series No. 14. Birmingham, England: University of Birmingham, Dept. of Geography.

TÓMASSON H. et al. (1981): Comparison of sediment load transport in the Skeiðará jökulhlaups in 1972 and 1976. Jökull, vol. 30, p. 21-33.

III.1. Vestfirdir:

GLUE D. E. (1970): The bird communities of two contrasting valleys in north-west Iceland. Bird Study, vol. 17, No. 3, p. 247-59.

HANSOM G. (1983): Variation in meltwater characteristics at Kaldalónsjökull, Iceland. Jökull, vol. 31, p. 95-99.

JOHN B. S. and SUGDEN D. E. (1962): The morphology of Kaldalón: a recently deglaciated valley in Iceland. Geografiska Annaler, vol. 64., no. 3-4, p. 347-65.

JOHN B. S. (1978): Fish for survival in Vestfirðir. Geographical Magazine, vol. 51, no. 1, p. 63-66.

SMÁRASON O. B. (1980): The geology of the Arnes volcano — a Tertiary volcanic centre, N.W. Iceland. Journal Geological Society of London, vol. 137, no. 1, p. 111.

III.2. Northern Highlands:

BJARNASON A. (1980): The history of woodland in Fnjóskadalur. Acta Phytogeog. Suec. vol. 68 p. 31-42.

BJÖRNSSON H. (1971): Baegisarjökull, N. Iceland: results of glaciological investigations 1967-68. Part I. Jökull, vol. 21, p. 1-23. (Pt. II in Jökull vol. 22).

CASELDINE C. J. (1983): Resurvey of the margins of Gljúfurárjökull and the chronology of recent deglaciation. Jökull, vol. 33, p. 111-118.

EIRKISSON J. (1980): Tjörnes, North Iceland: a bibliographical review of the geological research history. Jökull, vol. 30, p. 1-20.

EIRIKSSON J. (1981): Lithostratigraphy of the upper Tjórnes sequence, N. Iceland: the Breiðavík group. Reykjavík: Náttúrufraeðistofnun íslands.

ESCRITT E. A. (1974): North Iceland Glacier Inventory: manual for field survey parties. London: Young Explorers's Trust.

HALLGRÍMSSON H. and KRISTINSSON K. (1965): Um haeðarmörk plantna á Eyjafjarðarsvaeðinu (Altitudinal distribution of plants). Acta Botanica Islandica, vol. 3, p. 9-74.

VÍKINGSSON S. (1980): The deglaciation of the southern part of the Skagafjörður district, northern Iceland. Jökull, vol. 28, p. 1-17.

III.3. **Eastern Highlands:**

BLAKE D. H. (1970): Geology of the Álftafjörður volcano: a tertiary volcanic centre. Science in Iceland, vol. 2, p. 43-63.

GIBSON I. L. et al. (1966): The Geology of the Fáskruðsfjörður area. Greinar, vol. 4, no. 2, p. 53-122.

ROOBOL M. J. (1972) Size-graded, igenous layering in an Icelandic intrusion. Geological Magazine Vol. 109, no. 5, p. 393-404.

SIGBJARNARSON G. (1983): The Quaternary alpine glaciation and marine erosion in Iceland. Jökull, vol. 33, p. 87-98.

WALKER, G. P. L. (1962): Tertiary welded tuffs in Eastern Iceland. Quart. Jour. Geol. Soc. London, vol. 118, p. 275-93.

WALKER G. P. L. (1983): Topographic evolution of eastern Iceland. Jökull, vol. 33, p. 13-20.

IV.1. **Central plateau:**

KALDAL I. (1980): The deglaciation of the area north and north-east of Hofsjökull, central Iceland. Jökull, vol. 28, p. 18-31.

PRIESNITZ K. and SCHUNKE E. (1978): An approach to the ecology of permafrost in central Iceland. Proceedings of the 3rd International Conference on Permafrost. Vol 1 473-79.

IV. 2. **West central plateau:**

ASHWELL I. Y. (1977): Arnarvatnsheiði and its regional geomorphology. Jökull, vol. 25, p. 39-45.

IV.3. **Central Highlands:**

ASHWELL I. Y. (1972): Dust storms in an ice desert. Geographical Magazine, vol. 44, no. 5, p. 322-27.

EINARSSON T. (1967): The Great Geysir and the hot-spring area of Haukadalur, Iceland. Reykjavík: Geysir Committee.

KRISTINSSON H. (1974): The Vegetation of Thjórsarver, central Iceland.

SCOTT P. (1953): A thousand geese. London: Collins.

IV.4. **North-east Iceland:**

GRIFFITHS M. E. et al (1973): Selection for food concentration in Víkingavatn by diving duck. Newcastle, England: University of Newcastle Expedition Report. (9 articles)

MORRISON A. (1938): Notes on the birds of N.E. Iceland. Ibis, January, p. 129-36.

V.1. **Snaefellsnes:**

INGÓLFSSON A. (1969): Behaviour of gulls robbing eiders. Bird Study, vol. 16, no. 1, p. 45-52.

RUTTEN M. G. and WENSINK H. (1959) Geology of the Hvalfjörður-Skorradalur area. Geologie en Mijubouw. Vol. 21 p. 172-80.

SIGURDSSON H. (1966): Geology of the Setback area. Greinar, vol. 4, no. 2, p. 1-52.

STEINDÓRSSON S. (1968) Flóra Snaefellsnes. Flóra Vol. 6. p. 41-44.

UPTON B. G. J. and WRIGHT J. B. (1961) Intrusions of gabbro and granophyre in Snaefellsnes, W. Iceland. Geological Magazine Vol. 98, p. 488-92.

VI.1. **South-west young volcanics:**

ASHWELL I. Y. and HANNEL F. G. (1959) The recession of an Icelandic glacier. Geographical Journal Vol. 125, no. 1, p. 84-8.

FRIDLEIFSSON I. B. (1973): Quaternary volcanics in south-west Iceland. Journal of Geology vol. 129 no. 3 p. 393-420.

PIPER J. D. A. (1973) Volcanic history of the north Langjökull area, central Iceland. Canadian Journal of Earth Sciences Vol. 10, no. 2, p. 164-179.

SIGBJARNARSSON G. (1967) The changing levels of Hagavatn and glacial recession in this century. Jökull Vol. III, no. 17, p. 263-79.

THORARINSSON S. (1966) The age of the maximum post-glacial advance of Hagafellsjökull eystri. A tephrachronological study. Jökull Vol. 3, p. 207-10.

VI.2. South central young volcanics:

EINARSSON T. et al (1949-74): The Eruption of Hekla, 1947-1948. Reykjavík: Vísindafélag Íslendinga. 5 vols.

THORARINSSON S. (1970): Hekla — a Notorious Volcano. Reykjavik: Almenna Bókafélagid.

THORARINSSON S. (1970): The Lakagígar eruption of 1783. Bulletin Volcanologique, vol. 33, no. 3, p. 910-29.

THORARINSSON S. and SIGVALDASON G. E. (1973): Hekla eruption 1970. Bulletin Volcanologique. vol. 36, no. 2, p. 269-288.

VI.3. Mývatn-Gjastykki:

BENGTSSON S-A (1966): Field studies on the harlequin duck in Iceland. Slimbridge, England: Wildfowl Trust Annual Report no. 17.

BENGTSON S-A. (1971): Food and feeding of diving ducks breeding at Lake Mývatn, Iceland. Acta Ornithol. Fennica.

BENGTSON S-A. (1971): Habitat selection of duck broods in Lake Mývatn area, N.E. Iceland. Ornis Scandinavica 2 17-26.

BENGTSON S-A. and ULFSTRAND S. (1971): Food resources and breeding frequency of the harlequin duck (histrionicus histrionicus) in Iceland. Oikos 22. 235-239.

BENGTSON S-A. (1972) Reproduction and fluctuation in the size of duck populations at Lake Mývatn, Iceland. Oikos 23 p. 35-58.

BJÖRNSSON A. et al. (1977): Current rifting episode in north Iceland. Nature, vol. 266, p. 318-23.

EINARSSON T. (1965): The ring-mountains Hverfjall, Ludent, and Hrossaborg in Northern Iceland. Greinar vol. 4, no. 1, p. 1-28.

ESCRITT E. A. (1982): Krafla's wintry awakening. Geographical Magazine vol. 54, no. 1, p. 2-3. (fourth in a series: vol. 48, no. 7, p. 392-93, vol. 52, no. 8, p. 521-22, vol. 53, no. 1, p. 1-12).

GARDARSSON A. (1980); Long-term studies of duck populations at Mývatn. Nord Ecol. Newsletter 12. 4-6.

GISLASON G. M. (1980): Ecological studies on the blackfly (Simulium vittatum) in the River Laxá, N.E. Iceland. Nord Ecol. newsletter 12. p. 11-12.

JÓNASSON P. M. (Ed) (1979): Ecology of eutrophic, subarctic Lake Mývatn and the river Laxá. Copenhagen: Íslenzk Fraedafélag.

KRISTJÁNSSON J. (1980): Population dynamics of the char stock in Lake Mývatn. Nord Ecol. Newsletter 12. p. 6-8.

SIGURDSSON H. and SPARKS R. S. J. (1978): Rifting episode in N. Iceland in 1874-75 and the eruptions of Askja and Sveinagjá. Bull. Volcanologique vol. 41, no. 3, p. 1-19.

SNORRASSON S. (1980): The ecology of Lymnaea peregra (Gastropoda) in Lake Thingvallavatn and its status in the lake food web. Nord Ecol. Newsletter 12 8-9.

VI.4. Odadahraun:

BEMMELEN R. W. and VAN RUTTEN M. G. (1955): Table Mountains of northern Iceland. Leiden: Brill.

CLARKE G. (1970): The formation and landscapes of deserts in Iceland. Journal of Durham University Geographical Society, Vol. 12, p. 52-64.

THORARINSSON S. (1963): Askja on Fire. Reykjavik: Almenna Bókafélagid.

VI.5. Palagonite Ridge Highlands:

VI.6. **Jökulsá á Fjöllum:**

GUNNLAUGSSON T. (1975): Jökulsárgljúfur: íslenzkur undraheimur. (Jökulsá Canyon: an Icelandic wonderland) Akureyri: Bókaforlag Odds Björnssonar.

VANDER MOLEN P. (1984): Running the wild Jökulsá á Fjöllum. National Geographic Magazine, vol. 166, No. 3, p. 306-21.

VANDER-MOLEN P. (1985): Iceland Breakthrough. Sparkford, England: The Oxford Illustrated Press.

VII. **Glaciers:**

AHLMANN H. W. (1938): Land of Ice and Fire. London: Routledge & Kegan Paul.

BJÖRNSSON H. (1974): Explanation of jökulhlaups from Grímsvötn, Vatnajökull, Iceland. Jökull, vol. 24, p. 1-26.

BOULTON G. S. and VIVIAN R. (1973): Underneath the glaciers. Geographical Magazine, January, p. 311-16.

DOWDESWELL J. A. (1982): Supraglacial re-sedimentation from melt-water streams on to snow overlying glacier ice, Sylgjujökull, west Vatnajökull, Iceland. Journal of Glaciology, vol. 28, no. 99, p. 365-75.

ESCRITT, E. A. (1972): The map of Falljökull. Jökull, vol. 22, p. 62-4.

EYLES, N. (1980): Rock glaciers in Esjufjöll nunatak area, south-east Iceland. Jökull, vol. 28, p. 53-56.

FISHWICK A. B. (1974): Kálfafellsdalur, south-east Iceland: a study of landform and depostional assemblages associated with the wastage of a valley glacier. Ambleside: Brathay Exploration Group.

GALON R. (1973): Scientific Results of the Polish geographical expedition to Iceland (Vatnajökull, 1968). Geographica Polonica, vol. 26, 312p.

MILLER K. (1979): Under ice volcanoes. Geographical Journal, vol. 145, no. 1, p. 36-55.

THORARINSSON S. (1958): The Öraefajökull eruption of 1362. Acta Naturalia Islandica, vol. 2, no. 2.

THORARINSSON S. (1956): The Kingdom of Vatnajökull, in "The thousand years struggle against ice and fire." Reykjavík: Bókaútgafa Menningarsjóðs.

VIII. **Islands:**

BJÖRNSSON S. (1968): Iceland and Mid-Ocean Ridges. Reykjavík: Vísindafélag Íslendinga.

CLAPPERTON C. M. (1973): Eruption on Helgafell. Geographical Magazine, vol. 45, no. 7-9 and vol. 46, no. 2 (Four articles).

GROVE N. (1973): Volcano overwhelms an Icelandic village. National Geographic Magazine, vol. 144, no. 1, p. 40-67.

FRIDRIKSSON S. (1975) Vegetation of the outer Westman Islands. In "Surtsey — evolution of life on a volcanic island". London: Butterworths.

GUNNARSSON A. (1973): Volcano: ordeal by fire in Iceland's Westmann Islands. Reykjavík: Iceland Review.

HOLMES P. F. and KEITH D. B. (1936): Observations on the birds of Grímsey and North Iceland. Ibis, April, p. 322-30.

JACK R. (1957): Arctic Living: the story of Grímsey. London: Hodder.

THORARINSSON S. (1964): Surtsey, the New Island in the North Atlantic. Reykjavík: Almenna Bókafélagið.

THORARINSSON S. (1965): Surtsey: island born of fire. National Geographic Magazine, vol. 127, no. 5, p. 713-726.

APPENDICES

APPENDIX A PROTECTED PLANT SPECIES
The following list of vascular plants are totally protected by law in Iceland:
1. Botrychium simplex E. Hitchc.
2. Asplenium septentrionale (L.) Hoffm.
3. Asplenium trichomanes L.
4. Asplenium viride Hudson
5. Blechnum spicant (L.) Roth f. fallax Lge.
6. Cryptogramma crispa (L.) R. Br.
7. Lycopodium clavatum L.
8. Sieglingia decumbens (L.) Bernh.
9. Carex heleonastes L.
10. Carex flava L.
11. Allium oleraceum L.
12. Paris quadrifolia L.
13. Listera ovata (L.) R. Br.
14. Stellaria calycantha (Led.) Bong.
15. Spergula marina (J. & C. Presl.) D. Dietr.
16. Papaver radicatum Rottb. spp. Stefanssonii A. Love
17. Crassula aquatica (L.) Schonl.
18. Galium palustre
19. Saxifraga foliolosa R. Br.
20. Rosa pimpinellifolia L.
21. Rosa vosagiaca
22. Oxalis acetosella L.
23. Viola riviniana Rchb.
24. Primula egaliksensis Wormskj.
25. Ajuga pyramidalis L.
26. Hymenophyllum wilsonii
27. Juncus gerardi
28. Polygonum amphibium
29. Potentilla erecta
30. Callitriche brutia
31. Euphrasia calida

APPENDIX B
LIST OF PROTECTED NATURAL AREAS IN ICELAND

By Special Law	Character	Hectares
1. Mývatn-Laxá	geological, biological	440,000
National Parks		
2. Thingvellir	old parliament site, geology	4,200
3. Skaftafell	glaciological, biological	50,000
4. Jökulsárgljúfur	geological, biological	15,100
Reserves (Landscape)		
5. Hvannalindir	highland oasis	4,300
6. Herdubreidarfridland	highland oasis	17,000
7. Hornstrandir	remote uninhabited area	58,000
8. Vatnsfjördur	fjord, lake and woodland	20,000
9. Lónsöraefi	wild mountain/lowland area	32,500
10. Dýrholaey	coastal scenery	510
11. Esjufjöll	nunatuk	27,000
12. Gullfoss	waterfall	160
13. Stapa and Hellna	coast	75
14. Fjallabak	desert	47,000
Reserves (Biotype)		
15. Eldey	gannets	2
16. Melrakkey	divers	9
17. Svarfadardal	wetland	540
18. Grotta	eider/coastal ecology	5
19. Húsafellskógur	woodland	440
20. Íngólfshöfdi	bird life	90
21. Surtsey	ecology	270
22. Flatey	grey phalarope	100
23. Kringilsarráni	reindeer	8,500
24. Salthöfdi	wetland	220
25. Vestmannsvatn	wetland	600
26. Miklavatn	wetland	1,550
27. Budahraun	lava vegetation	915
28. Hrísey	island ecology	40
29. Ástjörn	bird life	25
30. Varmarósa		10
31. Pjórsarver	pink footed goose	37,500
Natural Monuments		
32. Geysir	geothermal	15
33. Hveravellir	geothermal	170
34. Grábrókargígar	craters	34
35. Eldborg í Bláfjöll	crater	50
36. Lakagígar	crater row	16,000
37. Skútustadagígar	pseudocraters	28
38. Staupasteinn	rock formation	7
39. Eldborg í Hnappa	crater	150

40. Surtarbrandsgil	petrified forest	150
41. Álftaversgîgar	pseudocraters	3,650
42. Kattarauga	floating island	1
43. Helgustaðanáma	old calcite mine	1
44. Teigarhorn	zeolites	120
45. Dîma î Lóni	rock formation	8
46. Háalda î Öraefum	kettle-hole	46
47. Askja (Dyngjufjöll)	caldera	5,000
48. Barðarlaug	hotspring (Snaefells)	50
49. Fjallfoss	waterfall (Dynjandisvógur)	700
50. Borgir (Kópavogur)		3
51. Laugarás (Reykjavík)		1
52. Tröllaborg	(Laekjarbotna)	5
53. Haubakkar	(Elliðárvógur)	2
54. Vighólar	(Kópavógur)	1

Nature Parks

55. Rauðhólar î Reykjavîk	45
56. Folkvangur Neskaupstaðar	300
57. Bláfjöll ski area	8,400
58. Holmanes	260
59. Hrutey î Blöndu	10
60. Reykjanesfólkvangur	30,000
61. Álfaborg î Borgafirði eystra	10
62. Spákonufellshöfdi	30
63. Ósland î Hornafirði	15

APPENDIX C. LIST OF BREEDING BIRDS IN ICELAND

I. Breeding Birds

Scientific name	English name	Icelandic name
Gavia immer	Great Northern Diver	Himbrimi
Gavia stellata	Red-throated Diver	Lómur
Podiceps auritus	Slavonian Grebe	Flórgoði
Fulmarus glacialis	Fulmar	Fýll
Puffinus puffinus	Manx Shearwater	Skrofa
Hydrobates pelagicus	Storm Petrel	Stormsvala
Oceanodroma leucorrhoa	Leach's Petrel	Sjósvala
Sula bassana	Gannet	Súla
Phalacrocorax carbo	Cormorant	Dílaskarfur
Phalacrocorax aristotelis	Shag	Toppskarfur
Cygnus cygnus	Whooper Swan	Álft
Anser Anser	Grey-lag Goose	Grágæs
Anser brachyrhynchus	Pink-footed Goose	Heiðagæs
Branta leucopsis	Barnacle Goose	Helsingi
Anas platyrhynchos	Mallard	Stokkönd
Anas crecca	Teal	Urtönd
Anas strepera	Gadwall	Gargönd
Anas penelope	Widgeon	Rauðhöfðaönd
Anas acuta	Pintail	Grafönd
Anas clypeata	Shoveler	Skeiðönd
Aythya ferina	Pochard	Skutulönd
Aythya fuligula	Tufted Duck	Skúfönd
Aythya marila	Scaup	Duggönd
Somateria mollissima	Eider	Æður
Melanitta nigra	Common Scoter	Hrafnsönd
Histrionicus histrionicus	Harlequin Duck	Straumönd
Clangula hyemalis	Long-tailed Duck	Hávella
Bucephala islandica	Barrow's Goldeneye	Húsönd
Mergus serrator	Red-breasted Merganser	Toppönd
Mergus merganser	Goosander	Gulönd
Haliaetus albicilla	White-tailed Eagle	Haförn
Falco rusticolus	Gyrfalcon	Fálki
Falco columbarius	Merlin	Smyrill
Lagopus mutus	Ptarmigan	Rjúpa
Rallus aquaticus	Water Rail	Keldusvin
Haematopus ostralegus	Oystercatcher	Tjaldur
Pluvialis apricaria	Golden Plover	Heiðlóa
Charadrius hiaticula	Ringed Plover	Sandlóa
Numenius phaeopus	Whimbrel	Spói
Limosa limosa	Black-tailed Godwit	Jaðrakan
Tringa totanus	Redshank	Stelkur
Gallinago gallinago	Snipe	Hrossagaukur
Calidris maritima	Purple Sandpiper	Sendlingur
Calidris alpina	Dunlin	Lóuþræll
Phalaropus fulicarius	Grey Phalarope	Þórshani
Phalaropus lobatus	Red-necked Phalarope	Óðinshani
Stercorarius skua	Great Skua	Skúmur
Stercorarius parasiticus	Arctic Skua	Kjói
Larus canus	Common Gull	Stormmáfur
Larus argentatus	Herring Gull	Silfurmáfur
Larus fuscus	Lesser Black-backed Gull	Sílamáfur
Larus marinus	Great Black-backed Gull	Svartbakur
Larus hyperboreus	Glaucous Gull	Hvítmáfur
Larus ridibundus	Black-headed Gull	Hettumáfur

Rissa tridactyla	Kittiwake	Rita
Sterna paradisaea	Arctic Tern	Kría
Alle alle	Little Auk	Haftyrðill
Alca torda	Razorbill	Álka
Uria lomvia	Brünnich's Guillemot	Stuttnefja
Uria aalge	Common Guillemot	Langvía
Cepphus grylle	Black Guillemot	Teista
Fratercula arctica	Puffin	Lundi
Nyctea scandiaca	Snowy Owl	Snæugla
Asio flammeus	Short-eared Owl	Brandugla
Anthus pratensis	Meadow Pipit	Þúfutittlingur
Motacilla alba	White Wagtail	Maríuerla
Troglodytes troglodytes	Wren	Músarrindill
Oenanthe oenanthe	Wheatear	Steindepill
Turdus iliacus	Redwing	Skóarpröstur
Plectrophenax nivalis	Snow Bunting	Snjótittlingur
Carduelis flammea	Redpoll	Auðnutittlingur
Sturnus vulgaris	Starling	Stari
Corvus corax	Raven	Hrafn

II. Common Passage Migrants or Winter Visitors

Anser albifrons	White-fronted Goose	Blesgæs
Branta leucopsis	Barnacle Goose	Helsingi
Branta bernicla	Brent Goose	Margæs
Arenaria interpres	Turnstone	Tildra
Calidris canutus	Knot	Rauðbrystingur
Calidris alba	Sanderling	Sanderia
Larus glaucoides	Iceland Gull	Bjartmáfur

APPENDIX D. FARM QUESTIONNAIRE

This questionnaire was compiled for use by Evesham High School while undertaking a study of a valley in the north of Iceland. The questions will not be applicable to all farms. In any case, as suggested in Chapter 1, it is advisable to have Icelandic assistance on a survey of this kind.

A translation follows the Icelandic.

Við erum nemendur við menntaskóla í Englandi og erum að vinna að rannsókna vegna landafræði. Við værum yður mjög þakklát ef þér vilduð svara spurningunum á þessum lista.

1. Hver er stærð ræktaðs lands (hektarar)?

2. Hve mörg húsdýr   (a) kindur
                                (b) nautgripir   þar af mjólkurkýr
                                (c) hestar
                                (d) geitur
                                (e) hænur
                                (f) svín?

3. Hvað er ræktað   (a) hey (taða)   (e) rófur
                                (b) bygg   (f) annað grænmeti
                                (c) hafrar   (g) foðurkál
                                (d) kartöflur   (h) annað?

4. Hver mikil er   (a) mjólkurframleiðslan
                              (b) ullarframleiðslan
                              (c) kjötframleiðslan — kinda
                                              nauta?

5. Er framleitt   (a) smjör
                        (b) ostur
                        (c) skyr   á bænum?

6. Hve stór hluti vetrarfóðurs er framleiddur á bænum?

7. Hvernig eru afurðirnar fluttar á markað?

8. Hve lengi hefur verið búið á jörðinni?

9. Hefur húsið alltaf verið á þessum stað?

10. Hve lengi hefur ætt yðar búið hér?

11. Við hvaða störf eru vélar notaðar á bænum (mjaltir, slátt, o.s.f.)?

12. Eru notaðar einhverjar gamlar vinuaðferðir (t.d. slegið með orfi og ljá o.s. frv)?

13. Fáið þér leigðar/lánaðar vílar í einhverjum tilgangi (t.d. frá K.E.A. Bunaðarsambandinu, nágrenni eða öðrum)?

14. Hve margir vinna á bænum á sumrin?

15. Hve marga mánuði er snjór á raektarlandi yðar? Frá . . . til . . .

16. Er landareign yðar snjóþyngri eða snjólettari en aðrar í hreppnum?

TRANSLATION OF FARM QUESTIONNAIRE

We are students from a school in England making a study for our geography course. We would be grateful if you are able to help us by answering this questionnaire.

1. What is the area of cultivated land (hectares))

2. How many farm animals (a) sheep
    (b) cattle   of which milch cows
    (c) horses
    (d) goats
    (e) poultry
    (f) pigs?

3. What is cultivated (a) hay (all types)   (e) turnips
    (b) barley   (f) other vegetables
    (c) oats   (g) kale
    (d) potatoes   (h) others?

4. How great is the (a) milk production
    (b) wool production
    (c) meat production — mutton
                              — beef?

5. Do you produce (a) butter
    (c) cheese
    (c) skyr   on the farm?

6. What proportion of winter feed is produced on the farm?

7. How is produce taken to market?

8. How long has the farm been in this location?

9. Has the house always been on this site?

10. How long has your family lived here?

11. For what purposes do you use machinery on the farm?

12. Do you still use any methods that you would describe as traditional?

13. Do you hire/borrow machinery for any purpose (eg. from KEA, farmers' group, locally or any other place?)

14. How many people work on the farm in the summer?

15. For how many months is the cultivated land under snow? From ... to ...

16. Is your land under snow for a longer or shorter period than others in the parish (hreppur)?

APPENDIX E: ICELAND TOUR OPERATORS

The principal office of ICELANDAIR is listed at the top of every section

Main UK Operators specialising in expedition groups

ICELANDAIR, 73 Grosvenor Street, London W1X 9DD (Tel. 01-499 9971)

ARCTIC EXPERIENCE, 29 Nork Way, Banstead, Surrey SM7 1PB (Tel. 07373 62321)

DICK PHILLIPS, Whitehall House, Nenthead, Alston, Cumbria CA9 3PS (Tel. 0498 81440)

DONALD MACKENZIE (Travel) LTD., 144 St. Vincent Street, Glasgow G2 5LH (Tel. 041-248 7781)

EXPEDITION EXPERIENCE LTD., 165 Northmoor Way, Wareham, Dorset BH20 4EH (Tel. 09295 51280)

FRED OLSEN TRAVEL LTD, 11 Conduit Street, London W1R 0LS (Tel. 01-409 2019)

REGENT HOLIDAYS LTD, 66 Regent Street, Shanklin, Isle of Wight PO37 7AE (Tel. 098-386 4212)

SCANSCAPE HOLIDAYS, 68 1/2 Upper Thames Street, London EC4V 3BJ (Tel. 01-248 0431)

TWICKENHAM TRAVEL LTD., 33 Notting Hill Gate, London W11 3JQ (Tel. 01-221 7278)

TWICKERS WORLD, 22 Church Street, Twickenham, Middlesex (Tel. 01-892 7606)

Principal European and North American Operators and agents:

Austria:

ICELANDAIR, Stampfenbachstr. 117, 8006 Zurich (Tel. 01-373-0000)

VERKEHRSBURO FUR DANEMARK UND ISLAND, Munsterhof 14, 8001 Zurich.

AIRTOUR AUSTRIA, Mollwaldplatz 5, A-1040 Vienna.

PAUL BRAUN, 16 Rue du Mont Blanc, 1211 Geneva (Tel. 022-314335)

REISBURO HUMMER, Makartplatz 9, A-5020 Salzburg.

SAB TOURS — NATURE & REISEN, Marcusstr. 4, A-4600 Wels (Tel. 07242-21626)

Belgium:

AVIA SALES, Centre International Rogier/Boite 33, B-1000 Brussel (Tel. 02-218-0880)

VOYAGES DE KEYSER THORT, Rue de la Madeleine, B-1000 Brussels.

Canada:

GOWAY TRAVEL, 53 Yong Street, Suite 101, Toronto M5E 1J3 (Tel. 416-863-0799)

GOWAY TRAVEL, 402 West Pender Street, Suite 716, Vancouver, British Columbia V6B 1T9 (Tel. 604-687-4004)

Denmark:

ICELANDAIR, Vester Farimagsgade 1, DK-1606 Copenhagen (Tel. 01-123388)

France:

ICELANDAIR, 9 Boulevard des Capuchines, 75002 Paris (Tel. 742-5226)

ALANT'S TOURS, 5 Rue Danielle Casanova, 75001 Paris France (Tel. 296-59-78)

KUONI, 3 Boulevard Victor Hugo, 6000 Nice.

VOYAGES AGREPA, 42 Rue Etienne Marcel, 75002 Paris.

VOYAGES BENNET, 5 Rue Scribe, 75009 Paris.

VOYAGES GALLIA, 12 Rue Auber, 75009 Paris.

VOYAGES KUONI, 33 Boulevard Malesherbes, 75008 Paris.

VOYAGES UTA, 3 Rue Meyerbeer, 75442 Paris.

Greece:

KEY TRAVEL, 6 Kriezotou St, Athens (Tel. 3603 134)

Luxembourg:

ICELANDAIR, Luxembourg Airport, P.O. Box 2101, 1021 Luxembourg (Tel. 4798-2470)

KEISER TOURS, Centre Commercial Louvigny, 34 Rue Phillipe 2, Luxembourg.

Italy:

HOTUR, Via Larga 26, 20122 Milan (Tel. 805-3031)

HOTUR, Via Ludovisi, 3600187 Roma (Tel. 475-6558)

A.T.O.L. 856B

REGENT Holidays (U.K.) Ltd.

TOUR OPERATORS

REGENT HOUSE, REGENT STREET, SHANKLIN, I.O.W.
PO37 7AE, ENGLAND. Tel. 4212/4225 (STD 098386)
Telex 81619

REGENT HOLIDAYS

15 YEARS EXPERIENCE IN OPERATING EXPEDITIONS
AND EXCLUSIVE TOURS TO:
ICELAND, GREENLAND, FAROE ISLANDS, SPITSBERGEN

FOR ALL YOUR REQUIREMENTS IN THESE COUNTRIES
CONTACT **REGENT:** It is to your advantage.

REGENT HOLIDAYS (U.K.) LTD
REGENT HOUSE
REGENT STREET
SHANKLIN
ISLE OF WIGHT
Tel. 0983 86 4212/4225

A.B.T.A.   I.A.T.A.   A.T.O.L.

Also at
13 Small Street, Bristol BS1 1DE
Tel. 211711/2 Telex 449242 Cables: Regentrav - Bristol

HOLIDAYS FOR THINKING PEOPLE
AGENTS THROUGHOUT THE WORLD

Netherlands:

AIR AGENCIES HOLLAND, Vliegfeldweg 30, 3045 ns Rotterdam (Tel. 010-379911)

ARKE REIZEN, Deurningerstraat 15, Postbus 365, 7500 aj Enchede (Tel. 053-353535)

BURGER AND ZOON b.v., Wiliamskade 14, 3016 dk Rotterdam (Tel. 053-145044)

HOLLAND INTERNATIONAL, PO Box 58, 2000 A B Haarlem.

INFO SKANDIC, Pottebakkersrijge 12, 9718 ae Groningen (Tel. 050-143200)

MY WAY, Meent 84e, 3011 ln Rotterdam (Tel. 010-331666)

REISBUREAU BBI, Meerstraat 22, Emmen.

REISEBUREAU MUELLER b.v., Damrak 90, 1012 Amsterdam (Tel. 020-264624)

SCANDINAVIAN ARCTIC SUNWAY, Saxen Weimarlaan 58, 1075 ce Amsterdam (Tel. 020-769011)

STICHTING NEDERLANDSE JEUGDHERBERGCENRALE, Prof. Tulpplein 4, 1018 gx Amsterdam (Tel. 020-264433)

Norway:

ICELANDAIR, Fridthof Nansens Plass 8, 3rd Floor, Oslo 1. (Tel. 02-423975)

Sweden:

ICELANDAIR, Humlegaardsgatan 6, 4th Floor, 114 46 Stockholm (Tel. 08-249930)

Spain:

TREKKING Y AVENTURA, Ramon de la Cruz 93, Madrid 6.

Switzerland:

ARCATOUR, Bahnhofstr. 23, CH-6301 Zug (Tel. 042-219779)

HANS IMHOLZ TRAVEL AGENCY, Zentrastrasse 2, 8036 Zurich.

J. BAUMELLER REISEN AG, Grendel 11, CH-6000 Luzern 6 (Tel. 041-509960)

JUGI TOURS, Postfach 132, Hochhaus 9, Shopping Centre, CH8958 Spreitenbach.

REISBURO KUONI AG, Bärenplatz, CH 3001 Bern.

REISBURO KUONI AG, Neugasse 231, CH-8037 Zurich (Tel. 01-441261)

SAGA REISEN AG, Bärenstutz, CH-3507 Biglen (Tel. 031-902122)

United States:

ICELANDAIR: 610b Fifth Avenue, Rockefeller Center, New York, N.Y. 10111-0334 (Tel.(212) 757-8585) Telephone the New York Toll Free number for details of your nearest agent: (800) 442 5910.

ICELAND TOURIST BOARD, 655 Third Avenue, New York, NY 10017.

West Germany:

ICELANDAIR, Rossmarkt 10, 6000 Frankfurt am Main 1 (Tel. 069-299978)

ICELAND TOURIST BOARD, 5 Laboisen, 200 Hamburg 1.

AIRTOURS INTERNATIONAL, Kurfurstendamm 65, 1 Berlin 15.

AIRTOURS INTERNATIONAL, Adalbertstr. 44-48, 6000 Frankfurt 90 (Tel. 0611-79281)

AIRTOURS INTERNATIONAL, Rodingsmarkt 31-33, 2 Hamburg 11.

AIRTOURS INTERNATIONAL, Prinzregentstrasse 12, 8 Munich 22.

AIRTOURS INTERNATIONAL, Heilmannstrasse 4, 4 Stuttgart 1.

ATHENA REISEN GmbH, Adenauerallee 10, 2000 Hamburg 1 (Tel. 0490-245243)

BURO FUR LANDER- UND VÖLKERKUNDE, KARAWANE STUDENTREISEN, Friedrichstr. 167, 7140 Ludwigsburg (Tel. 07141-83026)

EVANGELISHCHER REISEDIENST, Schutzenbuhlstrasse 81, 7000 Stuttgart 40.

FAHRTENRING DES KATHOLISCHEN BILDUNGSWEKES ESSEN e.V, Kettwiger Str. 2-10, 4300 Essen 1 (Tel. 0201-230862)

INTER AIR VOSS REISEN GmbH, Triftstr. 28-30, 6000 Frankfurt 71 (Tel. 0611-67031)

IRENE SCHMIDT REISEN, Allerseeweg 37, 8706 Höchberg (Tel. 0931-48681)

KONTAKT REISEN - KATHOLISCHES FERIENWERK WUPPERTAL e.V, Laurentiustr. 7, 5600 Wuppertal 1 (Tel. 0202-304410)

MENZELL TOURS, Alter Wall 67-69, 2000 Hamburg 11 (Tel. 040-370070)
NEUBAUER RESIEN GmbH, Grosse Str. 4, 2390 Flensburg (Tel. 0461-17175)
REISEAGENTUR WALDEMAR FAST, Alstertor 21, 2000 Hamburg 1.
REISEBÜRO NORDEN, Ost-West-Str. 70, 2000 Hamburg 11 (Tel. 040-363211)
NORDWEST REISEBÜRO PEKOL, Markt 7, 2900 Oldenburg (Tel. 0441-26655)
SHR-REISEN GmbH. Bismarckallee 2a, 7800 Freiburg (Tel. 0761-210077/78)
SEVEN OCEAN TOURS GmbH, Tizianstr. 3, 8200 Rosenheim (Tel. 08031-66616)
WIKINGER REISEN GmbH, Buddinghardt 9, 5800 Hagen 7 (Tel. 02331-40881)
WOLTERS REISEN GmbH, Postfach 100147, 2800 Bremen 1 (Tel. 0421-89991)
WOLTERS REISEN, Bremerstrasse 48, 2805 Stuhr 1.

APPENDIX F: USEFUL ADDRESSES IN BRITAIN

See also Appendix E. for addresses of Tour Operators.

Key Addresses:
EXPEDITION ADVISORY CENTRE, Royal Geographical Society, 1 Kensington Gore, London SW7 2AR (Tel. 01-581 2057)

ICELAND UNIT, Kennet Cottage, Harrow Park, Harrow on the Hill, Middlesex HA1 3JE (Tel. 01-422 2825) (or via the Young Explorers' Trust - see below)

YOUNG EXPLORERS' TRUST, Royal Geographical Society, 1 Kensington Gore, London SW7 2AR (Tel. 01-589 9724)

General:
ICELAND FREEZING PLANTS Ltd., Estate Road No. 2, S. Humberside Industrial Estate, Grimsby, S. Humberside DV31 2TG (Tel: 0472 44181)

ICELAND EMBASSY, 1 Eaton Terrace, London SW1 (Tel. 01-730 5131)

SAMBAND of ICELAND, 16 Eastcheap, London EC3M 1BH (Tel. 01-623 9283)

Airport Information:
LONDON (HEATHROW): Tel. 01-745 7051

GLASGOW: Tel. 041-887 1111 ext. 488

Books and Maps:
DICK PHILLIPS, Whitehall House, Nenthead, Alston, Cumbria (Tel. 0498 81440)

ICELAND UNIT, Kennet Cottage, Harrow Park, Harrow on the Hill, Middlesex HA1 3JE (Tel. 01-422 2825) (or via the Young Explorers' Trust - see above)

Equipment:
FIELD AND TREK (Equipment) LTD, 3 Wates Way, Brentwood, Essex CM15 9TB (Tel. 0277 233122)

MOUNTAIN LOGISTICS LTD, 26/28 Park Road, Chesterfield, Derbyshire S40 1XZ (Tel. 0246 201437)

Expeditions:
BRATHAY EXPLORATION GROUP, Old Brathay, Ambleside, Cumbria LA22 0HP (Tel. 09663 3042)

BRITISH SCHOOLS EXPLORING SOCIETY, Royal Geographical Society, 1 Kensington Gore, London SW7 2AR (Tel. 01-584 0710)

SAIL TRAINING ASSOCIATION, Bosham, Chichester, Sussex

SCOUT ASSOCIATION, Gilwell Park, Chingford, London E4 7QW

YOUNG EXPLORERS' TRUST regional exploring societies. Contact the YET office above.

Libraries:
SCOTT POLAR RESEARCH INSTITUTE, Lensfield Road, Cambridge, CB2 1ER (Tel. 0223 66499)

ROYAL GEOGRAPHICAL SOCIETY, 1 Kensington Gore, London SW7 2AR (Tel. 01-589 5466)

Shipping:
BRANTFORD INTERNATIONAL Ltd., Queens House, Paragon Street, Hull HU1 3NQ (Tel. 0482 27756) (Agents for Samband Line)

McGREGOR, GOW AND HOLLAND, Trelawny House, The Dock, Felixstowe, Suffolk (Tel. 039-42 85651) (Agents for Eimskip)

McGREGOR, GOW AND HOLLAND, Dock Offices, Immingham Dock, Immingham, S. Humberside DN40 2LZ (Tel. 0469 72261)

McGREGOR, GOW AND HOLLAND, Stanton Grove Warehouse, Merseyside Trading Park, Speke Hall Road, Speke, Liverpool L24 9CQ (Tel. 051-486 0668) (Agents for Eimskip)

P & O FERRIES, Orkney and Shetland Service, P & O Terminal, Aberdeen AB9 8DL. (Agents for Smyrill Line)

APPENDIX G: USEFUL ADDRESSES IN ICELAND

Accommodation:
YOUTH HOSTEL ASSOCIATION (Bandalag Íslenzkra Farfuglar), Laufasvegi 41, Reykjavík (Tel. 2-49-50)
EDDA HOTELS, Iceland Tourist Bureau, Reykjanesbraut 6, Reykjavík (Tel. 2-58-55)

Aircraft (Domestic and International):
EAGLE AIR, Lagmula 7, Reykjavík (Tel. 2-95-11)
ICELANDAIR: Bookings: Domestic (Innanlandsflug) (Tel. 2-66-22); International (Millilandaflug) (Tel. 2-51-00). Enquiries: Domestic (Tel. 2-60-11); International (Tel. 2-78-00).

Aircraft (Light):
ARNARFLUG (Eagle Air), Reykjavík Airport (Tel. 2-95-77)
ERNIR h.f., Ísafjörður Airport (Tel. (94) 4200)
FLUGFÉLAG AUSTURLANDS, Egilsstaðir Airport (Tel. (97) 1122)
FLUGFÉLAG NORÐURLANDS, Akureyri Airport (Tel. (96) 2-18-24)
HELGI JÓNSSON, Air Taxi, Reykjavík Airport (Tel. 1-08-80).
SVERRIR THORODDSSON, Reykjavík Airport (Tel. 2-80-11)

Books, maps and air photographs:
LANDMAELINGAR ÍSLANDS (Icelandic Geodetic Survey), Laugavegi 178, Reykjavík (Tel. 8-16-11) (maps and air photographs)
MÁLS OG MENNINGAR, Laugavegi 18, Reykjavík (Tel. 2-42-42)
SIGFÚS EYMUNDSSON, Austurstraeti 18, Reykjavík (Tel. 1-42-81)
SNAEBJÖRN JÓNSSON, Hafnarstraeti 4, Reykjavík (Tel. 1-19-36)

Bus Travel and Tour Operators:
ARENA TOURS, Hvassaleiti 26, Reykjavík (Tel. 68-56-86)
B.S.Í. TRAVEL, Umferðamiðstöðinni (Long-distance bus station), Hringbraut, Reykjavík (Tel. 2-23-00)
ELDÁ h.f., Reykjahlíð við Mývatn (Tel. (96)'4-42-20)
FERÐASKRIFSTOFA AKUREYRAR, Raðhústorgi 3, Akureyri (Tel. (96) 25-00-00)
FERÐASKRIFSTOFAN MIDNÆTURSÓL, Laugavegi 62, 101 Reykjavík (Tel. 2-80-60)
GUÐMUNDUR JÓNASSON h.f., Borgartúni 34, Reykjavík (Tel. 8-32-22)
REYKJAVÍK EXCURSIONS, Hotel Loftleiðir, Reykjavík (Tel. 62-10-11)
THE NEW TOURING CLUB (Rafts, snowmobiles, climbing), Flókagata 5, Reykjavík (Tel. 1-98-28)
ÚLFAR JACOBSEN, Austurstraeti 9, Reykjavík (Tel. 1-34-99)

Customs Offices:
TOLLGAESLAN, Tollhúsinu, Tryggvagata 19, Reykjavík (Tel. 1-85-00)

Eating out (Reykjavík):
HOTEL GARÐUR (University Student Centre), Hringbraut (Tel. 1-59-18)
HRESSINGARSKÁLINN, Austurstraeti 20 (Tel. 1-43-53)
KAFFIVAGNINN, Grandargarði 10 (Tel. 1-59-32)
KOKKHÚSIÐ, Laekjargata 8 (Tel. 1-03-40)
MULAKAFFI, Hallamuli (Tel. 3-77-37)
ÓÐINSVÉ, Odinstorg (Tel. 2-52-24)
POTTURINN OG PANNAN, Brautarholt 22 (Tel. 1-16-90)
ULFAR OG LJÓN, Grensásvegur, Reykjavík.

Embassies:
BRITISH EMBASSY, Laufásvegur 49, Reyjavík (Tel. 1-58-83)
DANISH EMBASSY, Hverfisgötu 29, Reykjavík (Tel. 1-37-47)
FINNISH EMBASSY, Kringlumýrarbraut, Reykjavík (Tel. 8-20-40)
FRENCH EMBASSY, Tungata 22, Reykjavík (Tel. 1-76-21)
NORWEGIAN EMBASSY, Fjölugata 17, Reykjavík (Tel. 1-30-65)

SWEDISH EMBASSY, Lagmuli 7, Reykjavík (Tel. 8-20-22)
UNITED STATES, Laufásvegur 21, Reykjavík (Tel. 2-91-00)
WEST GERMANY, Æssíða 78, Reykjavík (Tel. 1-99-84)

Emergencies:
See page 143 for police, hospitals, lost property etc.

Film Companies:
SAGA FILM, Háaleitisbraut 1, Reykjavík (Tel. 68-50-85)

Freight Transfer:
LANDFLUTNINGAR h.f., Skútuvógi 8, Reykjavík (Tel. 8-46-00)
SENDIBILASTÖDIN h.f., Borgartúni 21, Reykjavík (Tel. 2-50-50)
VÖRUFLUTNINGARMIDSTÖDIN h.f., Borgartúni 21, Reykjavík (Tel. 1-04-40)

Rafting and Climbing Tours:
THE NEW TOURING CLUB, Flókagata 5, 105 Reykjavík (Tel. 1-98-28)

Rescue Services:
SLYSAVARNARFÉLAG ÍSLANDS (National Life-saving Society), Grandagarði 14, Reykjavík (Tel. 2-70-00)

Research Enquiries:
HÖLLUSTUVERND (National Centre for Hygiene and Environmental Pollution), Siðamuli 13, Reykjavík (Tel. 8-18-44)
JÖKLARANNSÓKNAFÉLAG ÍSLANDS (Iceland Glaciological Society), P.O. Box 5128, Reykjavík.
NÁTTÚRUFRAEÐISTOFNUN ÍSLANDS (Icelandic Museum of Natural History), Laugavegi 105, Reykjavík (Tel. 2-98-22)
NÁTTÚRUVERNDARRÁD (Nature Conservation Council), Hverfisgötu 26, Reykjavík (Tel. 2-78 -55)
ORKUSTOFNUN (Power Authority), Grensásvegur 9, Rekjavík (Tel. 8-36-00)
RANNSÓKNARÁD RÍKISINS (National Research Council), Laugavegi 13, Reykjavík (Tel. 2-13- 20)
RAUNVÍSINDASTOFNUN HÁSKOLANS (University Science Research Institute), Dunhaga 3, Reykjavík (Tel. 2-13-40)
ÚTANRÍKISRÁDUNETTID (Ministry of Foreign Affairs), Hverfisgötu 115, Reykjavík.
VEÐURSTOFNUN ÍSLANDS (Weather Bureau), Bústaðavegi 9, Reykjavík (Tel. 68-60-00)

Shipping Companies:
EIMSKIPAFÉLAG ÍSLANDS (Iceland Steamship Company), Posthússtraeti, Reykjavík (Tel. 2-71- 00)
SKIPADEILD SAMBANDSINS (SAMBAND LINE), Samband House, Sólvhólsgötu 4, Reykjavík (Tel. 2-82-00)

Societies:
FERDAFÉLAG ÍSLANDS (Iceland Travel Club), Öldugata 3, Reykjavik (Tel. 1-95-33)
FERDAFELAG ÍSLENZKRA BIFREIDAEIGENDA (Federation of Icelandic motorists), Borgartúni 33, Reykjavík (Tel. 2-99-99)
ÍSALP (Iceland Alpine Club), P.O. Box 4186, Reykjavík.
KIWANIS INTERNATIONAL, Brautarholt 26, Reykjavík (Tel. 1-44-60)
LIONS CLUB INTERNATIONAL, Háaleitisbraut 68, Reykjavík (Tel. 3-31-22)
ROTARY INTERNATIONAL, Skólavörðustig 21, Reykjavík (Tel. 2-64-33)
BANDALAG ÍSLENSKRA SKÁTA (Iceland Scout Association), P.O. Box 831, 121 Reykjavík (Tel. 2-31-90)

Supplies:
ÓSTABUDIN (cheese etc), Snorrabraut 54, Reykjavík (Head Office: Bitruhálsi 2, Reykjavík) (Tel. 8-25-11)
RENT-A-TENT (Tjaldaleigan), Hringbraut v/Umferðamiðstöðina, 101 Reykjavík (Tel. 1-30-72)
SKÁTABUDIN (Scout Shop), Snorrabraut 60, Reykjavík (Tel. 1-20-45)
SLÁTURFÉLAG SUDERLANDS (meat), Skúlagata 20, Reykjavík (Tel. 2-53-55)

Taxis:

Borgarbilastödin:	2-24-40
Baejarleiđir:	3-35-00
Hreyfill:	8-55-22
B.S.R.:	1-17-20
Steindór:	1-15-80

Vehicle Hire:
GEYSIR CAR HIRE, Borgartuni 24, Reykjavík (Tel. 1-10-15)
HÚSAVíK CAR RENTAL, Garđarsbraut 66, Husavík (Tel. (96)4-18-88)
INTER-RENT, Skeifan 9, Reykjavík (Tel. 8-69-15)
INTER-RENT, Tryggvabraut 14, Akureyri (Tel. (96)2-35-15)

Vehicle Repairs:
BILANAUST, Siđamula 7-9, Reykjavík (Tel. 8-27-22) (spare parts)
HEKLA h.f., Laugavegi 170, Reykjavík (Tel. 2-12-40) (Land Rover)
HÖLDUR h.f., Fjölnisgötu 18, Akureyri (Tel. (96) 2-13-65) (Land Rover)
SVEINN EGILSSON, Skeifunni 17, Reykjavík (Tel. 68-51-00) (Ford)

APPENDIX H. FILMS ABOUT ICELAND

It may be useful to hire some films to help with both the launching of your expedition and the provision of background information for the expedition members. It is important to realise that in most cases the number of copies is limited and that the hirers or loaners are not equipped to maintain films. The quality of the copy cannot be guaranteed.

Films: (Distributor in brackets)
Air Rover (Icelandair) Video 20 mins (C, D, E)
Birth of an Island (Surtsey) 22 mins (B)
Conservation in Iceland Video 20 mins (C)
Days of Destruction 20 mins (B, C, D, H)
Exploring in Iceland 20 mins (G)
Fire on Heimaey 20 mins (B)
Iceland — Nature's Wonderland (B, D, E)
Iceland Story 20 mins (B)
Looking at Glaciers 15 mins (I)
On Top of the World 20 mins (B)
See How the Hot Springs Bubble 15 mins (C)
Spring in Iceland 15 mins (B)
The British Schools Exploring Society in Iceland 28 mins (A)
The Iceland Safari Video 20 mins (F)
The Living Sea 15 mins (B)
They shouldn't call Iceland 'Iceland' 20 mins (D, H)
Three Faces of Iceland 25 mins (B, D)
The Scientific Work of the British Schools Exploring Society (G)

Distributors:
(A) Stewart Film Distributors Ltd., 82-84 Clifton Hill, LONDON NH8 0JT (01-624 7296/1238)
(B) Icelandic Embassy, 1 Eaton Terrace, LONDON SW1 (01-730 5131)
(C) The Iceland Information Centre, Kennet Cottage, Harrow Park, HARROW ON THE HILL, Middlesex HA1 3JE (01-422 2825)
(D) Icelandair, 73 Grosvenor Street, LONDON WC1 9DD (01-499 9971)
(E) Twickenham Travel, 84 Hampton Road, TWICKENHAM, Middlesex TW2 5QS (01-898 9684)
(F) Fred Olsen Travel, 11 Conduit Street, London W1 (01-409 3275)
(G) Explorer Films, 7 Thulborn Close, Teversham, CAMBRIDGE CB1 5AU (02205 4336)
(H) Viscom Ltd., Parkhall Road Trading Estate, LONDON SE21 8EL (01-761 3035)
(I) Guild Sound and Vision, Oundle Road, PETERBOROUGH, Northants (0733)

APPENDIX I: SOME ICELANDIC and ICELAND-RELATED PERIODICALS

Most of the periodicals mentioned below are to be found in the library of the Scott Polar Research Institute in Cambridge.

> Árbók   = annual, yearbook.
> Greinar   = articles.
> Rit   = papers, writings, treatises.
> Timarit · = periodical, magazine, review.

Acta Botanica Islandica: Journal of Iceland Botany. Replaced the journal Flora (viz) in 1972. Articles in Icelandic, English, German and French. Always with an English summary.

Acta Naturalia Islandica: (1946 onwards). Predominantly geological but natural history generally. Mostly in English.

Árbók, Ferðafélag Akureyrar: Annually. Report of the Akureyri Travel Association's excursions.

Árbók, Ferðafélag Íslands: Iceland Travel Association. Each yearbook deals with a different area. In Icelandic.

Árbók, Landsbókasafn Íslands: National Library publication including list of works published in Iceland.

Ársrit Skógraektarfélags Íslands: Iceland Forestry Commission paper.

Aegir: (Rit Fiskifélags Íslands) Small paper bulletin of the Fisheries Association. In Icelandic.

Directory of Iceland: The Icelandic Yearbook Ltd., Information Service, P.O. Box 1396, Reykjavik. Annually. English. Useful articles on geography and economy.

Ferðahandbókinn: Annually. Touring guide to Iceland Icelandic and English.

Flóra: (1963-1968) Journal of Icelandic Botany. In Icelandic. Now superceded by Acta Botanica Islandica (viz).

Hagskýrslur Íslands: (Statistics of Iceland) Published by Hagstofa Íslands, (Statistical Bureau of Iceland), Hverfisgötu 8-10, Reykjavîk.

Hagtiðindi: Import-Export statistics published by Hagstofa Íslands.

Heilbrigðisskýrslur: (Public Health in Iceland) Icelandic with English summary.

Iceland Review: English articles of a general nature. Well illustrated.

Iceland: Published by the Central Bank of Iceland. A very good account of the economic and geography of Iceland.

Ísland: Bulletin of the Iceland Unit of the Young Explorers' Trust.

Island-Berichte: Newsletter of the Friends of Iceland, Hamburg. In German.

Jökull: (Journal of the Iceland Glaciological Society) Articles in Icelandic and English. Contains useful statistics on annual glacier measurements. Joined with the Geoscience Society of Iceland in 1977.

Leidabók: Bus timetables. Available from post offices and from the long-distance bus station in Reykjavík.

Náttúrufraedingurinn: Annually. Icelandic. Chiefly botany and geology. Some very short English summaries where important — eg. new species added to list.

News from Iceland: Monthly newspaper in English published by Iceland Review.

Rit Fiskideildar: (Hafrannsóknastofnunin — Marine Research Institute, Reykjavík) Mostly in English. Each edition devoted to a separate topic.

Saga-Book: Proceedings of the Viking Society for Northern Research. University College London.

Seismological Bulletin: Reykjavík.

Símaskráinn: Telephone book. Available from post offices, or Dick Phillips.

Statistical Bulletin: Thin paper bulletin. English.

Timaritid Týli: Journal of Natural History. Icelandic. Published by the Museum of Natural History, Akureyri.

Timarit Verkfraedingafélags Íslands: Icelandic. Good articles on engineering in Iceland. Maps. Diagrams. Occasional subtitle to diagrams.

Vedrátten: Iceland Meteorological reports.

Vedrid: Journal of Icelandic Meteorology. Icelandic.

Visindafélag Íslendinga (Societas Scientiarum Islandica): Periodic works on geology, botany, zoology, etc. Three separate types of papers: Rit, Greinar, and the magazine Science in Iceland. Mainly in English.

Vidskiptaskráinn: Commercial directory. Annually. Lists of firms in Iceland. Brief accounts of economic geography.

APPENDIX J. THE YOUNG EXPLORERS' TRUST

The Young Explorers' Trust is the association of British youth exploring societies whose expressed aims are to increase the opportunities for young people to take part in exploration, discovery and challenging adventure, and to make these expeditions safer and more worthwhile.

The Trust:

- Advises on all aspects of expedition planning.
- Links members with others who have run similar expeditions.
- Organises seminars, lectures and other training and discussion meetings.
- Publishes a quarterly magazine YETMAG full of information for expeditions.
- Produces manuals and leaflets with practical advice.
- Maintains study groups of members with common expedition interests.
- Grants YET APPROVAL to expeditions which meet its standards of planning.
- Makes financial grants to many expeditions of young people each year.

For further details contact the Administrative Officer, Y.E.T., Royal Geographical Society, 1 Kensington Gore, London SW7 2AR.

APPENDIX K. EXPEDITION ADVISORY CENTRE

The Expedition Advisory Centre provides an information and training service for those planning an expedition. It was founded, and is jointly administered by the Royal Geographical Society and the Young Explorers' Trust and is financed by The British Land Company Plc as a sponsorship project.

In addition to the organisation of a variety of seminars and publications, including the annual "Planning a Small Expedition" Seminar, the Centre provides a number of specialist services to explorers and expedition organisers. At its offices on the second floor of the Royal Geographical Society in London, a wide range of information sources are available including reports of past expeditions, a register of planned expeditions, lists of expedition consultants and suppliers, and of members available for expeditions as well as access to information on expedition organisation in all climates.

The Centre is open from 1000 to 1700 Monday to Friday and welcomes enquiries from the general public. For further information contact the Information Officer, E.A.C., Royal Geographical Society, 1 Kensington Gore, London SW7 2AR (01-581 2057)

APPENDIX L. POST-EXPEDITION QUESTIONNAIRE

The answers to this questionnaire will be analysed for publication in the Iceland Unit Bulletin ISLAND. The contents will be invaluable to future expeditions who will greatly appreciate the time taken to fill it in. Thank you.

NAME OF EXPEDITION:) DATES:

LEADER'S NAME AND ADDRESS:) PHONE: DAY:
) PHONE: PM:

TYPE OF PARTY: (Delete)

(a)   School/University/Youth Group/Scouts/Other: ....

(b) Research/Educational/Recreational/Cultural

NUMBERS: Male:)   Female:
       Leaders:
       Members:

WORKING AREAS:

FIELDWORK:
Subject: Brief description:

TRAVEL:

1. UK Travel Operator/Agent:

2. If your equipment travelled by sea:

                          Outward: Return:

       Name of Port:
              Weight:
             Volume:
   Basic Freight cost:
      Cost of extras:

3. If you hired a self-drive vehicle:

                Company:
          Type of vehicle:
 Basic cost per day/week:
      Free Km allowed:
        Extra cost/Km:
        Any problems:

4. If you hired a bus:Company:
                  Route:
                  Cost:
            Any problems:

5. If you used public transport:
     Routes: Time Taken: Cost:

6. If you used your own vehicle please comment on any difficulties experienced that would be useful for future leaders to know about:

7. If you used any other form of transport (eg. private aircraft) please give similar details if appropriate:

8. Between what points did you encounter:
   - (a) Tarmac road surface:
   - (b) Very poor road conditions:
   - (c) Changes in road alignment:
   - (d) Improved road surface:

ACCOMMODATION

1. Camp Sites used:
   Site: Cost: Comments:

2. Other accommodation used:
   Type: Location: Cost: Comments:

FOOD SUPPLIES

1. Approx. what percentage of food was bought in Iceland?

2. Approx. how much did food cost/head/day?

3. If you can recall the cost of any food items purchased in Iceland please list them at the end on a separate sheet.

INSURANCE ETC

1. Insurance Company:
2. Cost of Basic Holiday Insurance:
3. Cost of Mountaineering Insurance:
4. Cost of Mountain Rescue Insurance (if extra):
5. Any Claims?/Amount?:

6. If you made contingency plans for evacuation or had to make use of them can you give details of methods, emergency landing strips, nearest doctor, hospital, telephone, and an account of the procedures:

COSTS

Can you give us some indication of the cost/head for your expedition:

```
           (  in Britain:
Travel -(      by sea:
           (      by air:
           ( in Iceland:
              Freight:
Personal insurance:
  Vehicle insurance:
      Food and Fuel:
         Equipment:
             Other:
```

LITERATURE

1. What reading material did you find especially helpful in preparing your expedition?

2. Did you come across any new articles or books that might be of interest to expeditions (general or regional material):

3. Please comment on amendments or additions to our Broadsheets or the Handbook in the light of your experiences this year (especially customs procedures and regulations). If necessary continue on a separate sheet of paper.

THE FUTURE

Are you planning a follow-up expedition to   (a) the same area:

                                                           (b) another area:

2. If you are not planning a follow-up can you recommend any fieldwork that might usefully be carried out by another group?

3. Are you able to recommend any useful contacts at home or Iceland for specific purposes (see Note 1)?

4. Do you know the names and addresses of any forthcoming expeditions to Iceland?

FINALLY

1. Will you be producing a report of your expedition?
2. If so, may we please have a copy (preferably two) for our library?

NOTES

1. We realise from our own experience that there are facts and connections that one must of necessity keep to oneself. However, may we invite you to place a large asterisk against any information that you feel should not be disclosed without prior consultation with yourself.

2. To save removing this questionnaire from the Handbook, please do photocopy and enlarge it before filling in the details.

3. Please return this questionnaire to:
The Iceland Information Centre
Expedition Advisory Centre
Royal Geographical Society
Kensington Gore
London SW7 2AR

THANK YOU VERY MUCH FOR YOUR HELP

ICELAND EXPLORER

ARENA

*Challenge
the forces of nature
with the thrill
of Iceland Explorer*

ICELAND EXPLORER

Explore Iceland

Feel the excitement that the Viking explorers felt when they first set eyes on the unbelievable landscapes of Iceland's interior. Breathe the invigorating fresh air born of rugged mountains and chilling glaciers. Enjoy the freedom and independence of Iceland's open spaces.

Our heavy-duty buses and well-equipped kitchen wagons will take you to places which you never dreamed or hoped to find for yourself.

We specialize in camping explorations and are in a unique position to operate itineraries for groups with general or special interests.

Travelling in comfort, we traverse magnificent mountains and ford glacial rivers.

Icelandic Style

Accommodation is in two-person tents with air mattresses.
Sleeping bags are available as extras.

Meals are prepared by our own staff and include many Icelandic favorites, such as fish, smoked lamb and skyr.

Our prices include: vehicles, tents, air mattresses and meals. We will even do the washing up.

*On our explorations, **you** can concentrate on your projects, while **we** look after your well being.*

Write to: Arena Tours Hvassaleiti 26
108 Reykjavík Iceland

APPLICATION FORM (BLOCK CAPITALS PLEASE)

NAME: ....

ADDRESS: ....

....

.... POST CODE: ....

YET MEMBERSHIP No. .... (where appropriate)

Please indicate whether: Payment by Bankers Order
        (tick)   Appropriate Fee enclosed*

*Cheques to be made payable to ICE-AD.

Send this form to: The Iceland Centre, 3 Deynecourt, Harrow Park, Harrow on the Hill, Middlesex, HA1 3JE.

SUBSCRIPTION RATES

YET Members   £ 3.50 per annum
Non-YET Members   £ 6.00 per annum (individuals)
                         £10.00 per annum (corporate)

BANKERS ORDER Please forward to your own bank

TO .... BANK

ADDRESS ....

....

Please transfer from my/our account No. .... the payments quoted below to the NATIONAL WESTMINSTER BANK PLC (60-10-09) 92 HIGH STREET, HARROW, MIDDLESEX, HA1 3LR for the credit of ICE-AD (A/C No. 37905678.

the sum of £ .... on receipt of this form, and thereafter from 1st January 198 .... annually unless cancelled by me/us in writing, this replaces any previous standing order for transfer to the above stated bank account.

Name .... Signature ....

Address...

.... Date ....